AF758217

PRACTICE - ASSESS - DIAGNOSE

180 Days of MATH for Sixth Grade

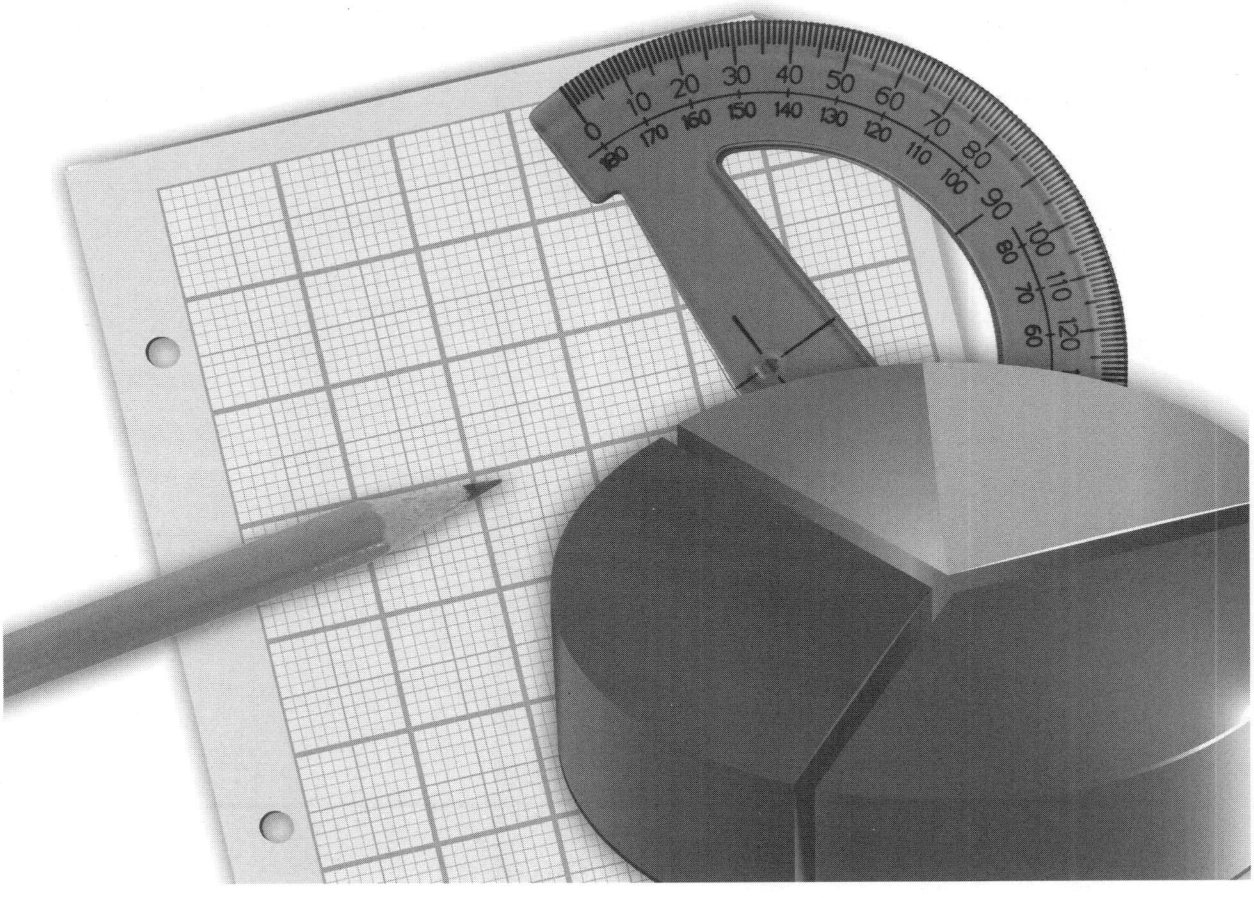

Developed by
Jodene Smith

Shell Education

Publishing Credits

Dona Herweck Rice, *Editor-in-Chief*; Lee Aucoin, *Creative Director*;
Don Tran, *Print Production Manager;* Timothy J. Bradley, *Illustration Manager*;
Chris McIntyre, M.A.Ed., *Editorial Director*; Sara Johnson, M.S.Ed., *Senior Editor*;
Aubrie Nielsen, M.S.Ed., *Associate Education Editor*; Juan Chavolla, *Cover/Interior Layout Designer;*
Grace Alba, *Production Artist;* Corinne Burton, M.A.Ed., *Publisher*

Shell Education
5482 Argosy Avenue
Huntington Beach, CA 92649-1030
www.tcmpub.com/shell-education

ISBN 978-1-4258-0802-0

Printed by: 465482
Printed in: Malaysia
PO#: 25082

TABLE OF CONTENTS

INTRODUCTION AND RESEARCH

The Need for Practice

In order to be successful in today's mathematics classroom, students must deeply understand both concepts and procedures so that they can discuss and demonstrate their understanding. Demonstrating understanding is a process that must be continually practiced in order for students to be successful. According to Marzano (2010, 83), "practice has always been, and will always be, a necessary ingredient to learning procedural knowledge at a level at which students execute it independently." Practice is especially important to help students apply their concrete, conceptual understanding to a particular procedural skill.

Understanding Assessment

In addition to providing opportunities for frequent practice, teachers must be able to assess students' understanding of mathematical procedures, terms, concepts, and reasoning (Kilpatrick, Swafford, and Findell 2001). This is important so that teachers can adequately address students' misconceptions, build on their current understanding, and challenge them appropriately.

Assessment is a long-term process that often involves careful analysis of student responses from a lesson discussion, project, practice sheet, or test. When analyzing the data, it is important for teachers to reflect on how their teaching practices may have influenced students' responses and to identify those areas where additional instruction may be required. In short, the data gathered from assessments should be used to inform instruction: slow down, speed up, or reteach. This type of assessment is called *formative assessment* and is used to provide a seamless connection between instruction and assessment (McIntosh 1997).

HOW TO USE THIS BOOK

180 Days of Math for Sixth Grade offers teachers and parents a full page of daily mathematics practice activities for each day of the school year.

Easy to Use and Standards-Based

These activities reinforce grade-level skills across a variety of mathematical concepts. The questions are provided as a full practice page, making them easy to prepare and implement as part of a classroom morning routine, at the beginning of each mathematics lesson, or as homework.

Every sixth-grade practice page provides 12 questions, each tied to a specific mathematical concept. Students are given the opportunity for regular practice in each mathematical concept, allowing them to build confidence through these quick standards-based activities.

Question	Mathematics Concept	NCTM Standards
1	**Addition or Subtraction**	Understands numbers, ways of representing numbers, relationships among numbers, and number systems; Understands the meanings of operations and how they relate to one another; Computes events and makes reasonable estimates
2	**Multiplication**	
3	**Division**	
4	**Place Value or Number Sense**	
5	**Fractions, Decimals, and Percents**	Works flexibly with fractions, decimals, and percents to solve problems; Compares and orders fractions, decimals, and percents efficiently; Understands the meaning and effects of arithmetic operations with fractions and decimals
6	**Order of Operations and Patterns**	Understands the meanings of operations and how they relate to one another
7	**Algebra and Algebraic Thinking**	Understands patterns, relations, and functions; Represents and analyzes mathematical situations and structures using algebraic symbols
8		
9	**Measurement**	Understands measurable attributes of objects and the units, systems, and processes of measurement; Applies appropriate techniques and formulas to determine measurements
10	**Geometry**	Uses visualization and spacial reasoning to solve problems; Analyzes characteristics and properties of two- and three-dimensional geometric shapes
11	**Data Analysis/Probability**	Selects and uses appropriate statistical methods to analyze data; Understands and applies basic concepts of probability
12	**Word Problem/Logic Problem or Mathematical Reasoning**	Solves problems that arise in mathematics and in other contexts; Applies and adapts a variety of appropriate strategies to solve problems

Standards are listed with the permission of the National Council of Teachers of Mathematics (NCTM). NCTM does not endorse the content or validity of these alignments.

HOW TO USE THIS BOOK *(cont.)*

Using the Practice Pages

As outlined on page 4, every question is aligned to a mathematics concept and standard.

Practice pages provide instruction and assessment opportunities for each day of the school year.

Each question ties student practice to a specific mathematics concept.

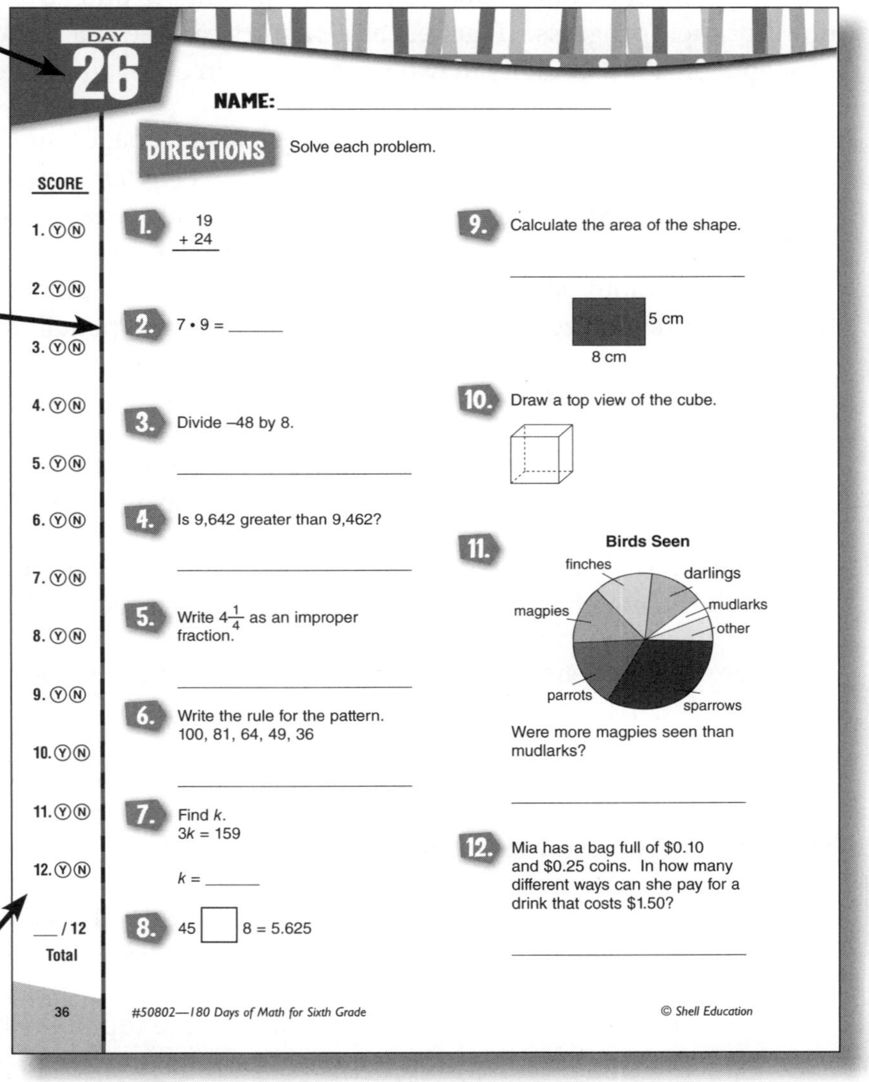
DAY 26

NAME: ____________

DIRECTIONS Solve each problem.

SCORE

1. Ⓨ Ⓝ
2. Ⓨ Ⓝ
3. Ⓨ Ⓝ
4. Ⓨ Ⓝ
5. Ⓨ Ⓝ
6. Ⓨ Ⓝ
7. Ⓨ Ⓝ
8. Ⓨ Ⓝ
9. Ⓨ Ⓝ
10. Ⓨ Ⓝ
11. Ⓨ Ⓝ
12. Ⓨ Ⓝ

___ / 12 Total

1. $19 + 24$

2. $7 \cdot 9 =$ ______

3. Divide –48 by 8.

4. Is 9,642 greater than 9,462?

5. Write $4\frac{1}{4}$ as an improper fraction.

6. Write the rule for the pattern. 100, 81, 64, 49, 36

7. Find k. $3k = 159$

$k =$ ______

8. 45 ☐ 8 = 5.625

9. Calculate the area of the shape.

5 cm

8 cm

10. Draw a top view of the cube.

11. Birds Seen

finches

darlings

mudlarks

other

magpies

parrots

sparrows

Were more magpies seen than mudlarks?

12. Mia has a bag full of \$0.10 and \$0.25 coins. In how many different ways can she pay for a drink that costs \$1.50?

36

#50802—180 Days of Math for Sixth Grade

© Shell Education

Using the Scoring Guide

Use the scoring guide along the side of each practice page to check answers and see at a glance which skills may need more reinforcement.

Fill in the appropriate circle for each problem to indicate correct (Y) or incorrect (N) responses. You might wish to indicate only incorrect responses to focus on those skills. (For example, if students consistently miss numbers 2 and 6, they may need additional help with those concepts as outlined in the table on page 4.) Use the answer key at the back of the book to score the problems, or you may call out answers to have students self-score or peer-score their work.

HOW TO USE THIS BOOK *(cont.)*

Diagnostic Assessment

Teachers can use the practice pages as diagnostic assessments. The data analysis tools included with the book enable teachers or parents to quickly score students' work and monitor their progress. Teachers and parents can see at a glance which mathematics concepts or skills students may need to target in order to develop proficiency.

After students complete a practice page, grade each page using the answer key (pages 191–206). Then, complete the *Practice Page Item Analysis* (page 7) for the whole class, or the *Student Item Analysis* (page 8) for individual students. These charts are also provided in the digital resources (filenames: G6_practicepage_analysis.pdf, G6_student_analysis.pdf). Teachers can input data into the electronic files directly on the computer, or they can print the pages and analyze students' work using paper and pencil.

To complete the Practice Page Item Analysis:

- Write or type students' names in the far-left column. Depending on the number of students, more than one copy of the form may be needed or you may need to add rows.
- The question numbers are included across the top of the chart. Each item correlates with the matching question number from the practice page.
- For each student, record an *X* in the column if the student has the item incorrect. If the item is correct, leave the item blank.
- Count the *X*s in each row and column and fill in the correct boxes.

To complete the Student Item Analysis:

- Write or type the student's name on the top row. This form tracks the ongoing progress of each student, so one copy per student is necessary.
- The question numbers are included across the top of the chart. Each item correlates with the matching question number from the practice page.
- For each day, record an *X* in the column if the student has the item incorrect. If the item is correct, leave the item blank.
- Count the *X*s in each row and column and fill in the correct boxes.

Practice Page Item Analysis

Directions: Record an *X* in cells to indicate where students have missed questions. Add up the totals. You can view: (1) which questions/concepts were missed per student; (2) the total correct score for each student; and (3) the total number of students who missed each question.

Day: ______	Question #	1	2	3	4	5	6	7	8	9	10	11	12	# Correct
Student Name														
Sample Student			X			X	X						X	8/12
# of Students Missing Each Question														

HOW TO USE THIS BOOK *(cont.)*

Student Item Analysis

Directions: Record an *X* in cells to indicate where the student has missed questions. Add up the totals. You can view: (1) which questions/concepts the student missed; (2) the total correct score per day; and (3) the total number of times each question/concept was missed.

Student Name: Sample Student													
Question	**1**	**2**	**3**	**4**	**5**	**6**	**7**	**8**	**9**	**10**	**11**	**12**	**# Correct**
Day													
1		X			X	X						X	8/12
Total													

HOW TO USE THIS BOOK *(cont.)*

Using the Results to Differentiate Instruction

Once data is gathered and analyzed, teachers can use the results to inform the way they differentiate instruction. The data can help determine which concepts are the most difficult for students and which need additional instructional support and continued practice. Depending on how often the practice pages are scored, results can be considered for instructional support on a daily or weekly basis.

Whole-Class Support

The results of the diagnostic analysis may show that the entire class is struggling with a particular concept or group of concepts. If these concepts have been taught in the past, this indicates that further instruction or reteaching is necessary. If these concepts have not been taught in the past, this data is a great pre-assessment and demonstrates that students do not have a working knowledge of the concepts. Thus, careful planning for the length of the unit(s) or lesson(s) must be considered, and extra frontloading may be required.

Small-Group or Individual Support

The results of the diagnostic analysis may show that an individual or small group of students is struggling with a particular concept or group of concepts. If these concepts have been taught in the past, this indicates that further instruction or reteaching is necessary. Consider pulling aside these students while others are working independently to instruct further on the concept(s). Teachers can also use the results to help identify individuals or groups of proficient students who are ready for enrichment or above-grade level instruction. These students may benefit from independent learning contracts or more challenging activities. Students may also benefit from extra practice using games or computer-based resources.

Digital Resources

Reference page 208 for information about accessing the digital resources and an overview of the contents.

HOW TO USE THIS BOOK *(cont.)*

NCTM Standards

The lessons in this book are aligned to the National Council of Teachers of Mathematics (NCTM) standards. The standards listed on page 4 support the concepts and skills that are consistently presented on each of the practice pages.

Standards Correlations

Shell Education is committed to producing educational materials that are research and standards based. In this effort, we have correlated all of our products to the academic standards of all 50 states, the District of Columbia, and the Department of Defense Dependent Schools, as well as to the college and career readiness standards.

How to Find Standards Correlations

To print a customized correlation report of this product for your state, visit our website at **www.tcmpub.com/shell-education** and follow the on-screen directions. If you require assistance in printing correlation reports, please contact Customer Service at 1-877-777-3450.

Purpose and Intent of Standards

The No Child Left Behind legislation mandates that all states adopt academic standards that identify the skills students will learn in kindergarten through grade twelve. While many states had already adopted academic standards prior to NCLB, the legislation set requirements to ensure the standards were detailed and comprehensive.

Standards are designed to focus instruction and guide adoption of curricula. Standards are statements that describe the criteria necessary for students to meet specific academic goals. They define the knowledge, skills, and content students should acquire at each level. Standards are also used to develop standardized tests to evaluate students' academic progress.

Teachers are required to demonstrate how their lessons meet state standards. State standards are used in development of all of our products, so educators can be assured they meet the academic requirements of each state.

NAME: ______________________________

DIRECTIONS Solve each problem.

1.
$$\begin{array}{r} 30 \\ +\ 16 \\ \hline \end{array}$$

2. 7 x 8 = ______

3. 30 ÷ 6 = ______

4. What is the place value of 6 in the number 6,029?

____

5. Write 0.31 as a fraction.

____

6. What number comes next in the sequence? 1,475; 1,575; 1,675;

____

7. 59 + ______ = 66

8. ______ – 14 = 38

9. What is the volume of the prism?

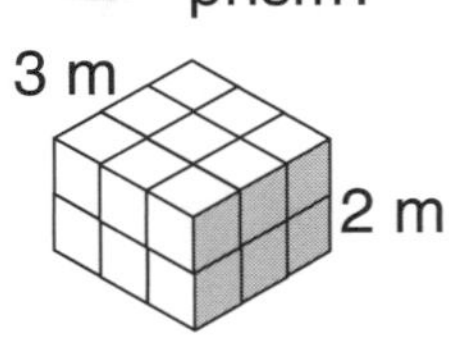

____

10. Name the shape that is located at (F,4).

____

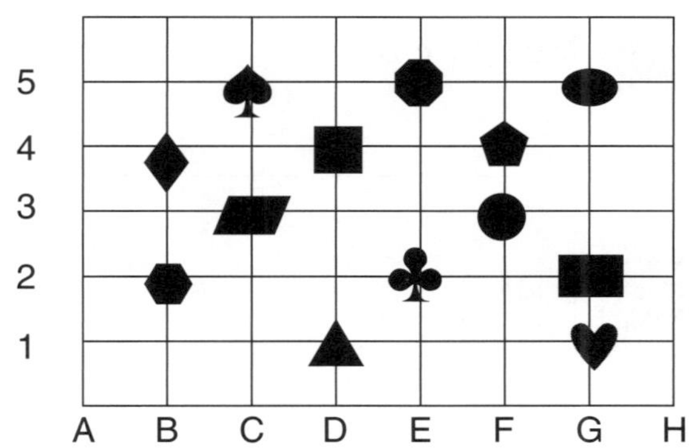

11. Record the data in the table.

Mrs. Cally's class sold boxes of cookies to raise money.

On day 1, 32 boxes were sold.
On day 2, 29 boxes were sold.
On day 3, 30 boxes were sold.
On day 4, 32 boxes were sold.

12. In magic squares, each row, column, and diagonal adds up to the same number. Complete the magic square, using 1–9 only once.

	3	
	5	
6	7	

SCORE

1. Ⓨ Ⓝ
2. Ⓨ Ⓝ
3. Ⓨ Ⓝ
4. Ⓨ Ⓝ
5. Ⓨ Ⓝ
6. Ⓨ Ⓝ
7. Ⓨ Ⓝ
8. Ⓨ Ⓝ
9. Ⓨ Ⓝ
10. Ⓨ Ⓝ
11. Ⓨ Ⓝ
12. Ⓨ Ⓝ

___ / 12 Total

DAY 2

NAME: ____________________

DIRECTIONS Solve each problem.

SCORE

1. Ⓨ Ⓝ
2. Ⓨ Ⓝ
3. Ⓨ Ⓝ
4. Ⓨ Ⓝ
5. Ⓨ Ⓝ
6. Ⓨ Ⓝ
7. Ⓨ Ⓝ
8. Ⓨ Ⓝ
9. Ⓨ Ⓝ
10. Ⓨ Ⓝ
11. Ⓨ Ⓝ
12. Ⓨ Ⓝ

___ / 12
Total

1. 60 – 8 = ______

2. Multiply 6 and 4.

____

3. $5\overline{)45}$

4. 8,000 + 500 + 40 + 9 = ______

5. How many tenths are in $\frac{3}{10}$?

____

6. What number comes next in the sequence? 448, 438, 428,

____

7. ______ + 36 = 125

8. 65 – ☐ = 46

9. Write the time shown.

____

10. Name the triangle with three equal sides.

____

11. Using the spinner below, what is the probability you will spin red?

____

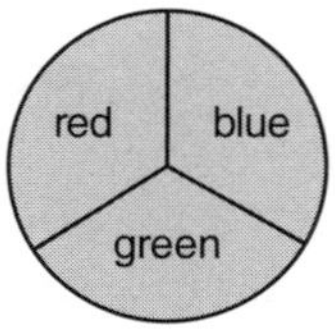

12. A welder can make 2 cuts in a metal bar in 6 minutes. At the same speed, how long will it take him to make 5 cuts in the bar?

____

DAY 3

NAME: ____________________

DIRECTIONS Solve each problem.

1. 29 + 35 = ______

2. 5 • 4 = ______

3. 42 ÷ 6 = ______

4. Round 1,654 to the nearest hundred.

____

5. Is $\frac{1}{4}$ greater than, less than, or equal to $\frac{3}{8}$?

____

6. 45 ÷ 9 + 7= ______

7. 6 ☐ 5 = 30

8. 180 ÷ ☐ = 9

9. Do you use A.M. or P.M. to write 6:35 in the evening?

____

10. How many centimeters are in 39 millimeters?

____

11.

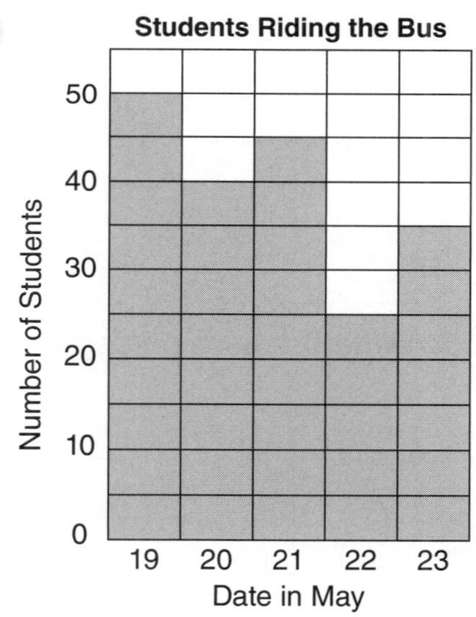

How many students rode the bus on May 20th?

____

12. A small bag of pretzels costs $0.99 and contains 4 ounces. A large bag of pretzels costs $2.99 and contains 15 ounces. Which is the better buy?

____

SCORE

1. Ⓨ Ⓝ
2. Ⓨ Ⓝ
3. Ⓨ Ⓝ
4. Ⓨ Ⓝ
5. Ⓨ Ⓝ
6. Ⓨ Ⓝ
7. Ⓨ Ⓝ
8. Ⓨ Ⓝ
9. Ⓨ Ⓝ
10. Ⓨ Ⓝ
11. Ⓨ Ⓝ
12. Ⓨ Ⓝ

___ / 12

Total

DAY 4

NAME: ____________________

DIRECTIONS Solve each problem.

SCORE

1. Ⓨ Ⓝ
2. Ⓨ Ⓝ
3. Ⓨ Ⓝ
4. Ⓨ Ⓝ
5. Ⓨ Ⓝ
6. Ⓨ Ⓝ
7. Ⓨ Ⓝ
8. Ⓨ Ⓝ
9. Ⓨ Ⓝ
10. Ⓨ Ⓝ
11. Ⓨ Ⓝ
12. Ⓨ Ⓝ

___ / 12 Total

1.
$$\begin{array}{r} 32 \\ -\ 19 \\ \hline \end{array}$$

2. $4 \times 7 =$ ______

3. $270 \div 3 =$ ______

4. $6^2 =$ ______

5. Write 0.1 as a percentage.

____

6. $6 + 1 \cdot 24 =$ ______

7. $149 - \square = 72$

8. $95 \ \square \ 23 = 118$

9. How many days are in one year?

____

10. Complete the chart for the shape below.

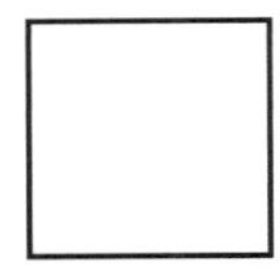

Name the polygon.	
How many sides does the shape have?	
How many angles does the shape have?	
Does the shape have symmetry?	
Is it a plane shape or solid shape?	

11. Imagine that you write each letter of the word *EXCELLENT* on a different card and then shuffle the cards. You turn the deck facedown on a table and turn over the top card. What is the probability that you will turn over a *T*?

____

12. Trena's jump rope is 3.5 feet long. Jackie's is 3.8 feet long. How much longer is Jackie's jump rope than Trena's?

____

DAY 5

NAME: ______________________________

DIRECTIONS Solve each problem.

1.

$$\begin{array}{r} 20 \\ +\ 12 \\ \hline \end{array}$$

2. 9 x 9 = ______

3. $5\overline{)35}$

4. What is the numeral for fifteen?

____

5. $\frac{1}{8}$ of 32 is ______.

6. Find the missing number.

3,296; 3,286; ______; 3,266

7. 140 ÷ ☐ = 10

8. Solve for *x* when *x* + 9 = 49.

x = ______________

9. Calculate the area of a square with 7 cm sides.

____

10. Use a protractor to measure the angle. Then identify it as either *acute*, *reflex*, *obtuse*, or *straight*.

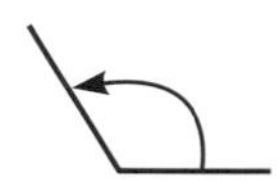

Size	
Name	

11. What is the mean of this set of data?

45, 31, 26, 46

____

12. A snail is climbing a brick wall that is 15 m high. It climbs up 3 m every day but slides down 1 m every night. How many days will it take to reach the top of the wall?

____

SCORE

1. Ⓨ Ⓝ
2. Ⓨ Ⓝ
3. Ⓨ Ⓝ
4. Ⓨ Ⓝ
5. Ⓨ Ⓝ
6. Ⓨ Ⓝ
7. Ⓨ Ⓝ
8. Ⓨ Ⓝ
9. Ⓨ Ⓝ
10. Ⓨ Ⓝ
11. Ⓨ Ⓝ
12. Ⓨ Ⓝ

___ / 12
Total

DAY
6

NAME: ____________________

DIRECTIONS Solve each problem.

SCORE

1. Ⓨ Ⓝ
2. Ⓨ Ⓝ
3. Ⓨ Ⓝ
4. Ⓨ Ⓝ
5. Ⓨ Ⓝ
6. Ⓨ Ⓝ
7. Ⓨ Ⓝ
8. Ⓨ Ⓝ
9. Ⓨ Ⓝ
10. Ⓨ Ⓝ
11. Ⓨ Ⓝ
12. Ⓨ Ⓝ

___ / 12
Total

1. $40 - 9 =$ ______

2. $7 \times 6 =$ ______

3. $42 \div 7 =$ ______

4. What is 1,000 less than 1,416?

____

5. Is $\frac{3}{5}$ greater than, less than, or equal to $\frac{6}{10}$?

____

6. $27 - 13 + 18 =$ ______

7. Solve for *x*.
$x - 25 = 53$

$x =$ ______

8. $\frac{12}{20} = \frac{3}{\square}$

9. How many minutes pass from 4:21 P.M. to 4:59 P.M.?

____

10. Draw a top view of the cylinder.

11. Which spinner has a 25% probability of landing on red?

____

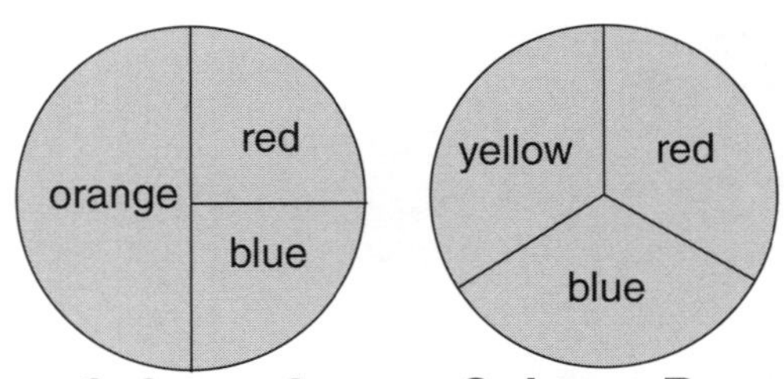

Spinner A **Spinner B**

12. Compare a triangular pyramid with a triangular prism.

	Faces	Edges	Vertices
Triangular Pyramid			
Triangular Prism			

NAME: ____________________

DIRECTIONS Solve each problem.

1. 45 + 27 = ______

2.

$$\begin{array}{r} 6 \\ \times\ 8 \\ \hline \end{array}$$

3. Calculate 36 divided by 6.

____

4. List the factors of 40.

____

5. Write 0.61 as a fraction.

____

6. 126 ÷ 9 • 2 = ______

7. Solve for *n*.

$\frac{1}{4} \cdot n = 4$

$n =$ ______

8. ☐ x 10 = 30

9. Calculate the perimeter of the shape.

____

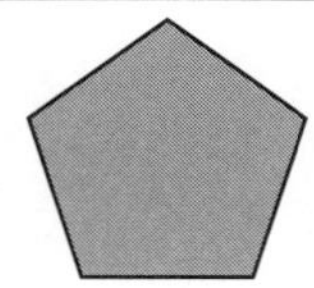

4 cm

10. How many faces are on the solid?

____

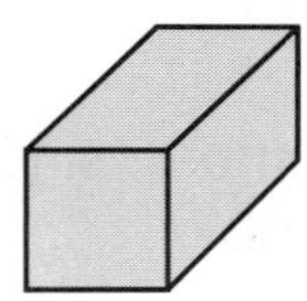

11. Two red cubes, two green cylinders, and three yellow rectangular prisms were put in a bag. If you reach into the bag and pull out an object, what is the probability that you will pull out a green cylinder?

____

12. Shaundra is 5 years older than her brother. If the sum of their ages is 31, how old is Shaundra?

____

SCORE

1. Ⓨ Ⓝ
2. Ⓨ Ⓝ
3. Ⓨ Ⓝ
4. Ⓨ Ⓝ
5. Ⓨ Ⓝ
6. Ⓨ Ⓝ
7. Ⓨ Ⓝ
8. Ⓨ Ⓝ
9. Ⓨ Ⓝ
10. Ⓨ Ⓝ
11. Ⓨ Ⓝ
12. Ⓨ Ⓝ

___ / 12 Total

DAY
8

NAME: ____________________________________

DIRECTIONS Solve each problem.

SCORE

1. Ⓨ Ⓝ
2. Ⓨ Ⓝ
3. Ⓨ Ⓝ
4. Ⓨ Ⓝ
5. Ⓨ Ⓝ
6. Ⓨ Ⓝ
7. Ⓨ Ⓝ
8. Ⓨ Ⓝ
9. Ⓨ Ⓝ
10. Ⓨ Ⓝ
11. Ⓨ Ⓝ
12. Ⓨ Ⓝ

___ / 12 Total

1. $\begin{array}{r} 37 \\ -\ \ 8 \\ \hline \end{array}$

2. $4 \cdot 9 =$ ______

3. $280 \div 4 =$ ______

4. What number is 10 more than 8,358?

____

5. $\frac{1}{3}$ of 15 is ______.

6. Write the rule for this pattern.
3, 6, 9, 12, 15

____

7. 84 ☐ 56 = 28

8. Find a when $120 \div a = 12$.

$a =$ ______

9. How many grams are in 9.5 kilograms?

____

10. Are opposite sides equal in length on a rectangle?

____

11. Which number is the outlier in this data set?
9, 12, 32, 8, 11

____

12. The Handy family drinks 20 pints of milk each week. How many gallons of milk do they drink each week?

____

DAY 9

NAME: ______________________

DIRECTIONS Solve each problem.

1. 38 + 6 = ______

2. 5 x 9 = ______

3. What is the quotient when 63 is divided by 9?

____

4. List the first four multiples of 2.

____

5. Is $\frac{2}{3}$ equal to $\frac{6}{10}$?

____

6. Write the rule for this pattern.
5, 20, 80, 320

____

7. 9 x ☐ = 99

8. 35 ☐ 26 = 61

9. How many millimeters are in 6.5 centimeters?

____

10. What is the diameter of a circle with a 4.2 cm radius?

____

11. **Cookies Baked**

Molly	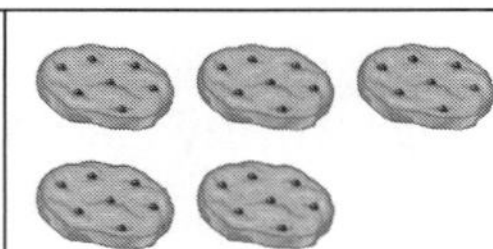
Jake	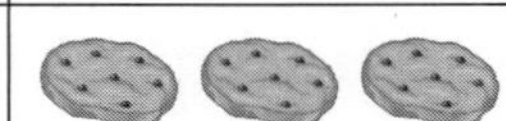
Lucas	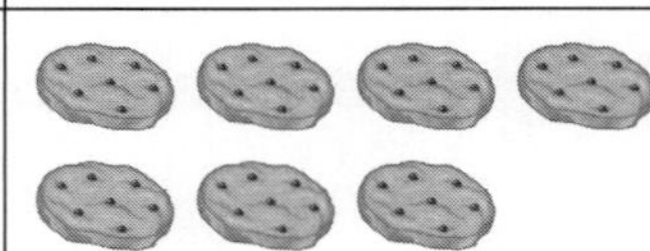
Mindy	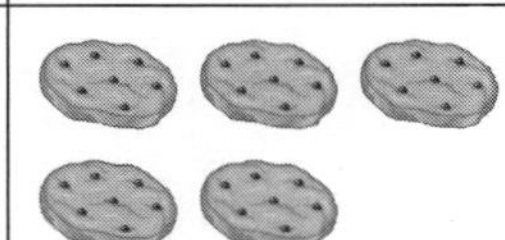

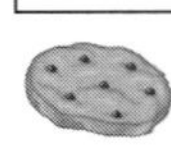 = 1 dozen cookies

Who baked the most cookies?

____

12. Nine children join hands to form a circle. How many hands are joined?

____

SCORE

1. Ⓨ Ⓝ
2. Ⓨ Ⓝ
3. Ⓨ Ⓝ
4. Ⓨ Ⓝ
5. Ⓨ Ⓝ
6. Ⓨ Ⓝ
7. Ⓨ Ⓝ
8. Ⓨ Ⓝ
9. Ⓨ Ⓝ
10. Ⓨ Ⓝ
11. Ⓨ Ⓝ
12. Ⓨ Ⓝ

___ / 12 Total

NAME: ______________________

DIRECTIONS Solve each problem.

SCORE

1. Ⓨ Ⓝ
2. Ⓨ Ⓝ
3. Ⓨ Ⓝ
4. Ⓨ Ⓝ
5. Ⓨ Ⓝ
6. Ⓨ Ⓝ
7. Ⓨ Ⓝ
8. Ⓨ Ⓝ
9. Ⓨ Ⓝ
10. Ⓨ Ⓝ
11. Ⓨ Ⓝ
12. Ⓨ Ⓝ

___ / 12
Total

1. $-5 + 10 =$ ______

2. $9 \times 6 =$ ______

3. $8\overline{)40}$

4. How many digits are in 35,920?

____

5. Write 0.7 as a percentage.

____

6. $192 \div 2 + 20 =$ ______

7. Solve for *s*.
$26s = 78$

$s =$ ______

8. 160 ☐ 10 = 16

9. Record the line length shown.

____

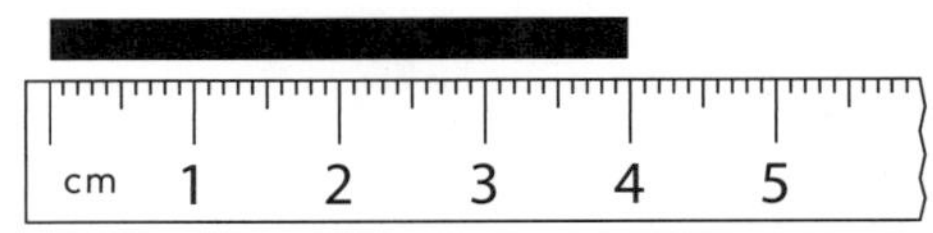

10. Use a protractor to measure the angle.

____

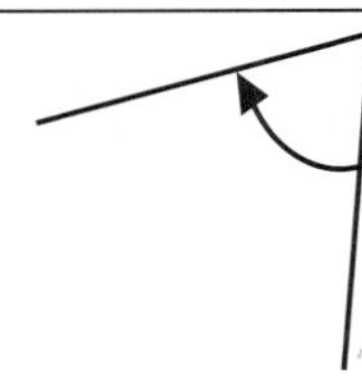

11. A box of a dozen donuts contains 5 chocolate donuts, 4 sprinkled donuts, 2 lemon donuts, and 1 raspberry-filled donut. If you reach in a box and grab one donut, what is the probability that it will be a raspberry-filled donut?

____

12. Complete the addition table.

+	22	26	33	35	41	46
19						
29						
39						
49						

NAME: ____________________

DIRECTIONS Solve each problem.

1. $99 + 27$

2. 4×4

3. $72 \div 9 =$ ______

4. What digit is in the tens place in 69,321?

______

5. Write $\frac{9}{4}$ as a mixed number.

______

6. What number comes next?
120, 140, 160, 180,

______

7. 40 x ☐ = 80

8. 69 ☐ 58 = 127

9. Use A.M. or P.M. to write 3:47 in the morning.

______

10. How many vertices does an octagon have?

______

11. Is it *impossible*, *unlikely*, *likely*, or *certain* that you will blink in the next two minutes?

______

12. Round each item on the bill to the nearest nickel to estimate the total.

______

$3.21
$1.26
$2.55
$0.86
$1.93
$0.21

SCORE

1. Ⓨ Ⓝ
2. Ⓨ Ⓝ
3. Ⓨ Ⓝ
4. Ⓨ Ⓝ
5. Ⓨ Ⓝ
6. Ⓨ Ⓝ
7. Ⓨ Ⓝ
8. Ⓨ Ⓝ
9. Ⓨ Ⓝ
10. Ⓨ Ⓝ
11. Ⓨ Ⓝ
12. Ⓨ Ⓝ

___ / 12
Total

NAME: ______________________________

DIRECTIONS Solve each problem.

SCORE

1. Ⓨ Ⓝ
2. Ⓨ Ⓝ
3. Ⓨ Ⓝ
4. Ⓨ Ⓝ
5. Ⓨ Ⓝ
6. Ⓨ Ⓝ
7. Ⓨ Ⓝ
8. Ⓨ Ⓝ
9. Ⓨ Ⓝ
10. Ⓨ Ⓝ
11. Ⓨ Ⓝ
12. Ⓨ Ⓝ

___ / 12
Total

1. 96 – 14 = ______

2. –9 x 3 = ______

3. Divide 320 into 8 equal groups.

____

4. Write the expanded notation for 15,729.

____

____

5. $\frac{1}{2}$ of 24 is ______.

6. 12 – 8 ÷ 4 = ______

7. 73 – ☐ = 48

8. $\frac{1}{\square}$ of 150 is 15.

9. How many kilograms are in 5,000 grams?

____

10. How many sides does a parallelogram have?

____

11. What is the probability you will spin a blue?

____

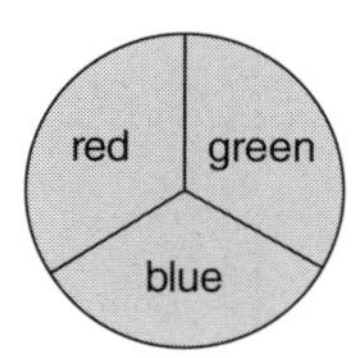

12. Hillary spent $23.45 on new mats for her car. She spent $9.99 on a car wash. How much did she spend on her car?

____

NAME: ________________________

DIRECTIONS Solve each problem.

1. –59 + 37 = ______

2. 8 • 6 = ______

3. $7\overline{)42}$

4. Is 7,890 closer to 7,000 or 8,000?

____

5. How many fifths are in $\frac{4}{5}$?

____

6. 4 • 7 ÷ 4 = ______

7. Find *w*.
$\frac{w}{3} = 5$

w = ______

8. 4 ☐ 22 = 88

9. Calculate the area of the shape.

____

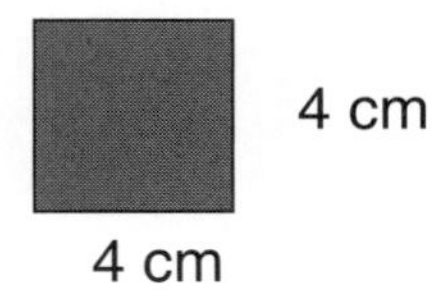

10. Name the solid shape.

____

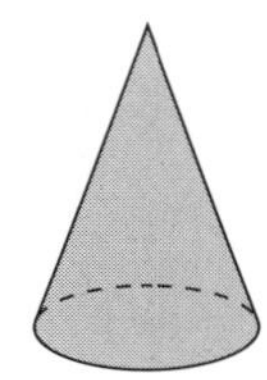

11.

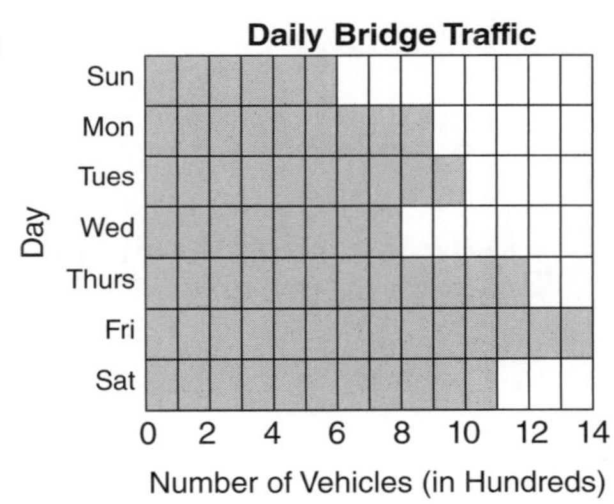

On which day were there 600 vehicles?

____

12. Complete the chart to show your understanding of fractions, decimals, and percents.

Fraction	Decimal	Percent
$\frac{2}{5}$		

SCORE

1. Ⓨ Ⓝ
2. Ⓨ Ⓝ
3. Ⓨ Ⓝ
4. Ⓨ Ⓝ
5. Ⓨ Ⓝ
6. Ⓨ Ⓝ
7. Ⓨ Ⓝ
8. Ⓨ Ⓝ
9. Ⓨ Ⓝ
10. Ⓨ Ⓝ
11. Ⓨ Ⓝ
12. Ⓨ Ⓝ

___ / 12
Total

NAME: ______________________

DIRECTIONS Solve each problem.

SCORE

1. Ⓨ Ⓝ
2. Ⓨ Ⓝ
3. Ⓨ Ⓝ
4. Ⓨ Ⓝ
5. Ⓨ Ⓝ
6. Ⓨ Ⓝ
7. Ⓨ Ⓝ
8. Ⓨ Ⓝ
9. Ⓨ Ⓝ
10. Ⓨ Ⓝ
11. Ⓨ Ⓝ
12. Ⓨ Ⓝ

___ / 12
Total

1. $40 + 36 =$ ______

2.
$$\begin{array}{r} 8 \\ \times\ 4 \\ \hline \end{array}$$

3. $56 \div (-7) =$ ______

4. Is 5 a prime number?

____

5. Write $\frac{10}{3}$ as a mixed number.

____

6. Write the rule for the pattern.
1, 5, 9, 13, 17

____

7. Solve for *x*.
$\frac{x}{10} = 7$

$x =$ ______

8. $70 \;\square\; 63 = 133$

9. What is the volume of a cube with 4 cm sides?

____

10. Complete the chart for the shape below.

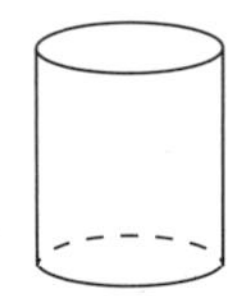

Name the figure.	
How many surfaces?	
How many vertices?	
Does it stack or roll?	
Is it a plane shape or a solid shape?	

11. The numbers 20 through 30 were written on individual cards and placed in a bag. If you take one card from the bag, what is the probability that it will have a 2 on it?

____

12. Ten blocks were placed in a line at 10 cm intervals. Ten pennies were placed between the first two blocks, 20 pennies were placed between the next two blocks, then 30 pennies, then 40 pennies, and so on. How much money was used to fill the spaces?

____

NAME: ____________________

DIRECTIONS Solve each problem.

1.
$$\begin{array}{r} 35 \\ -\ 19 \\ \hline \end{array}$$

2. 6 x 3 = ______

3. 81 ÷ 9 = ______

4. What is the next odd number after 31?

____

5. Write $\frac{72}{35}$ as a mixed number.

____

6. (17 – 7) + 6 = ______

7. 75 ☐ 80 = 155

8. Find f when $27f = 81$.

f = ______

9. How many seconds are in $2\frac{1}{2}$ minutes?

____

10. Is 69° less than a right angle?

____

11. Sue has blue pants, an orange skirt, and a yellow shirt. List all the possible outfits she can wear.

____

12. Complete the factor wheel to show all the factors of 10.

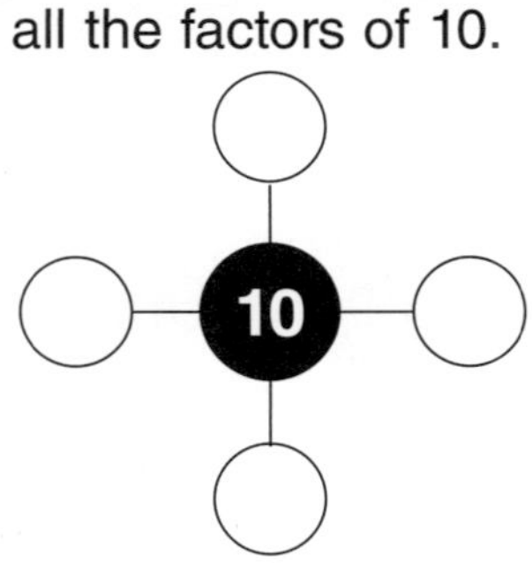

SCORE

1. Ⓨ Ⓝ
2. Ⓨ Ⓝ
3. Ⓨ Ⓝ
4. Ⓨ Ⓝ
5. Ⓨ Ⓝ
6. Ⓨ Ⓝ
7. Ⓨ Ⓝ
8. Ⓨ Ⓝ
9. Ⓨ Ⓝ
10. Ⓨ Ⓝ
11. Ⓨ Ⓝ
12. Ⓨ Ⓝ

___ / 12 Total

NAME: ____________________

DIRECTIONS Solve each problem.

SCORE

1. Ⓨ Ⓝ
2. Ⓨ Ⓝ
3. Ⓨ Ⓝ
4. Ⓨ Ⓝ
5. Ⓨ Ⓝ
6. Ⓨ Ⓝ
7. Ⓨ Ⓝ
8. Ⓨ Ⓝ
9. Ⓨ Ⓝ
10. Ⓨ Ⓝ
11. Ⓨ Ⓝ
12. Ⓨ Ⓝ

___ / 12 Total

1. 90 + (–8) = ______

2. $\begin{array}{r} 6 \\ \times\ 5 \\ \hline \end{array}$

3. 450 ÷ 5 = ______

4. Is –7 a negative or a positive number?

____

5. Write $\frac{14}{3}$ as a mixed number.

____

6. 7 • 8 + 6 • 5 = ______

7. 20 x ☐ = 400

8. Find *d*. *d* – 47 = 231

d = ______

9. 2 pints = ______ quarts

10. Draw a side view of the cone.

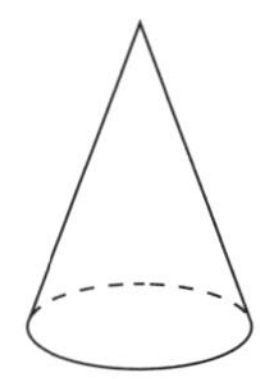

11. What is the probability the spinner will land on *soccer*?

____

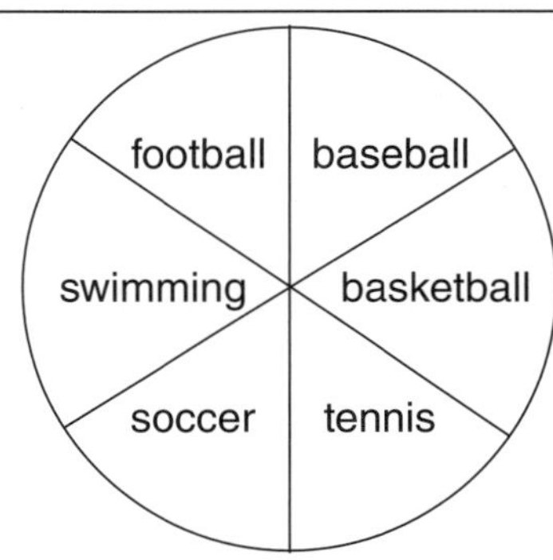

12. Mitch, Miranda, and Evan added their heights together. They got a total of 15 feet 3 inches. Convert that measurement to inches.

____

DAY 17

NAME: ______________________________

DIRECTIONS Solve each problem.

1. Calculate 35 less than 67.

____

2. $(-4) \times (-5) =$ ______

3. $6\overline{)36}$

4. Is 6 a factor of 30?

____

5. $\frac{3}{5}$ of 35 is ______.

6. $18 \div 3 - 6 \bullet 1 =$ ______

7. $\frac{3}{8}$ of ☐ is 9.

8. Find x. $x + 43 = 189$

$x =$ ______

9. How many months are in 3 years?

____

10. How many vertices are on the solid?

____

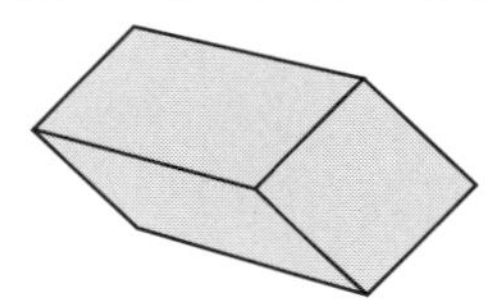

11. You have 2 bags. Each bag has 6 marbles. Bag One has 4 blue and 2 red marbles. Bag Two has 2 blue and 4 red marbles.

Do you have a greater probability of pulling a blue marble from Bag One or Bag Two?

____

12. Use the four shapes below to complete the grid so that the same shape does not appear twice in any row or column.

●	▲	⬢	■

SCORE

1. Ⓨ Ⓝ
2. Ⓨ Ⓝ
3. Ⓨ Ⓝ
4. Ⓨ Ⓝ
5. Ⓨ Ⓝ
6. Ⓨ Ⓝ
7. Ⓨ Ⓝ
8. Ⓨ Ⓝ
9. Ⓨ Ⓝ
10. Ⓨ Ⓝ
11. Ⓨ Ⓝ
12. Ⓨ Ⓝ

___ / 12 Total

DAY
18

NAME: ____________________

DIRECTIONS Solve each problem.

SCORE

1. Ⓨ Ⓝ
2. Ⓨ Ⓝ
3. Ⓨ Ⓝ
4. Ⓨ Ⓝ
5. Ⓨ Ⓝ
6. Ⓨ Ⓝ
7. Ⓨ Ⓝ
8. Ⓨ Ⓝ
9. Ⓨ Ⓝ
10. Ⓨ Ⓝ
11. Ⓨ Ⓝ
12. Ⓨ Ⓝ

___ / 12
Total

1. $58 + 6 =$ ______

2.
$$\begin{array}{r} 6 \\ \times\ 7 \\ \hline \end{array}$$

3. $-56 \div 7 =$ ______

4. What is one thousand less than 89,257?

____

5. Write 0.65 as a fraction.

____

6. Write the next number in this pattern. 10, 11, 20, 21, 30, 31,

____

7. Find h.
$59 + h = 129$

$h =$ ______

8. 91 ☐ 58 = 33

9. Calculate the perimeter of the shape.

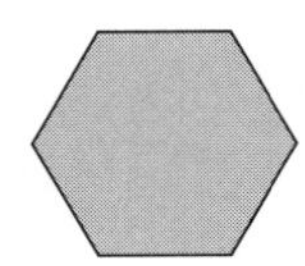
3 cm

10. A square has ______ diagonals.

11. Inside a bag of candy there are 16 lollipops, 12 pieces of chocolate, and 7 pieces of licorice. If you reach into the bag and grab a piece of candy, what is the probability you will grab a lollipop?

____

12. Use three of the numbers 3, 4, 5, 12, or 15 to complete the number sentence. Do not use any number more than once.

(______ – ______) ÷ ______ = 3

NAME: ______________________________

DIRECTIONS Solve each problem.

1. 95 + (–68) = ______

2. 9 x 4 = ______

3. Divide 72 by 9.

____

4. Is 72 evenly divisible by 4?

____

5. Write 0.45 as a percentage.

____

6. 225 ÷ 9 ÷ 5 = ______

7. Find *b*.

$\frac{b}{4} = 7.25$

b = ______

8. $\frac{1}{6}$ of ☐ = 5

9. How many millimeters are in 7.5 centimeters?

____

10. Do parallel lines meet at a 30° angle?

____

11. In a game, the probability of the spinner landing on a 2 is 1:3. How many times would you expect to land on a 2 if you spin the spinner 6 times?

____

12. An explorer walked 1 km west, 3 km south, 5 km west, 4 km north, 3 km east, 2 km north, 6 km west, and 4 km south to reach point D. At which point did he begin?

____

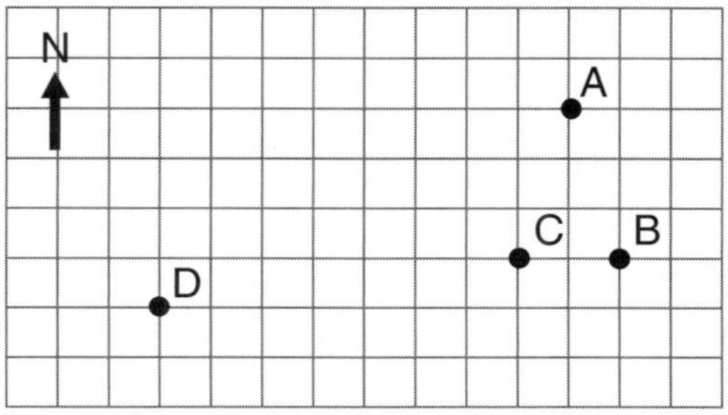

1 square = 1 square km

SCORE

1. Ⓨ Ⓝ
2. Ⓨ Ⓝ
3. Ⓨ Ⓝ
4. Ⓨ Ⓝ
5. Ⓨ Ⓝ
6. Ⓨ Ⓝ
7. Ⓨ Ⓝ
8. Ⓨ Ⓝ
9. Ⓨ Ⓝ
10. Ⓨ Ⓝ
11. Ⓨ Ⓝ
12. Ⓨ Ⓝ

___ / 12 Total

DAY 20

NAME: ____________________

DIRECTIONS Solve each problem.

SCORE

1. Ⓨ Ⓝ
2. Ⓨ Ⓝ
3. Ⓨ Ⓝ
4. Ⓨ Ⓝ
5. Ⓨ Ⓝ
6. Ⓨ Ⓝ
7. Ⓨ Ⓝ
8. Ⓨ Ⓝ
9. Ⓨ Ⓝ
10. Ⓨ Ⓝ
11. Ⓨ Ⓝ
12. Ⓨ Ⓝ

___ / 12 Total

1. $\begin{array}{r} 154 \\ +\ 20 \\ \hline \end{array}$

2. $-5 \times -5 =$ ______

3. $840 \div 10 =$ ______

4. Find the smallest possible two-digit number using the digits 2, 7, and 3.

____

5. Write $3\frac{2}{5}$ as an improper fraction.

____

6. $4 + 7 \cdot 9 =$ ______

7. 71 ☐ 48 = 23

8. Solve for r when $\frac{r}{4} = 0.75$.

$r =$ ______

9. What time is 16 minutes after 9:53 A.M.?

____

10. Is this angle acute, obtuse, or reflex?

____

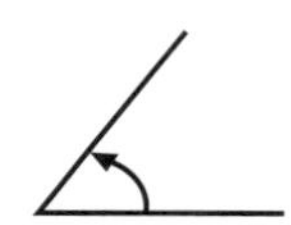

11. The numbers 0–9 are on the calculator. If you randomly push one number on the calculator, what is the probability that you will push 8?

____

12. On a skiing trip, there are five people but only three pairs of skis. How many different groups of three could ski?

____

NAME: ____________________

DIRECTIONS Solve each problem.

1. 92 – 37 = ______

2. 7 • 4 = ______

3. $9\overline{)54}$

4. What is the place value of 4 in the number 74,589?

____

5. Write $2\frac{2}{5}$ as an improper fraction.

____

6. What number comes next? 645, 545, 445,

____

7. $\frac{3}{\square}$ of 32 is 24.

8. 112 $\square$ 8 = 14

9. Write 25 past 7 on the digital clock.

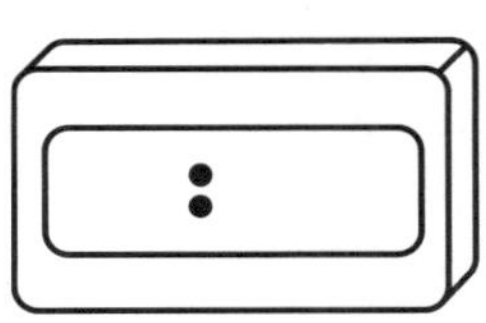

10. Which line segment is parallel to line *D*?

____

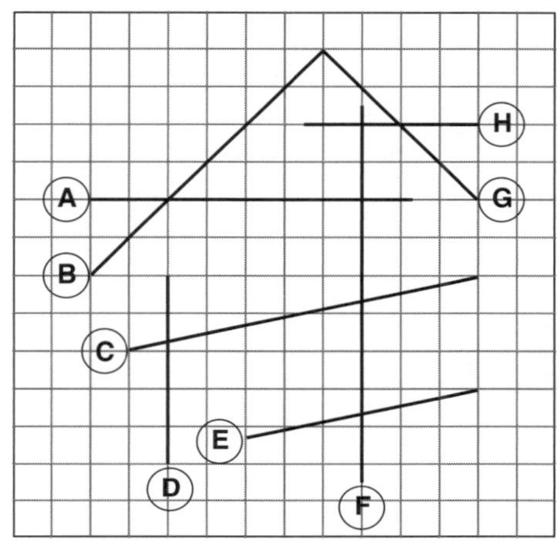

11. Record the following data in the table.

Mitch hit three home runs.

Sam hit two home runs.

Tim did not hit any home runs.

Dale hit three home runs.

Player	Home Runs

12. Michelle spent $52.46 at the grocery store. She spent $23.25 at the gas station. She spent $14.50 for lunch. If she started with a $100.00 bill, how much money does she have left?

____

SCORE

1. Y N
2. Y N
3. Y N
4. Y N
5. Y N
6. Y N
7. Y N
8. Y N
9. Y N
10. Y N
11. Y N
12. Y N

___ / 12 Total

DAY 22

NAME: ______________________

DIRECTIONS Solve each problem.

SCORE

1. Ⓨ Ⓝ
2. Ⓨ Ⓝ
3. Ⓨ Ⓝ
4. Ⓨ Ⓝ
5. Ⓨ Ⓝ
6. Ⓨ Ⓝ
7. Ⓨ Ⓝ
8. Ⓨ Ⓝ
9. Ⓨ Ⓝ
10. Ⓨ Ⓝ
11. Ⓨ Ⓝ
12. Ⓨ Ⓝ

___ / 12 Total

1. 45 – (–23) = ______

2.

$$\begin{array}{r} 4 \\ \times\ 2 \\ \hline \end{array}$$

3. 64 ÷ 8 = ______

4. 500 + 40 + 8 = ______

5. Write 97% as a decimal.

____

6. Write the rule for the pattern.
1, 2, 4, 7, 11

____

7. 253 ☐ 136 = 389

8. $\frac{1}{8}$ of ☐ is 5.

9. How many grams are in 7 kilograms?

____

10. What is the sum of the angles inside a square?

____

11. What is the probability that you will spin green?

____

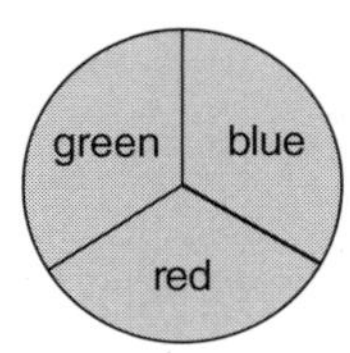

12. Place each number 1 through 9 in the circles so that the sum of the numbers along each side of the triangle is 20.

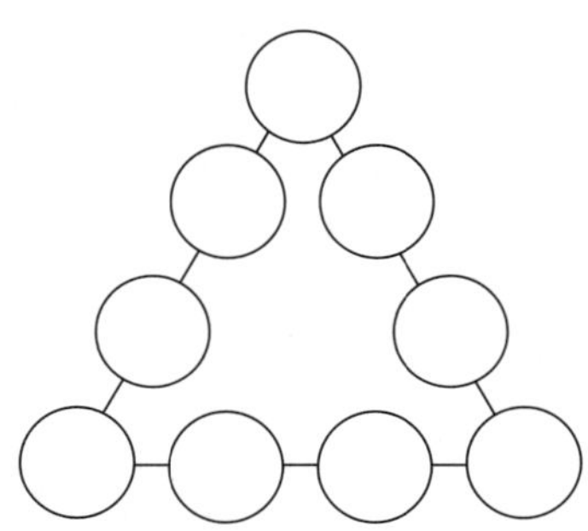

DAY 23

NAME: ______________________

DIRECTIONS Solve each problem.

1. 70 – 12 = ______

2. –4 x 8 = ______

3. What is the quotient when 72 is divided by 8?

____

4. Round the number 8,568 to the nearest thousand.

____

5. $\frac{9}{10}$ of 60 is ______.

6. 56 ÷ 7 • 3 = ______

7. 58 ☐ 35 = 23

8. Find *g*.
$g + 13 + 25 = 53$

g = ______

9. What is the volume of the prism if each cube is 1 cm³?

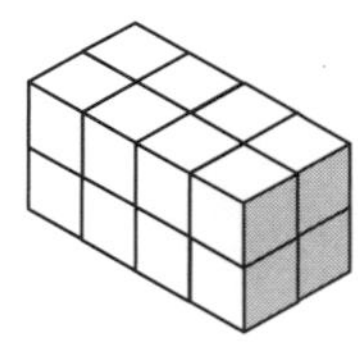

____

10. Circle the correct cross-section for the solid.

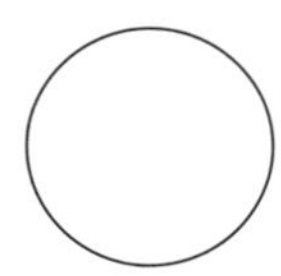

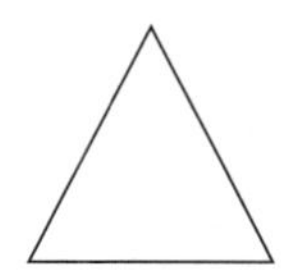

11. Steve, Mark, Melissa, Joe, and Mary are in a group. They randomly line up at the door. What is the probability that the first person in the line is a boy?

____

12. Circle the factors of the given product.

Possible Factors									Product
6	7	4	8	3	15	9	16	2	36

SCORE

1. Ⓨ Ⓝ
2. Ⓨ Ⓝ
3. Ⓨ Ⓝ
4. Ⓨ Ⓝ
5. Ⓨ Ⓝ
6. Ⓨ Ⓝ
7. Ⓨ Ⓝ
8. Ⓨ Ⓝ
9. Ⓨ Ⓝ
10. Ⓨ Ⓝ
11. Ⓨ Ⓝ
12. Ⓨ Ⓝ

___ / 12
Total

DAY
24

NAME: ____________________

DIRECTIONS Solve each problem.

SCORE

1. Ⓨ Ⓝ
2. Ⓨ Ⓝ
3. Ⓨ Ⓝ
4. Ⓨ Ⓝ
5. Ⓨ Ⓝ
6. Ⓨ Ⓝ
7. Ⓨ Ⓝ
8. Ⓨ Ⓝ
9. Ⓨ Ⓝ
10. Ⓨ Ⓝ
11. Ⓨ Ⓝ
12. Ⓨ Ⓝ

___ / 12

Total

1. Add 84 to 16.

____

2. Calculate the number of people in 5 groups with 8 people per group.

____

3. $950 \div 8 =$ ______

4. $3^2 =$ ______

5. Is $\frac{2}{5}$ equal to $\frac{3}{10}$?

____

6. $51 \div 3 - 54 \div 9 =$ ______

7. $148 \; \square \; 37 = 111$

8. Find *p*.
$52p = 208$.

$p =$ ______

9. How many meters are in $\frac{3}{4}$ kilometers?

____

10. Complete the chart for the shape.

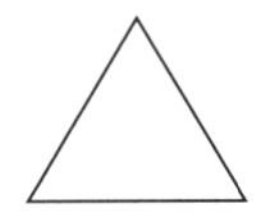

Name the figure.	
How many sides?	
How many angles?	
Does it have symmetry?	
Is it a plane shape or a solid shape?	

11. **Time Spent on Homework**

Day	Minutes
Monday	52
Tuesday	45
Wednesday	30
Thursday	45
Friday	0

How much time was spent on homework on Tuesday?

____

12. Faye bought 3 pizzas for lunch. Each pizza had 10 slices in it. If 90% of the lunch was eaten, how many slices were left?

____

DAY 25

NAME: ____________________

DIRECTIONS Solve each problem.

1. 95 – 68 = ______

2. $\begin{array}{r} 8 \\ \times\ 7 \\ \hline \end{array}$

3. $9\overline{)45}$

4. Write the ordinal number for thirty-one.

____

5. Is 95% equivalent to 0.95?

____

6. $8^2 + 7^2 =$ ______

7. Find *c*.
$3.4 + c = 8.1$

$c =$ ______

8. ☐ x 4 = 128

9. If it took you from 6:21 A.M. until 7:03 A.M. to get ready for school, how many minutes did it take you to get ready?

____

10. Is 145° an obtuse angle?

____

11. What is the mode of this set of numbers?

31, 28, 35, 31, 42

____

12. In magic squares, each row, column, and diagonal adds up to the same number. Complete the magic square. Use each number 1–9 only once.

2		4
	5	
		8

SCORE

1. Ⓨ Ⓝ
2. Ⓨ Ⓝ
3. Ⓨ Ⓝ
4. Ⓨ Ⓝ
5. Ⓨ Ⓝ
6. Ⓨ Ⓝ
7. Ⓨ Ⓝ
8. Ⓨ Ⓝ
9. Ⓨ Ⓝ
10. Ⓨ Ⓝ
11. Ⓨ Ⓝ
12. Ⓨ Ⓝ

___ / 12
Total

DAY 26

NAME: ______________________

DIRECTIONS Solve each problem.

SCORE

1. Ⓨ Ⓝ
2. Ⓨ Ⓝ
3. Ⓨ Ⓝ
4. Ⓨ Ⓝ
5. Ⓨ Ⓝ
6. Ⓨ Ⓝ
7. Ⓨ Ⓝ
8. Ⓨ Ⓝ
9. Ⓨ Ⓝ
10. Ⓨ Ⓝ
11. Ⓨ Ⓝ
12. Ⓨ Ⓝ

___ / 12 Total

1.
$$\begin{array}{r} 19 \\ +\ 24 \\ \hline \end{array}$$

2. $7 \cdot 9 =$ ______

3. Divide –48 by 8.

____

4. Is 9,642 greater than 9,462?

____

5. Write $4\frac{1}{4}$ as an improper fraction.

____

6. Write the rule for the pattern.
100, 81, 64, 49, 36

____

7. Find *k*.
$3k = 159$

$k =$ ______

8. 45 ☐ 8 = 5.625

9. Calculate the area of the shape.

____

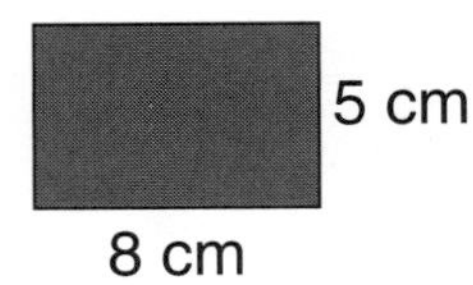

10. Draw a top view of the cube.

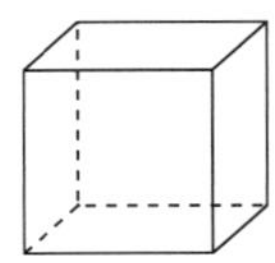

11.

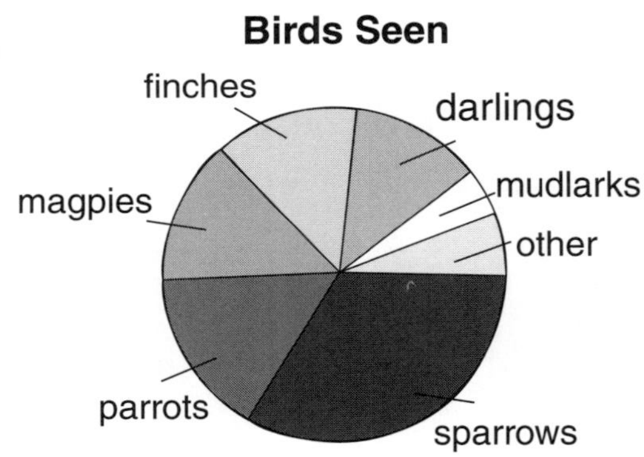

Were more magpies seen than mudlarks?

____

12. Mia has a bag full of $0.10 and $0.25 coins. In how many different ways can she pay for a drink that costs $1.50?

____

DAY 27

NAME: ______________________________

DIRECTIONS Solve each problem.

1.
$$\begin{array}{r} 52 \\ -\ 9 \\ \hline \end{array}$$

2. 8 x 3 = ______

3. $7\overline{)49}$

4. List all of the factors of 20.

____

5. Write the decimal equivalent of 80%.

____

6. 50 + 8 – 23 = ______

7. 9.9 ☐ 6.5 = 3.4

8. $\frac{5}{10} + \square = \frac{7}{10}$

9. What time is 15 minutes after 6:42?

____

10. How many vertices does a sphere have?

____

11. Two red cubes, two green cylinders, and three yellow pyramids were put into a bag. What is the probability that you will pull out a yellow pyramid from the bag?

____

12. The perimeter of a square room is 20 m. What is the cost of carpeting the room if carpet costs $10.00 per square meter?

____

SCORE

1. Ⓨ Ⓝ
2. Ⓨ Ⓝ
3. Ⓨ Ⓝ
4. Ⓨ Ⓝ
5. Ⓨ Ⓝ
6. Ⓨ Ⓝ
7. Ⓨ Ⓝ
8. Ⓨ Ⓝ
9. Ⓨ Ⓝ
10. Ⓨ Ⓝ
11. Ⓨ Ⓝ
12. Ⓨ Ⓝ

___ / 12 Total

NAME: ______________________

DIRECTIONS Solve each problem.

SCORE

1. Ⓨ Ⓝ
2. Ⓨ Ⓝ
3. Ⓨ Ⓝ
4. Ⓨ Ⓝ
5. Ⓨ Ⓝ
6. Ⓨ Ⓝ
7. Ⓨ Ⓝ
8. Ⓨ Ⓝ
9. Ⓨ Ⓝ
10. Ⓨ Ⓝ
11. Ⓨ Ⓝ
12. Ⓨ Ⓝ

___ / 12 Total

1. What is the sum of 175 and 89?

____

2. $6 \cdot -6 =$ _______

3. $28 \div 4 =$ _______

4. Is 27 a prime number? _______

5. $\frac{3}{8}$ of 40 is _______.

6. $100 - (9 - 3)^2 =$ _______

7. Find z.
$126 + z = 259$

$z =$ _______

8. Solve for a if $29a = 87$.

$a =$ _______

9. Calculate the perimeter of the regular octogon.

____

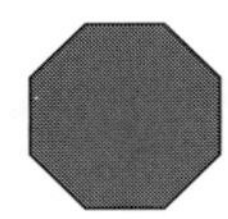

2 cm

10. How many sides does a quadrilateral have?

____

11. What is the outlier in this data set?

23, 31, 28, 73, 19

____

12. List the shapes in order of size from smallest area to largest area.

____

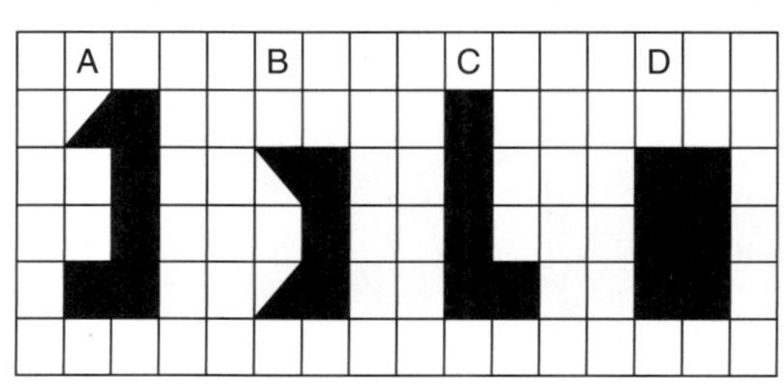

NAME: ______________________________

DIRECTIONS Solve each problem.

1. 54 – 28 = ______

2.

$$\begin{array}{r} 8 \\ \times\ 8 \\ \hline \end{array}$$

3. Divide 24 into 6 equal groups.

____

4. List the first three multiples of 7.

____

5. $5 \times \frac{2}{5} =$ ______

6. Fill in the missing numbers in this pattern.

11, ______, 27, 35, ______, 51

7. 325 ☐ 134 = 459

8. Find m when $m - 125 = 264$.

$m =$ ______

9. How many centimeters are in 3.7 meters?

____

10. Do perpendicular lines meet at a 90° angle?

____

11. **Cookies Baked**

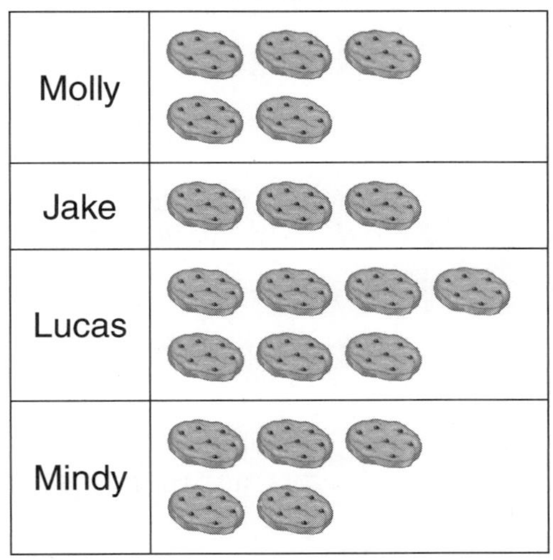

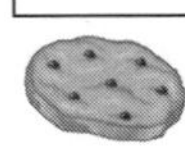 = 1 dozen cookies

How many cookies did Molly bake?

____

12. Frank bought 2 gallons of water. He drank $\frac{1}{4}$ of it today. How many quarts did he drink?

____

SCORE

1. Ⓨ Ⓝ
2. Ⓨ Ⓝ
3. Ⓨ Ⓝ
4. Ⓨ Ⓝ
5. Ⓨ Ⓝ
6. Ⓨ Ⓝ
7. Ⓨ Ⓝ
8. Ⓨ Ⓝ
9. Ⓨ Ⓝ
10. Ⓨ Ⓝ
11. Ⓨ Ⓝ
12. Ⓨ Ⓝ

___ / 12 Total

DAY
30

NAME: ______________________________

DIRECTIONS Solve each problem.

SCORE

1. Ⓨ Ⓝ
2. Ⓨ Ⓝ
3. Ⓨ Ⓝ
4. Ⓨ Ⓝ
5. Ⓨ Ⓝ
6. Ⓨ Ⓝ
7. Ⓨ Ⓝ
8. Ⓨ Ⓝ
9. Ⓨ Ⓝ
10. Ⓨ Ⓝ
11. Ⓨ Ⓝ
12. Ⓨ Ⓝ

___ / 12
Total

1. $64 + 27 =$ _______

2. $5 \times 3 =$ _______

3. $36 \div -4 =$ _______

4. How many digits are in 67,392?

____

5. Is $3\frac{3}{4}$ greater than, less than, or equal to $\frac{14}{4}$?

____

6. $(20 - 8)^2 =$ _______

7. Find x. $1.3 + x = 3.8$

$x =$ _______

8. $\frac{1}{\square}$ of 18 is 3.

9. How many days are in the month of December?

____

10. Circle the obtuse angle measurement.

48° 169° 295°

11. A box of a dozen donuts contains 5 chocolate donuts, 4 sprinkled donuts, 2 lemon donuts, and 1 raspberry-filled donut. If you reach in and grab a donut, what is the probability that it will be a lemon donut?

____

12. Haru needs to be at school at 8:15. If it takes him 20 minutes to walk to school, 15 minutes to eat breakfast, and 12 minutes to get dressed and brush his hair, what time should he get up?

____

NAME: ____________________

DIRECTIONS Solve each problem.

1. 364 – 38 = ______

2. Find the product of 5 and 6.

______

3. 6 $\overline{)48}$

4. What is the value of the digit 2 in the number 2,309?

______

5. Is 80% the same as $\frac{8}{10}$?

______

6. What number comes next?
3,700; 3,800; 3,900;

______

7. Find *w*. *w* – *28* = 37

w = ______

8. Find *b*. 87 – *b* = 45

b = ______

9. Use A.M. or P.M. to write 4:57 in the evening.

______

10. What shape is located at (G,1)?

______

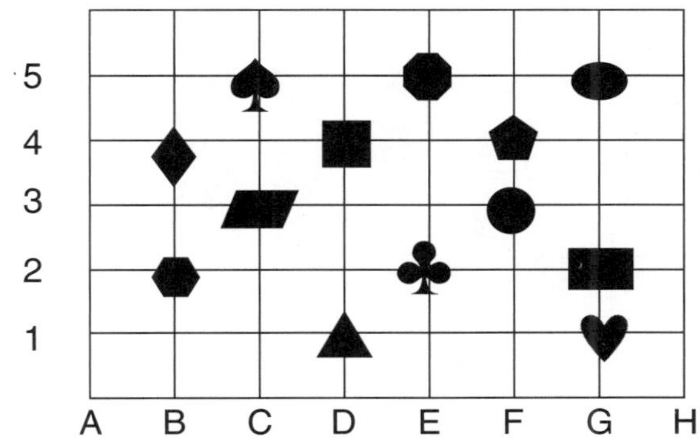

11. Write *blue*, *red*, or *orange* in each section of the circle graph based on the following data:
There are 32 children. 25% of the children like blue,16 children like red, and 8 children like orange.

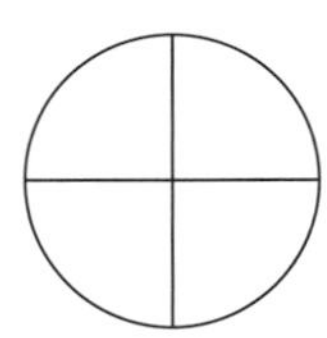

12. Betty goes to the movies. She spends equal amounts of money on her ticket and at the snack stand. If her total bill is $25.50, how much did she spend at the snack stand?

______

SCORE

1. Ⓨ Ⓝ
2. Ⓨ Ⓝ
3. Ⓨ Ⓝ
4. Ⓨ Ⓝ
5. Ⓨ Ⓝ
6. Ⓨ Ⓝ
7. Ⓨ Ⓝ
8. Ⓨ Ⓝ
9. Ⓨ Ⓝ
10. Ⓨ Ⓝ
11. Ⓨ Ⓝ
12. Ⓨ Ⓝ

___ / 12
Total

DAY 32

NAME: ____________________

DIRECTIONS Solve each problem.

SCORE

1. Ⓨ Ⓝ
2. Ⓨ Ⓝ
3. Ⓨ Ⓝ
4. Ⓨ Ⓝ
5. Ⓨ Ⓝ
6. Ⓨ Ⓝ
7. Ⓨ Ⓝ
8. Ⓨ Ⓝ
9. Ⓨ Ⓝ
10. Ⓨ Ⓝ
11. Ⓨ Ⓝ
12. Ⓨ Ⓝ

___ / 12 Total

1. $(-12) + (-14) =$ ______

2. $6 \cdot 9 =$ ______

3. $540 \div 6 =$ ______

4. Write 573 in expanded notation.

____

____

5. $\frac{1}{2} \cdot \frac{1}{3} =$ ______

6. $32 - 8 \cdot 2 =$ ______

7. Solve for *x*. $\frac{x}{7} = 7$

$x =$ ______

8. 30 ☐ 10 = 300

9. Calculate the volume of a cube in which each side measures 3 cm.

____

10. What is the sum of the angles in a triangle?

____

11. What is the probability you will spin red or green?

____

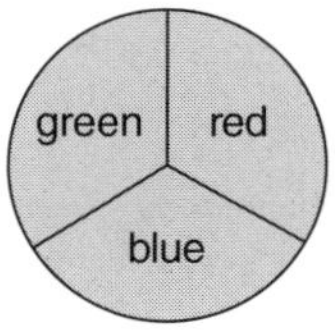

12. Complete the subtraction table.

–	72	76	81	85	93	97
19						
39						
59						
69						

NAME: ____________________________

DIRECTIONS Solve each problem.

1.
$$\begin{array}{r} 80 \\ -\ 14 \\ \hline \end{array}$$

2. $(-9) \times (-8) =$ ______

3. $5\overline{)40}$

4. Round 7,259 to the nearest ten.

____

5. $3 \times \frac{3}{4} =$ ______

6. Write the rule for the pattern.
85, 80, 75, 70, 65

____

7. 50% of ☐ is 36

8. 19.9 ☐ 8.5 = 11.4

9. Is 10:46 the same as 14 minutes to 10:00?

____

10. How many axes of symmetry does the shape have?

____

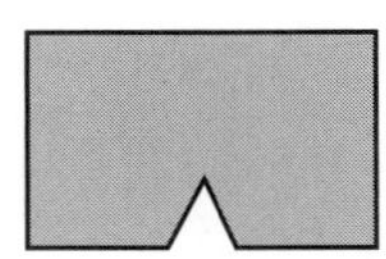

11. If you toss a 6-sided die, what is the probability you will get a 6?

____

12. Kiera is looking at birds and sees 48 legs. How many birds does she see?

____

SCORE

1. Ⓨ Ⓝ
2. Ⓨ Ⓝ
3. Ⓨ Ⓝ
4. Ⓨ Ⓝ
5. Ⓨ Ⓝ
6. Ⓨ Ⓝ
7. Ⓨ Ⓝ
8. Ⓨ Ⓝ
9. Ⓨ Ⓝ
10. Ⓨ Ⓝ
11. Ⓨ Ⓝ
12. Ⓨ Ⓝ

___ / 12
Total

NAME: ____________________

DIRECTIONS Solve each problem.

SCORE

1. Ⓨ Ⓝ
2. Ⓨ Ⓝ
3. Ⓨ Ⓝ
4. Ⓨ Ⓝ
5. Ⓨ Ⓝ
6. Ⓨ Ⓝ
7. Ⓨ Ⓝ
8. Ⓨ Ⓝ
9. Ⓨ Ⓝ
10. Ⓨ Ⓝ
11. Ⓨ Ⓝ
12. Ⓨ Ⓝ

___ / 12
Total

1. 186 + 97 = ______

2.

$$\begin{array}{r} 7 \\ \times\ 3 \\ \hline \end{array}$$

3. Divide 25 into 5 equal groups.

____

4. Is 6 a composite number?

____

5. Write $\frac{9}{10}$ as a decimal.

____

6. 25 + 5 − 6 = ______

7. 30 ☐ 5 = 6

8. Find *c* if 116 + *c* = 168.

c = ________

9. Write 1:24 P.M. in a 24-hour time format.

____

10. Complete the chart for the shape.

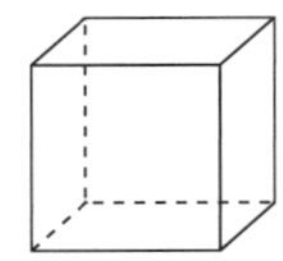

Name the figure.	
How many surfaces?	
How many vertices?	
Does it stack or roll?	
Is it a plane shape or a solid shape?	

11. **Boys and Girls in Class**

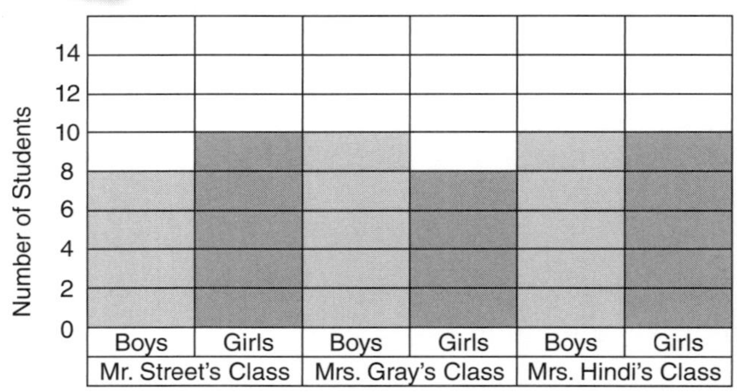

In which class is there a total of 20 students?

____

12. A family went on a vacation. They drove 120 miles. Dad drove 80% of the distance How many miles did Dad drive?

____

NAME: ______________________

DIRECTIONS Solve each problem.

1. $8 + (-10) =$ ______

2. $7 \times 5 =$ ______

3. $5\overline{)30}$

4. What is the even number right before 92?

____

5. Write 5 tenths + 7 hundredths as a decimal.

____

6. $72 \div 3 \div 6 =$ ______

7. Find *n*. $n - 7.3 = 8.5$

$n =$ ______

8. ☐ % of 68 = 34

9. How many days are in a leap year?

____

10. Is 107° an acute angle?

____

11. Every week, Colin mows the lawn, edges the lawn, and pulls the weeds. List all the possible orders in which he can take care of the yard.

____

____

____

____

____

____

____

____

12. There are 82 sixth graders at Morris School. If they are arranged in groups of 6, how many full groups would there be?

____

SCORE

1. Ⓨ Ⓝ
2. Ⓨ Ⓝ
3. Ⓨ Ⓝ
4. Ⓨ Ⓝ
5. Ⓨ Ⓝ
6. Ⓨ Ⓝ
7. Ⓨ Ⓝ
8. Ⓨ Ⓝ
9. Ⓨ Ⓝ
10. Ⓨ Ⓝ
11. Ⓨ Ⓝ
12. Ⓨ Ⓝ

___ / 12 Total

DAY 36

NAME: ____________________

DIRECTIONS Solve each problem.

SCORE

1. Ⓨ Ⓝ
2. Ⓨ Ⓝ
3. Ⓨ Ⓝ
4. Ⓨ Ⓝ
5. Ⓨ Ⓝ
6. Ⓨ Ⓝ
7. Ⓨ Ⓝ
8. Ⓨ Ⓝ
9. Ⓨ Ⓝ
10. Ⓨ Ⓝ
11. Ⓨ Ⓝ
12. Ⓨ Ⓝ

___ / 12 Total

1. $80 - 14 =$ ______

2. $10 \times 5 =$ ______

3. $-90 \div -10 =$ ______

4. What is the number 4 less than 2?

____

5. Is $\frac{3}{4}$ greater than, less than, or equal to $\frac{6}{8}$?

____

6. $29 \cdot 3 \div 3 =$ ______

7. Solve for v. $\frac{v}{7} = 22$

$v =$ ______

8. 4 ☐ 29 = 116

9. 2 yards = ______ inches

10. Draw a side view of the rectangular prism.

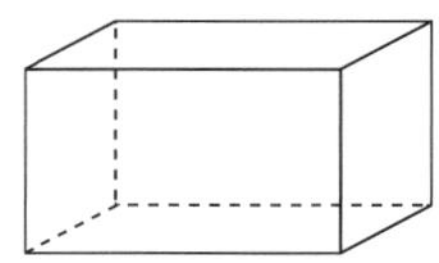

11. What is the probability that the spinner will land on a sport that uses a ball?

____

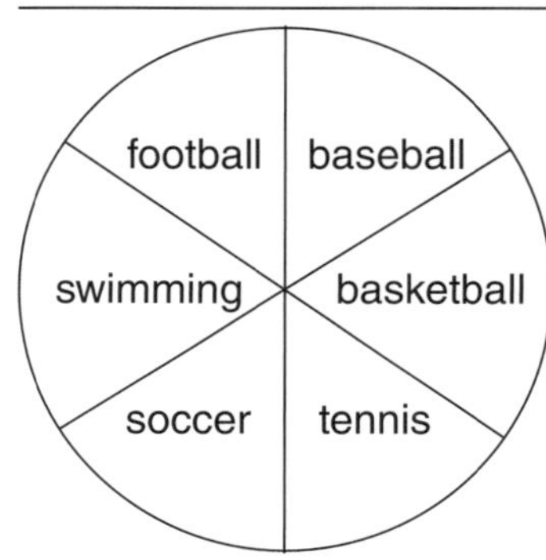

12. I am part of a whole. I am four times as large as one-fifth. I am a decimal. What am I?

____

NAME: ______________________

DIRECTIONS Solve each problem.

SCORE

1. $\begin{array}{r} 24 \\ +\ 45 \\ \hline \end{array}$

2. 10 x 17 = ______

3. $6\overline{)36}$

4. Is 6 a factor of 48? ______

5. Write $1\frac{45}{100}$ as a decimal.

____

6. What is the rule for the pattern? 1, 1, 2, 3, 5, 8

____

7. 348 ☐ 109 = 457

8. Find *x*. $x - 138 = 209$

$x =$ ______

9. What is the name for the perimeter of a circle?

____

10. How many faces are on the solid?

____

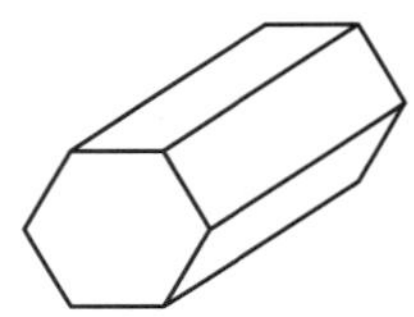

11. Look at the set of shapes. What is the probability of picking a triangle?

____

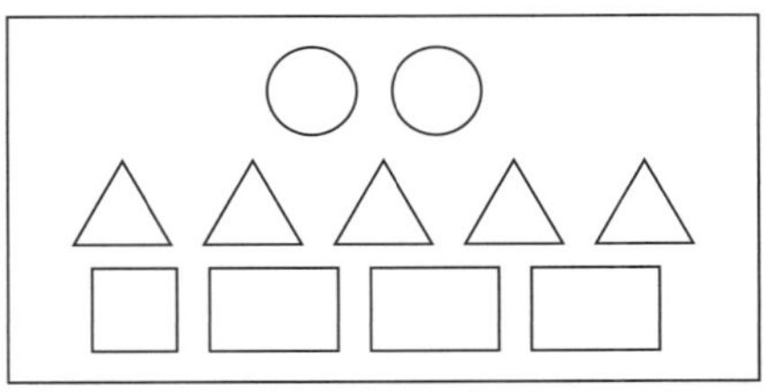

12. Compare a pentagonal pyramid with a pentagonal prism.

	Faces	Edges	Vertices
Pentagonal Pyramid			
Pentagonal Prism			

1. Ⓨ Ⓝ
2. Ⓨ Ⓝ
3. Ⓨ Ⓝ
4. Ⓨ Ⓝ
5. Ⓨ Ⓝ
6. Ⓨ Ⓝ
7. Ⓨ Ⓝ
8. Ⓨ Ⓝ
9. Ⓨ Ⓝ
10. Ⓨ Ⓝ
11. Ⓨ Ⓝ
12. Ⓨ Ⓝ

___ / 12
Total

DAY
38

NAME: ____________________________

DIRECTIONS Solve each problem.

SCORE

1. Ⓨ Ⓝ
2. Ⓨ Ⓝ
3. Ⓨ Ⓝ
4. Ⓨ Ⓝ
5. Ⓨ Ⓝ
6. Ⓨ Ⓝ
7. Ⓨ Ⓝ
8. Ⓨ Ⓝ
9. Ⓨ Ⓝ
10. Ⓨ Ⓝ
11. Ⓨ Ⓝ
12. Ⓨ Ⓝ

___ / 12
Total

1. What is the difference when you subtract 30 from 245?

____

2.
$$\begin{array}{r} 9 \\ \times\ 7 \\ \hline \end{array}$$

3. What is the quotient of 32 divided by 8?

____

4. Is 56,729 greater than 56,279?

____

5. Write 0.72 as a percentage.

____

6. What is the next number in the pattern? 5,627; 5,527; 5,427;

____

7. 20 ☐ 10 = 200

8. 125 ÷ ☐ = 5

9. Calculate the perimeter of a rectangle that is 8 cm by 3 cm.

____

10. What is the name for a triangle that has exactly two equal sides?

____

11. Inside a bag of candy there are 16 lollipops, 12 pieces of chocolate, and 7 pieces of licorice. If you reach into the bag and grab one item, what is the probability that it will be a piece of chocolate?

____

12. Circle the cube that could be made from this diagram.

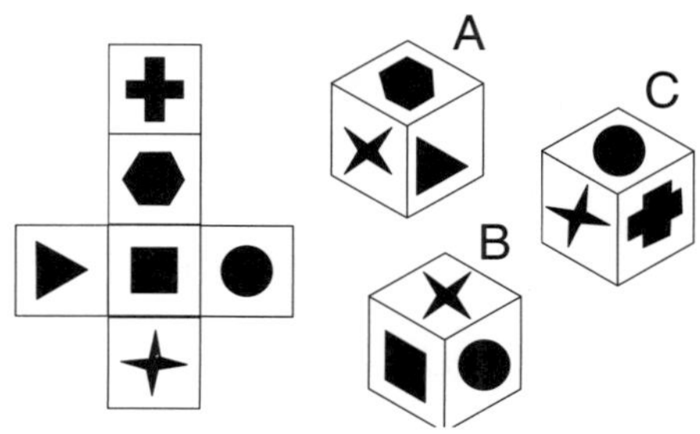

DAY
39

NAME: ____________________________

DIRECTIONS Solve each problem.

1. 36 + 9 = ______

2. –10 x 16 = ______

3. $4\overline{)20}$

4. Is 336 a multiple of 9?

____

5. Is $\frac{1}{2}$ greater than $\frac{2}{5}$?

____

6. 5 • 9 • 3 = ______

7. Find *d* when 95 – *d* = 52.

d = ______

8. Find *j* when *j* + 46 = 84.

j = ______

9. Calculate the area of the shape.

____

9 m

9 m

10. Are opposite sides of a rectangle parallel?

____

11.

Points Scored

	Game 1	Game 2	Game 3
Sara	14	15	14
Allison	19	13	11
Phillip	21	19	20
Sonia	16	13	15

How many fewer points did Sonia score in game 2 than in game 1?

____

12. Two numbers have a sum of 31 and a product of 228. What are the numbers?

____

SCORE

1. Ⓨ Ⓝ
2. Ⓨ Ⓝ
3. Ⓨ Ⓝ
4. Ⓨ Ⓝ
5. Ⓨ Ⓝ
6. Ⓨ Ⓝ
7. Ⓨ Ⓝ
8. Ⓨ Ⓝ
9. Ⓨ Ⓝ
10. Ⓨ Ⓝ
11. Ⓨ Ⓝ
12. Ⓨ Ⓝ

___ / 12
Total

DAY 40

NAME: ______________________

DIRECTIONS Solve each problem.

SCORE

1. Ⓨ Ⓝ
2. Ⓨ Ⓝ
3. Ⓨ Ⓝ
4. Ⓨ Ⓝ
5. Ⓨ Ⓝ
6. Ⓨ Ⓝ
7. Ⓨ Ⓝ
8. Ⓨ Ⓝ
9. Ⓨ Ⓝ
10. Ⓨ Ⓝ
11. Ⓨ Ⓝ
12. Ⓨ Ⓝ

___ / 12
Total

1.
$$\begin{array}{r} 232 \\ -\ \ 49 \\ \hline \end{array}$$

2. $12 \cdot 5 =$ ______

3. $80 \div (-8) =$ ______

4. What is the smallest possible two-digit number that can be made from the digits 4, 9, and 3?

____

5. Write $\frac{9}{4}$ as a mixed number.

____

6. $8 + 3 \cdot (9 + 1) =$ ______

7. 40 ☐ 10 = 400

8. Solve for *y*. $\frac{y}{4} = 12.5$

$y =$ ______

9. How many meters are in $1\frac{3}{4}$ kilometers?

____

10. Use a protractor to measure the angle.

____

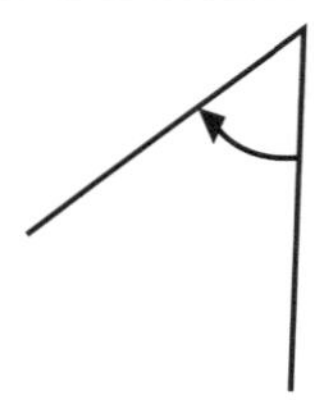

11.

	Regular Price	Discount
Pants	\$32	25%
Shirt	\$24	30%
Shoes	\$45	35%
Socks	\$4	10%

How much more are the shoes than the shirt after the discount?

____

12. Use three of the numbers 3, 4, 5, 12, and 15 to complete the number sentence. Do not use any number more than once.

(______ – ______) x ______ = 8

DAY 41

NAME: ____________________

DIRECTIONS Solve each problem.

SCORE

1. $\begin{array}{r} 97 \\ +\ 35 \\ \hline \end{array}$

2. 10 x 14 = ______

3. $4\overline{)32}$

4. What is the value of the digit 4 in 64,297?

____

5. Write 3 ones + 7 tenths + 9 hundredths as a decimal.

____

6. Write the next number in the pattern.

3, 2, 1, 0, –1, ______

7. Find *s*. $6s = 138$

s = ______

8. Solve for *x*. $\frac{x}{6} = 37$

x = ______

9. Draw 20 past 6 on the clock.

10. True or false? The angles of a triangle are always equal.

____

11. What is the probability of drawing one gray marble from the hat?

____

12. At a conference, 1 car was provided for every 4 people. If there were 17 cars, how many people were there? Provide all possible answers.

____

1. Ⓨ Ⓝ
2. Ⓨ Ⓝ
3. Ⓨ Ⓝ
4. Ⓨ Ⓝ
5. Ⓨ Ⓝ
6. Ⓨ Ⓝ
7. Ⓨ Ⓝ
8. Ⓨ Ⓝ
9. Ⓨ Ⓝ
10. Ⓨ Ⓝ
11. Ⓨ Ⓝ
12. Ⓨ Ⓝ

___ / 12
Total

DAY 42

NAME: ______________________

DIRECTIONS Solve each problem.

SCORE

1. Ⓨ Ⓝ
2. Ⓨ Ⓝ
3. Ⓨ Ⓝ
4. Ⓨ Ⓝ
5. Ⓨ Ⓝ
6. Ⓨ Ⓝ
7. Ⓨ Ⓝ
8. Ⓨ Ⓝ
9. Ⓨ Ⓝ
10. Ⓨ Ⓝ
11. Ⓨ Ⓝ
12. Ⓨ Ⓝ

___ / 12 Total

1. $96 - 38 =$ ______

2.

$$\begin{array}{r} 90 \\ \times\ 4 \\ \hline \end{array}$$

3. Divide 21 by 3.

____

4. 60,000 + 7,000 + 400 + 3 =

____

5. Is $\frac{4}{10}$ equal to $\frac{2}{3}$? ______

6. Write the next number in the pattern.

$\frac{1}{4}, \frac{1}{2}, \frac{3}{4}, 1, 1\frac{1}{4},$ ______

7. Find *n*. $28n = 84$

$n =$ ______

8. 135 ☐ 68 = 67

9. How many liters are in 10,500 milliliters?

____

10. Here are five views of the same cube.

Draw the shape that is on the face opposite the circle.

11. What is the probability that you will spin green or blue?

____

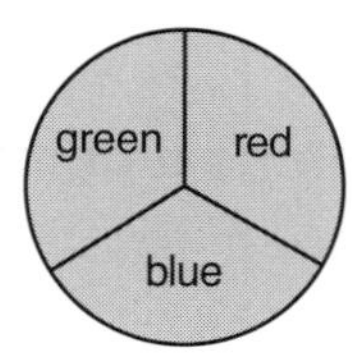

12. Greg worked for 4 hours and made $24. How much money would he make if he worked for 10 hours?

____

NAME: ____________________

DIRECTIONS Solve each problem.

1. 79 + 4 = ______

2. 10 x 13 = ______

3. $10\overline{)40}$

4. Round 2,449 to the nearest hundred.

____

5. $\frac{4}{5}$ of 30 is ______.

6. Write the missing numbers in the pattern.

–5, –4, ______, ______, –1, 0

7. ☐ % of 90 is 45.

8. 127 ☐ 56 = 183

9. How many millimeters are in 4.2 centimeters?

____

10. Name the solid figure.

____

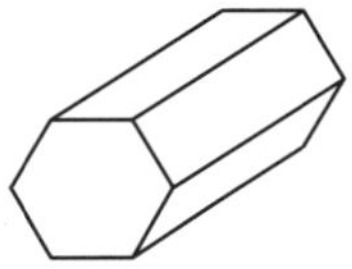

11. Steve, Mark, Melissa, Joe, and Mary are in a group. They randomly line up at the door. What is the probability that the name of the first person in line begins with *L*?

____

12. Jan doubled her starting number, added 5, subtracted 7, divided by 3, then squared the result. If her final answer was 36, what was her starting number?

____

SCORE

1. Ⓨ Ⓝ
2. Ⓨ Ⓝ
3. Ⓨ Ⓝ
4. Ⓨ Ⓝ
5. Ⓨ Ⓝ
6. Ⓨ Ⓝ
7. Ⓨ Ⓝ
8. Ⓨ Ⓝ
9. Ⓨ Ⓝ
10. Ⓨ Ⓝ
11. Ⓨ Ⓝ
12. Ⓨ Ⓝ

___ / 12 Total

DAY 44

NAME: ____________________

DIRECTIONS Solve each problem.

SCORE

1. Ⓨ Ⓝ
2. Ⓨ Ⓝ
3. Ⓨ Ⓝ
4. Ⓨ Ⓝ
5. Ⓨ Ⓝ
6. Ⓨ Ⓝ
7. Ⓨ Ⓝ
8. Ⓨ Ⓝ
9. Ⓨ Ⓝ
10. Ⓨ Ⓝ
11. Ⓨ Ⓝ
12. Ⓨ Ⓝ

___ / 12 Total

1.

$$\begin{array}{r} 58 \\ -\ 52 \\ \hline \end{array}$$

2. $7 \times 7 =$ ______

3. $(-20) \div (-5) =$ ______

4. Is 409 an odd or an even number?

____

5. Is $1\frac{1}{5}$ equal to $\frac{6}{5}$? ______

6. $5^2 \div 5 \cdot 2 =$ ______

7. 53 ☐ 28 = 25

8. Find *e*. $31e = 93$

$e =$ ______

9. How many minutes are in $3\frac{1}{4}$ hours?

____

10. Complete the chart for the shape.

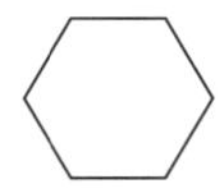

Name the figure.	
How many sides?	
How many angles?	
Does it have symmetry?	
Is it a plane shape or solid?	

11. Imagine you write each letter of the word *EXCELLENT* on a different card and then shuffle the cards. You turn the deck of cards facedown on a table and turn over the top card. What is the probability you will turn over a letter with only curved lines?

____

12. On a swim team of 20 people, one-fourth of the swimmers compete in the backstroke. How many swimmers compete in the backstroke event?

____

NAME: ______________________________

DIRECTIONS Solve each problem.

1.
$$\begin{array}{r} 63 \\ -\ 8 \\ \hline \end{array}$$

2. 61 • 10 = ______

3. $4\overline{)28}$

4. Write the ordinal number for sixteen.

____

5. Write 0.76 as a fraction.

____

6. (7 + 4) • (6 + 2) = ______

7. 50% of ☐ = 70

8. Find *m*. *m + 45* = 163

m = ______

9. What is the volume of the prism?

____

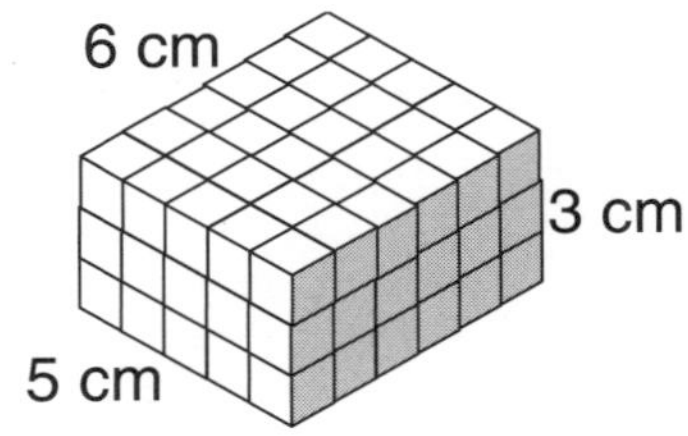

10. How many degrees are in a straight angle?

____

11. What is the median of this set of data?

40, 50, 60, 70, 80

____

12. Complete the factor wheel to show all the factors of the number 18.

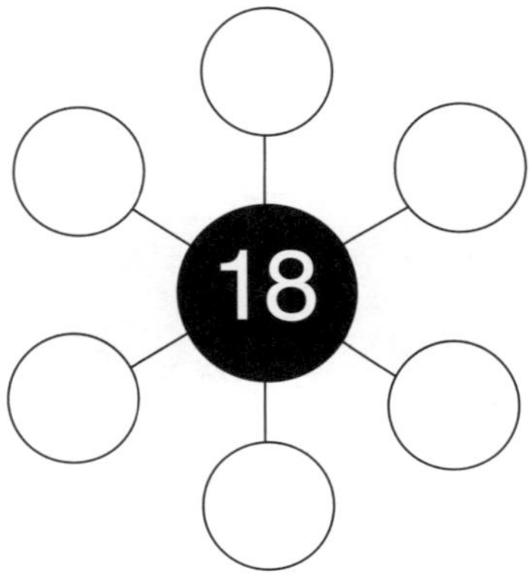

SCORE

1. Ⓨ Ⓝ
2. Ⓨ Ⓝ
3. Ⓨ Ⓝ
4. Ⓨ Ⓝ
5. Ⓨ Ⓝ
6. Ⓨ Ⓝ
7. Ⓨ Ⓝ
8. Ⓨ Ⓝ
9. Ⓨ Ⓝ
10. Ⓨ Ⓝ
11. Ⓨ Ⓝ
12. Ⓨ Ⓝ

___ / 12 Total

NAME: ____________________

DIRECTIONS Solve each problem.

SCORE

1. Ⓨ Ⓝ
2. Ⓨ Ⓝ
3. Ⓨ Ⓝ
4. Ⓨ Ⓝ
5. Ⓨ Ⓝ
6. Ⓨ Ⓝ
7. Ⓨ Ⓝ
8. Ⓨ Ⓝ
9. Ⓨ Ⓝ
10. Ⓨ Ⓝ
11. Ⓨ Ⓝ
12. Ⓨ Ⓝ

___ / 12 Total

1. $15 + 14 + 25 =$ ______

2. $-70 \times 9 =$ ______

3. What is half of 34? ______

4. True or false? $9{,}076 > 9{,}760$

____

5. $\frac{3}{4} \bullet \frac{10}{15} =$ ______

6. $5 + 2 \bullet 3 - 1 =$ ______

7. $\square \div 25 = 7$

8. Find *x*. $5x = 230$

$x =$ ______

9. Calculate the area of a rectangle that is 4 m by 7 m.

____

10. Draw a top view of the triangular prism.

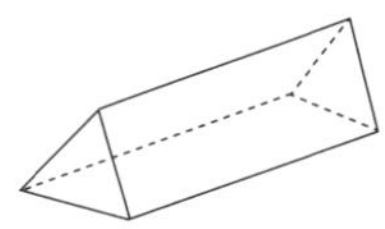

11. Which spinner would be best to use if you want to land on blue?

____

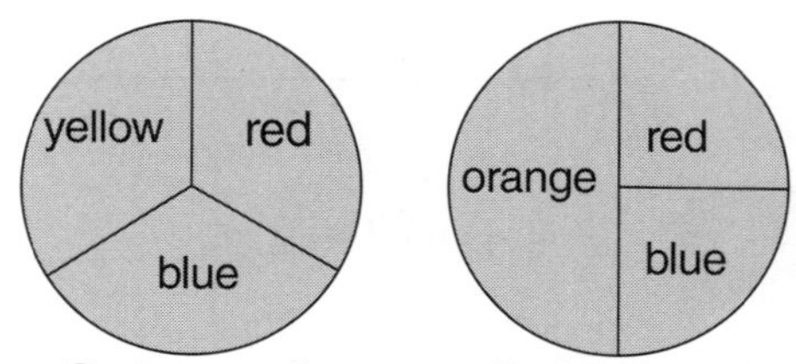

Spinner A **Spinner B**

12. Petra started with a number, added 3, multiplied the result by 4, subtracted 6, and multiplied that result by 3. If her final answer was 90, with what number did she begin?

____

NAME: ____________________

DIRECTIONS Solve each problem.

1. 46 – 8 = ______

2.

$$\begin{array}{r} 80 \\ \times\ 7 \\ \hline \end{array}$$

3. 54 ÷ –9 = ______

4. List all the factors of 18.

____

5. $\frac{9}{10}$ of 30 is ______.

6. –1 + 4 – 2 = ______

7. 30 x ☐ = 600

8. Find *h*. $h \div 4 = 31$

h = ______

9. Write 5:46 P.M. in a 24-hour time format.

____

10. How many edges are on a cylinder?

____

11. There are two red pencils, two green pencils, and two yellow pencils in a drawer. If you reach in the drawer and grab a pencil, what is the probability that it will be red?

____

12. Circle the factors of the given product.

Possible Factors									Product
8	5	4	3	7	15	12	9	17	45

SCORE

1. Ⓨ Ⓝ
2. Ⓨ Ⓝ
3. Ⓨ Ⓝ
4. Ⓨ Ⓝ
5. Ⓨ Ⓝ
6. Ⓨ Ⓝ
7. Ⓨ Ⓝ
8. Ⓨ Ⓝ
9. Ⓨ Ⓝ
10. Ⓨ Ⓝ
11. Ⓨ Ⓝ
12. Ⓨ Ⓝ

___ / 12 Total

DAY 48

NAME: ______________________________

DIRECTIONS Solve each problem.

SCORE

1. Ⓨ Ⓝ
2. Ⓨ Ⓝ
3. Ⓨ Ⓝ
4. Ⓨ Ⓝ
5. Ⓨ Ⓝ
6. Ⓨ Ⓝ
7. Ⓨ Ⓝ
8. Ⓨ Ⓝ
9. Ⓨ Ⓝ
10. Ⓨ Ⓝ
11. Ⓨ Ⓝ
12. Ⓨ Ⓝ

___ / 12 Total

1. $$\begin{array}{r} 135 \\ +\ \ 34 \\ \hline \end{array}$$

2. $14 \cdot 3 =$ ______

3. $5\overline{)45}$

4. Circle the composite number.

5 35

5. Write $2\frac{5}{8}$ as an improper fraction.

____

6. $5 + (10 - 4) =$ ______

7. $\frac{1}{5} + \square = \frac{3}{5}$

8. Find c. $50c = 150$

$c =$ ______

9. What is one half hour after 25 minutes to 9:00?

____

10. Is a sphere a plane shape or a solid shape?

____

11. Which number is the outlier in this data set?

45, 52, 61, 48, 91

____

12. Shade half of each rectangle in a different way.

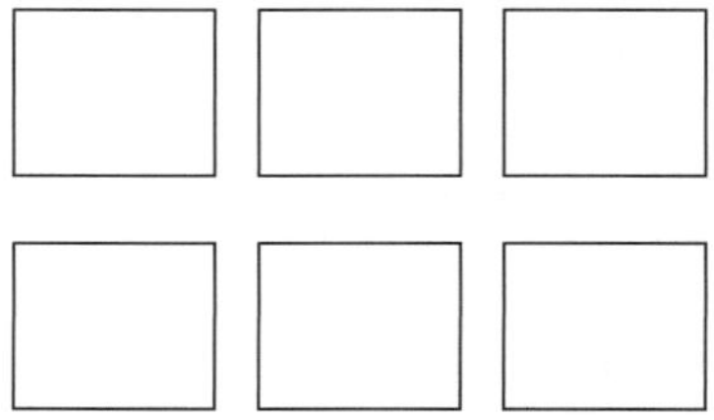

NAME: ____________________

DIRECTIONS Solve each problem.

1. 38 + 24 = ______

2. 73 x 10 = ______

3. 690 ÷ 5 = ______

4. List the first four multiples of 3.

____

5. $\frac{4}{5}$ of 30 is ______.

6. 5 – 6 + 2 = ______

7. ☐ – 85 = 67

8. Find *p*. $12 + p = 17$

p = ______

9. Record the line length shown.

____

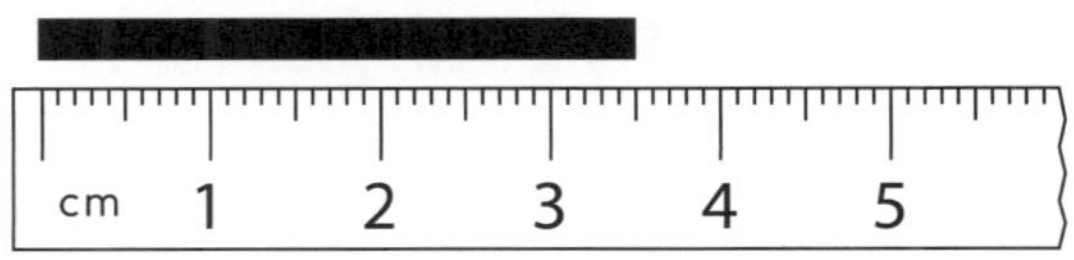

10. Does a square include perpendicular lines?

____

11. In a game, the probability of the spinner landing on yes is 1:2. How many times would you expect to land on yes if you spin the spinner 20 times?

____

12. Sheldon has $15 more than Colin. If Sheldon has $48, how much does Colin have?

____

SCORE

1. Ⓨ Ⓝ
2. Ⓨ Ⓝ
3. Ⓨ Ⓝ
4. Ⓨ Ⓝ
5. Ⓨ Ⓝ
6. Ⓨ Ⓝ
7. Ⓨ Ⓝ
8. Ⓨ Ⓝ
9. Ⓨ Ⓝ
10. Ⓨ Ⓝ
11. Ⓨ Ⓝ
12. Ⓨ Ⓝ

___ / 12 Total

DAY 50

NAME: ______________________________

DIRECTIONS Solve each problem.

SCORE

1. Ⓨ Ⓝ
2. Ⓨ Ⓝ
3. Ⓨ Ⓝ
4. Ⓨ Ⓝ
5. Ⓨ Ⓝ
6. Ⓨ Ⓝ
7. Ⓨ Ⓝ
8. Ⓨ Ⓝ
9. Ⓨ Ⓝ
10. Ⓨ Ⓝ
11. Ⓨ Ⓝ
12. Ⓨ Ⓝ

___ / 12 Total

1. 67 – 32 = ______

2.

$$\begin{array}{r} 35 \\ \times\ 10 \\ \hline \end{array}$$

3. What is half of 56?

____

4. How many digits are in the number 136,579?

____

5. 10% of 90 is ______.

6. Find the next number in the pattern.

60, 75, 90, ________

7. $\frac{1}{10} \times \square = 4$

8. Find *z*. $z - 78 = 65$

$z =$ ______

9. How many centimeters are in 25 millimeters?

____

10. Is a straight angle greater than a right angle?

____

11. A box of a dozen donuts contains 5 chocolate donuts, 4 sprinkled donuts, 2 lemon donuts, and 1 raspberry-filled donut. If you reach in and grab a donut, what is the probability that it will be a chocolate donut?

____

12. In magic squares, each row, column, and diagonal adds up to the same number. Complete the magic square. Use each number 0–8 only once.

1		5
8		0
3	2	

NAME: ______________________

DIRECTIONS Solve each problem.

1. 56 – 39 = ______

2. 9 x 40 = ______

3. $7\overline{)42}$

4. What is the value of the digit 9 in 4,729?

____

5. Is $1\frac{2}{3}$ less than or greater than $1\frac{3}{4}$?

____

6. 4 + 2 • 5 + 3 = ______

7. ☐ % of 80 is 20.

8. Solve for *f*. $f + \frac{3}{8} = \frac{5}{8}$

f = ________

9. How many pints are in a quart?

____

10. Which line is perpendicular to line B?

____

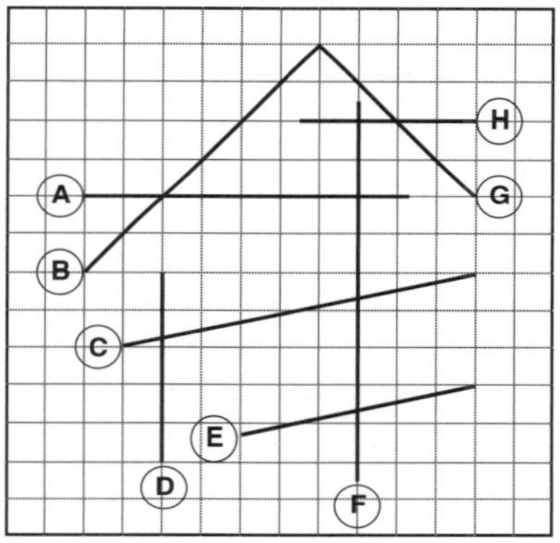

11. Record the data in the table.

Trish has 2 brothers and 1 sister. Max doesn't have any siblings. Melissa has 2 brothers. Allison has 1 sister. Trent has a brother and a sister.

Child's Name	Brothers	Sisters

12. A farmer sold 250 of his sheep, bought 35 more sheep, and then bought 68 more sheep. After 3 died, he sold another 260. If he now has 190 sheep, how many sheep did he have at the beginning?

____

SCORE

1. Ⓨ Ⓝ
2. Ⓨ Ⓝ
3. Ⓨ Ⓝ
4. Ⓨ Ⓝ
5. Ⓨ Ⓝ
6. Ⓨ Ⓝ
7. Ⓨ Ⓝ
8. Ⓨ Ⓝ
9. Ⓨ Ⓝ
10. Ⓨ Ⓝ
11. Ⓨ Ⓝ
12. Ⓨ Ⓝ

___ / 12 Total

DAY
52

NAME: ____________________

DIRECTIONS Solve each problem.

SCORE

1. Ⓨ Ⓝ
2. Ⓨ Ⓝ
3. Ⓨ Ⓝ
4. Ⓨ Ⓝ
5. Ⓨ Ⓝ
6. Ⓨ Ⓝ
7. Ⓨ Ⓝ
8. Ⓨ Ⓝ
9. Ⓨ Ⓝ
10. Ⓨ Ⓝ
11. Ⓨ Ⓝ
12. Ⓨ Ⓝ

___ / 12
Total

1. Calculate 49 more than 567.

____

2. 26 x 10 = _______

3. –670 ÷ 10 = _______

4. Write the expanded notation for 4,237.

____

5. $-\frac{1}{11} + -\frac{3}{11} =$ _______

6. Complete the input/output chart. Look for a pattern and write the rule.

Input	42	52	62	72	82	92
Output	56	66	76			

____

____

7. 30 ÷ ☐ = 5

8. Find *m*. $8m = 16$

m = _______

9. Write the time 4:39 P.M. in a 24-hour time format.

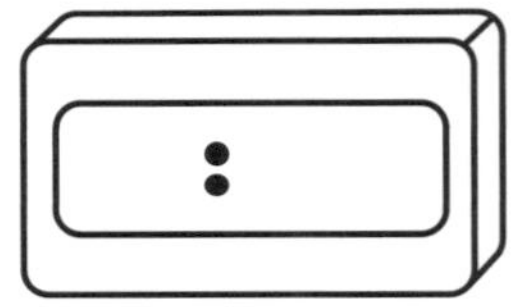

10. To make this pattern, has Tile A been *reflected*, *translated*, or *rotated*?

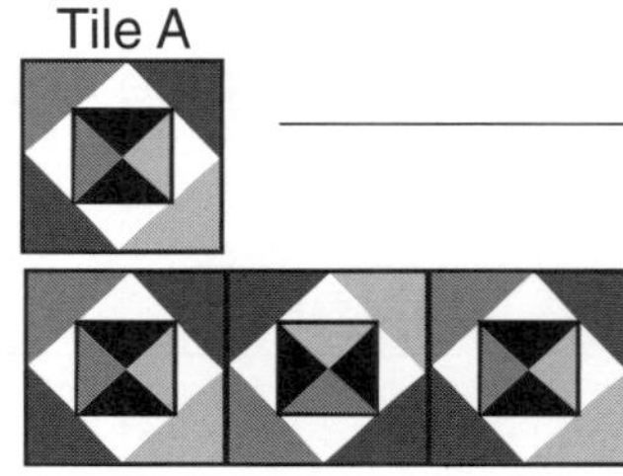

____

11.

Student	Savings Amount
Jack	$144
Trevor	$137
Brandon	$85
Michael	$202

Write the savings amounts in order from least to greatest.

____

12. Mr. Kendrik was 25 years old when his daughter Melissa was born. If Melissa was born in 2001, in what year was Mr. Kendrik born?

____

NAME: ____________________

DIRECTIONS Solve each problem.

1.

$$\begin{array}{r} 79 \\ -\ 46 \\ \hline \end{array}$$

2. 10 x 16 = ______

3. How many groups of 8 are in 56?

____

4. Is 4,283 closer to 4,000 or 5,000?

____

5. Is $1\frac{4}{5}$ less than or greater than $1\frac{7}{10}$?

____

6. $\frac{1}{5} = \frac{\square}{10}$

7. 42 $\square$ 6 = 7

8. $\square$ – 14 = 82

9. How many centimeters are in 7.5 meters?

____

10. Circle the correct cross-section for the solid.

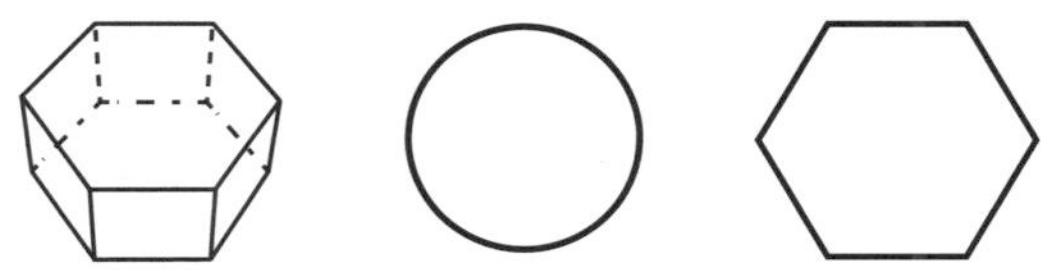

11. If you toss a 6-sided die, what is the probability you will get a 1?

____

12. Peaches cost $2 per pound. If Mrs. Myers spends $7 on peaches, how many pounds does she buy?

____

SCORE

1. Ⓨ Ⓝ
2. Ⓨ Ⓝ
3. Ⓨ Ⓝ
4. Ⓨ Ⓝ
5. Ⓨ Ⓝ
6. Ⓨ Ⓝ
7. Ⓨ Ⓝ
8. Ⓨ Ⓝ
9. Ⓨ Ⓝ
10. Ⓨ Ⓝ
11. Ⓨ Ⓝ
12. Ⓨ Ⓝ

___ / 12 Total

DAY
54

NAME: ____________________

DIRECTIONS Solve each problem.

SCORE

1. Ⓨ Ⓝ
2. Ⓨ Ⓝ
3. Ⓨ Ⓝ
4. Ⓨ Ⓝ
5. Ⓨ Ⓝ
6. Ⓨ Ⓝ
7. Ⓨ Ⓝ
8. Ⓨ Ⓝ
9. Ⓨ Ⓝ
10. Ⓨ Ⓝ
11. Ⓨ Ⓝ
12. Ⓨ Ⓝ

___ / 12
Total

1. $39 + 56 =$ ______

2. $31 \cdot 10 =$ ______

3. $72 \div 9 =$ ______

4. Is 16 a composite number?

____

5. Write $1\frac{3}{4}$ as an improper fraction.

____

6. $3 + (-2) + 4 =$ ______

7. $\square + 27 = 126$

8. Solve for r if $\frac{r}{2} = 12$.

$r =$ ______

9. How many kilograms are in 7,000 grams?

____

10. Complete the chart for the shape.

Name the figure.	
How many surfaces?	
How many vertices?	
Does it stack or roll?	
Is it a plane shape or a solid shape?	

11. The numbers 20 through 30 were written on individual cards and placed in a bag. If you take one card from the bag, what is the probability that it will be a multiple of 10?

____

12. On a bus, Mia watched 8 people get off and 4 get on at the first stop, 3 people get off and 10 get on at the second stop, and 5 people get off and 7 get on at the third stop. If there are now 25 passengers, how many people were on the bus when Mia started counting?

____

NAME: ______________________________

DIRECTIONS Solve each problem.

1. $-12 + 28 =$ ______

2. 10 x 13 = ______

3. $7\overline{)63}$

4. What number is 100 more than 5,739?

____

5. Is $\frac{2}{3}$ of 12 equal to 9? ______

6. 4 x 2 + 5 x 3 = ______

7. ☐ of 32 is 4.

8. Write the expression *x* increased by 12.

____

9. How many liters are in 4,580 milliliters?

____

10. Name the triangle.

____

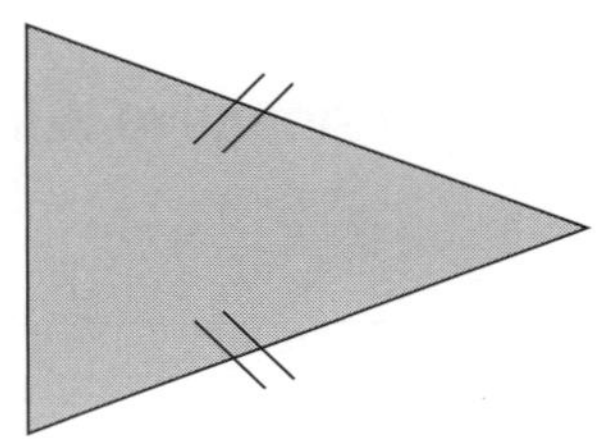

11. What is the mode of this set of data?

52, 40, 48, 42, 43, 48, 51

____

12. Complete the multiplication table.

×	8		9		7	4
					42	
8		48				
9				45		
						28

SCORE

1. Ⓨ Ⓝ
2. Ⓨ Ⓝ
3. Ⓨ Ⓝ
4. Ⓨ Ⓝ
5. Ⓨ Ⓝ
6. Ⓨ Ⓝ
7. Ⓨ Ⓝ
8. Ⓨ Ⓝ
9. Ⓨ Ⓝ
10. Ⓨ Ⓝ
11. Ⓨ Ⓝ
12. Ⓨ Ⓝ

___ / 12 Total

DAY 56

NAME: ____________________

DIRECTIONS Solve each problem.

SCORE

1. Ⓨ Ⓝ
2. Ⓨ Ⓝ
3. Ⓨ Ⓝ
4. Ⓨ Ⓝ
5. Ⓨ Ⓝ
6. Ⓨ Ⓝ
7. Ⓨ Ⓝ
8. Ⓨ Ⓝ
9. Ⓨ Ⓝ
10. Ⓨ Ⓝ
11. Ⓨ Ⓝ
12. Ⓨ Ⓝ

___ / 12 Total

1.

$$\begin{array}{r} 163 \\ +\ 25 \\ \hline \end{array}$$

2. Multiply 65 and 10.

____

3. $7\overline{)35}$

4. Is –5 a negative number?

____

5. Arrange the fractions in descending order.

$\frac{1}{3}, \frac{1}{2}, \frac{1}{4}$

_______ _______ _______

6. $-1 + 7 + (-3) =$ _______

7. 19 ☐ 24 = 43

8. Solve for *k*. $\frac{k}{7} = 5$

$k =$ _______

9. What is the elapsed time from 11:34 A.M. to 12:06 P.M.?

____

10. What is the sum of the interior angles of a triangle?

____

11.

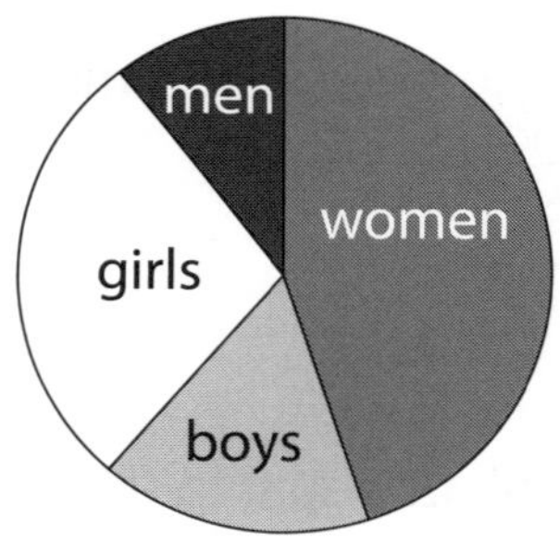

Order the size of each group from largest to smallest.

____

____

12. Conner has $3 more than Chi and $2 more than Cher. Jan has $1 less than Cher. Together they have $28. How much does Conner have?

____

NAME: ______________________________

DIRECTIONS Solve each problem.

1. 72 – 39 = ______

2. 29 x 2 = ______

3. 790 ÷ 10 = ______

4. Is 5 a factor of 30? ______

5. Does $0.75 = \frac{3}{4}$? ______

6. $1^2 + 2^2 + 3^2$ = ______

7. $\frac{3}{4}$ of 20 is ______.

8. Find *a*. 25 – *a* = 12

a = ______

9. How many centimeters are in 5.64 meters?

____

10. How many vertices are on the solid below?

____

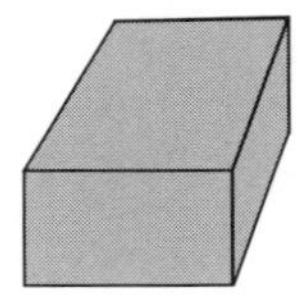

11. Look at the set of shapes below. What is the probability of picking a square?

____

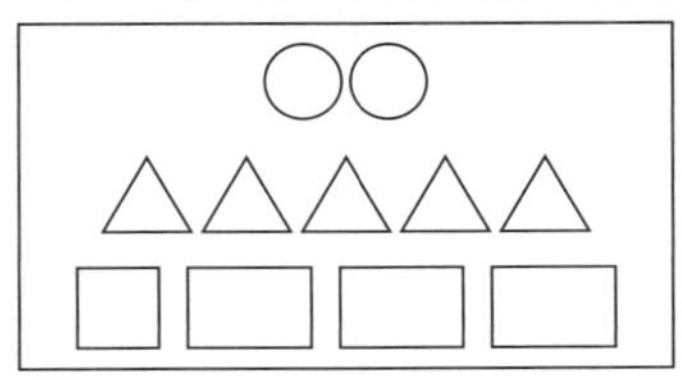

12. Add to find the total bill. Round the total to the nearest five cents and find the change from $20.00.

$1.98
$0.75
$3.96
$2.73
$2.64

Total ______

Change ______

SCORE

1. Ⓨ Ⓝ
2. Ⓨ Ⓝ
3. Ⓨ Ⓝ
4. Ⓨ Ⓝ
5. Ⓨ Ⓝ
6. Ⓨ Ⓝ
7. Ⓨ Ⓝ
8. Ⓨ Ⓝ
9. Ⓨ Ⓝ
10. Ⓨ Ⓝ
11. Ⓨ Ⓝ
12. Ⓨ Ⓝ

___ / 12 Total

DAY 58

NAME: ______________________________

DIRECTIONS Solve each problem.

SCORE

1. Ⓨ Ⓝ
2. Ⓨ Ⓝ
3. Ⓨ Ⓝ
4. Ⓨ Ⓝ
5. Ⓨ Ⓝ
6. Ⓨ Ⓝ
7. Ⓨ Ⓝ
8. Ⓨ Ⓝ
9. Ⓨ Ⓝ
10. Ⓨ Ⓝ
11. Ⓨ Ⓝ
12. Ⓨ Ⓝ

___ / 12 Total

1. $6 + 6 + 6 + 6 =$ ______

2. $8 \times (-30) =$ ______

3. $490 \div 49 =$ ______

4. List all of the prime numbers between 10 and 20.

____

5. 50% of 12 is ______.

6. $(-4) + (-3) + (-2) =$ ______

7. $\frac{3}{5}$ of $\square$ is 12

8. Find n. $\frac{1}{2}n = 21$

$n =$ ______

9. How many grams are there in 7.5 kilograms?

____

10. How many diagonals does a rectangle have?

____

11. Inside a bag of candy there are 16 lollipops, 12 pieces of chocolate, and 7 pieces of licorice. If you reach in the bag and grab a piece of candy, what is the probability that it will be licorice?

____

12. Mr. Wright is five times as old as his daughter, Lilly. Lilly is twice as old as her brother, Micah. If Micah is 3 years old, how old is Mr. Wright?

____

NAME: ____________________

DIRECTIONS Solve each problem.

1.
$$\begin{array}{r} 78 \\ -\ 49 \\ \hline \end{array}$$

2. 24 x 4 = ______

3. 305 ÷ 5 = ______

4. Is 163 divisible by 7? ______

5. Write one and seventy-six hundredths in decimal form.

____

6. $\frac{3}{6} = \frac{\square}{10}$

7. $\square - 19 = 13$

8. Find y when $10y = 25$.

$y =$ ______

9. Calculate the perimeter of a square with 12 m sides.

____

10. What is the radius of a circle with a 6.2 cm diameter?

____

11.

Points Scored

	Game 1	Game 2	Game 3
Sara	14	15	14
Allison	19	13	11
Phillip	21	19	20
Sonia	16	13	15

What was the total number of points Phillip scored in all three games?

____

12. Compare a rectangular pyramid to a rectangular prism.

	Faces	Edges	Vertices
Rectangular Pyramid			
Rectangular Prism			

SCORE

1. Ⓨ Ⓝ
2. Ⓨ Ⓝ
3. Ⓨ Ⓝ
4. Ⓨ Ⓝ
5. Ⓨ Ⓝ
6. Ⓨ Ⓝ
7. Ⓨ Ⓝ
8. Ⓨ Ⓝ
9. Ⓨ Ⓝ
10. Ⓨ Ⓝ
11. Ⓨ Ⓝ
12. Ⓨ Ⓝ

___ / 12 Total

DAY 60

NAME: ______________________

DIRECTIONS Solve each problem.

SCORE

1. Ⓨ Ⓝ
2. Ⓨ Ⓝ
3. Ⓨ Ⓝ
4. Ⓨ Ⓝ
5. Ⓨ Ⓝ
6. Ⓨ Ⓝ
7. Ⓨ Ⓝ
8. Ⓨ Ⓝ
9. Ⓨ Ⓝ
10. Ⓨ Ⓝ
11. Ⓨ Ⓝ
12. Ⓨ Ⓝ

___ / 12 Total

1. 45 + 62 = ______

2.

$$\begin{array}{r} 10 \\ \times\ 27 \\ \hline \end{array}$$

3. $3\overline{)369}$

4. What is the largest possible four-digit number you can make from the digits 2, 7, 9, and 6?

____

5. $\frac{2}{9} - \frac{5}{9} =$ ______

6. Write the next number in the pattern. 360, 450, 540,

____

7. $\frac{5}{8}$ of ☐ is 25.

8. Write the expression for the product of 7 and *h*.

____

9. How many meters are in $\frac{1}{4}$ kilometers?

____

10. Is the angle less than, greater than, or equal to 90 degrees?

____

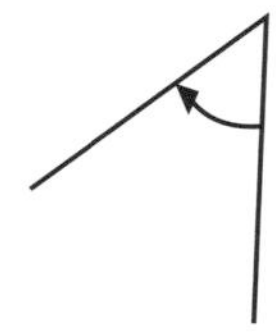

11. The numbers 0–9 are on the calculator. If you randomly push one number on the calculator, what is the probability that you will not push a 5 or 6?

____

12. A movie is 2 hours 23 minutes long. If the movie ends at 4:25, what time did the movie start?

____

NAME: ____________________

DIRECTIONS Solve each problem.

1. 683 – 39 = ______

2. 90 x 6 = ______

3. 670 ÷ (–10) = ______

4. What is the place value of 9 in the number 69,485?

____

5. Write 5 ones + 9 tenths + 4 hundredths as a decimal.

____

6. 10 + (–7) + 5 = ______

7. 45 ☐ 5 = 9

8. $\frac{1}{3} = \frac{\square}{6}$

9. Write 11:26 P.M. in a 24-hour time format.

____

10. How many faces does a square pyramid have?

____

11. What is the probability of drawing one black marble from the hat?

____

12. Amanda rents skis every day for a week while she is on vacation. If it costs $12 per day to rent the skis, how much does she pay for the whole week?

____

SCORE

1. Ⓨ Ⓝ
2. Ⓨ Ⓝ
3. Ⓨ Ⓝ
4. Ⓨ Ⓝ
5. Ⓨ Ⓝ
6. Ⓨ Ⓝ
7. Ⓨ Ⓝ
8. Ⓨ Ⓝ
9. Ⓨ Ⓝ
10. Ⓨ Ⓝ
11. Ⓨ Ⓝ
12. Ⓨ Ⓝ

___ / 12 Total

DAY 62

NAME: ____________________

DIRECTIONS Solve each problem.

SCORE

1. Ⓨ Ⓝ
2. Ⓨ Ⓝ
3. Ⓨ Ⓝ
4. Ⓨ Ⓝ
5. Ⓨ Ⓝ
6. Ⓨ Ⓝ
7. Ⓨ Ⓝ
8. Ⓨ Ⓝ
9. Ⓨ Ⓝ
10. Ⓨ Ⓝ
11. Ⓨ Ⓝ
12. Ⓨ Ⓝ

___ / 12 Total

1. $\begin{array}{r} 46 \\ +\ 29 \\ \hline \end{array}$

2. $10 \cdot 52 =$ ______

3. What is half of $5?

____

4. 80,000 + 5,000 + 30 + 8 =

____

5. $\frac{2}{3}$ of 18 is ______.

6. $\frac{1}{4} = \frac{\square}{8}$

7. 20% of $\square$ is 20.

8. Find *w*. $w - 10 = 48$

$w =$ ______

9. Write the digital time for the analog time shown.

____

10. How many sides does a parallelogram have?

____

11. What is the probability you will spin a word that has the letter *E* in it?

____

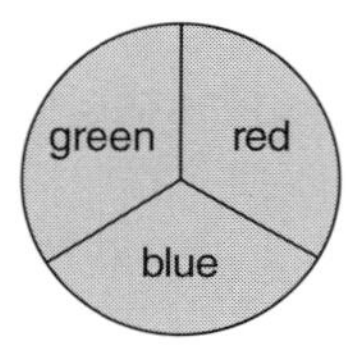

12. Use three of the numerals 3, 4, 5, 12, or 15 to complete the number sentence. Do not use any numeral more than once.

______ + ______ + ______ = 12

NAME: ____________________

DIRECTIONS Solve each problem.

1. $81 - 35 =$ ______

2. $\begin{array}{r} 13 \\ \times\ \ 4 \\ \hline \end{array}$

3. $7\overline{)147}$

4. Round 28,537 to the nearest thousand.

____

5. $\frac{3}{4} \div \frac{1}{4} =$ ______

6. $-8 + 20 - 4 =$ ______

7. $\square - 8 = 82$

8. $\frac{1}{2}$ of $\square$ is 12.

9. How many millimeters are in 9 centimeters?

____

10. How many axes of symmetry does the shape below have?

____

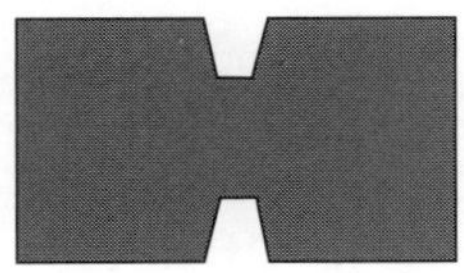

11. Steve, Mark, Melissa, Joe, and Mary are in a group. They randomly line up at the door. What is the probability that the first person in the line is a girl?

____

12. Without using the same digit twice in any number, how many two-digit numbers can be made using 1, 2, 3, and 4?

____

____

____

SCORE

1. Ⓨ Ⓝ
2. Ⓨ Ⓝ
3. Ⓨ Ⓝ
4. Ⓨ Ⓝ
5. Ⓨ Ⓝ
6. Ⓨ Ⓝ
7. Ⓨ Ⓝ
8. Ⓨ Ⓝ
9. Ⓨ Ⓝ
10. Ⓨ Ⓝ
11. Ⓨ Ⓝ
12. Ⓨ Ⓝ

___ / 12
Total

NAME: ____________________

DIRECTIONS Solve each problem.

SCORE

1. Ⓨ Ⓝ
2. Ⓨ Ⓝ
3. Ⓨ Ⓝ
4. Ⓨ Ⓝ
5. Ⓨ Ⓝ
6. Ⓨ Ⓝ
7. Ⓨ Ⓝ
8. Ⓨ Ⓝ
9. Ⓨ Ⓝ
10. Ⓨ Ⓝ
11. Ⓨ Ⓝ
12. Ⓨ Ⓝ

___ / 12
Total

1. $-15 + 22 =$ ______

2. $32 \times 10 =$ ______

3. $609 \div 3 =$ ______

4. $8^2 =$ ______

5. $\frac{3}{8} + \frac{2}{8} =$ ______

6. $2\ (5 + 3) =$ ______

7. $-5 \times \square = 10$

8. Solve for q. $\frac{1}{4}q = 10$

$q =$ ______

9. How many grams are in 9 kilograms?

______

10. Complete the chart for the shape.

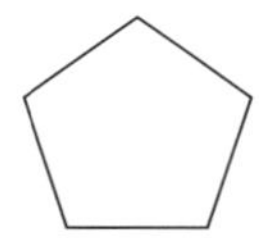

Name the figure.	
How many sides?	
How many angles?	
Does it have symmetry?	
Is it a plane shape or a solid shape?	

11. **Time Spent on Homework**

Day	Minutes
Monday	52
Tuesday	45
Wednesday	30
Thursday	45
Friday	0

How much more time was spent on homework on Thursday than on Wednesday?

______

12. Landon scored 80% on his math test. If there were 40 problems on the test, how many did he answer correctly?

______

NAME: ______________________________

DIRECTIONS Solve each problem.

1. 187 – 26 = ______

2. 35 x 10 = ______

3. 670 ÷ 10 = ______

4. Write the ordinal number for twenty-five.

____

5. Write 0.5 as a percentage.

____

6. Complete the input/output chart. Look for a pattern and write the rule.

Input	37	47	57	67	77	87
Output	74	94	114			

____

____

7. ☐ + 28 = 52

8. Write the expression for the sum of *m* and 10.

____

9. Calculate the area of the shape.

____

6 m

6 m

10. Use a protractor to measure the angle. Then identify it as either *acute*, *right*, *obtuse*, or *straight*.

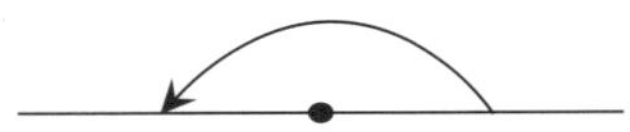

Name	
Size	

11. What is the mean of this set of data?

$1.30, $1.90, $1.60

____

12. Write the number that has these place values:

7 hundred thousands
4 ones
8 thousands
6 tens
2 ten thousands

____

SCORE

1. Ⓨ Ⓝ
2. Ⓨ Ⓝ
3. Ⓨ Ⓝ
4. Ⓨ Ⓝ
5. Ⓨ Ⓝ
6. Ⓨ Ⓝ
7. Ⓨ Ⓝ
8. Ⓨ Ⓝ
9. Ⓨ Ⓝ
10. Ⓨ Ⓝ
11. Ⓨ Ⓝ
12. Ⓨ Ⓝ

___ / 12
Total

DAY
66

NAME: ____________________

DIRECTIONS Solve each problem.

SCORE

1. Ⓨ Ⓝ
2. Ⓨ Ⓝ
3. Ⓨ Ⓝ
4. Ⓨ Ⓝ
5. Ⓨ Ⓝ
6. Ⓨ Ⓝ
7. Ⓨ Ⓝ
8. Ⓨ Ⓝ
9. Ⓨ Ⓝ
10. Ⓨ Ⓝ
11. Ⓨ Ⓝ
12. Ⓨ Ⓝ

___ / 12 Total

1. Calculate 85 more than 459.

____

2. $67 \times (-5) =$ ______

3. How many groups of 3 are in 24?

____

4. Is 6,875 greater than or less than 6,785?

____

5. $\frac{2}{3}$ of 12 is ______.

6. $(-3) + (-4) + (-5) =$ ______

7. $245 - \square = 215$

8. Find c. $c^2 = 25$

$c =$ ______

9. What is the volume of the prism?

____

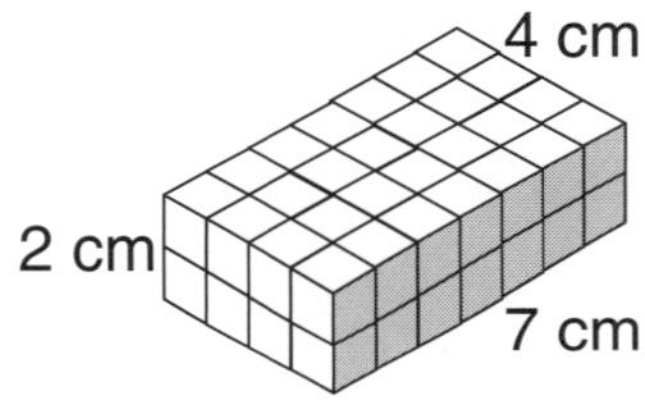

10. What is the term for a pair of angles that have a sum of 90°?

____

11. Which spinner would be best to use if you wanted to land on yellow?

____

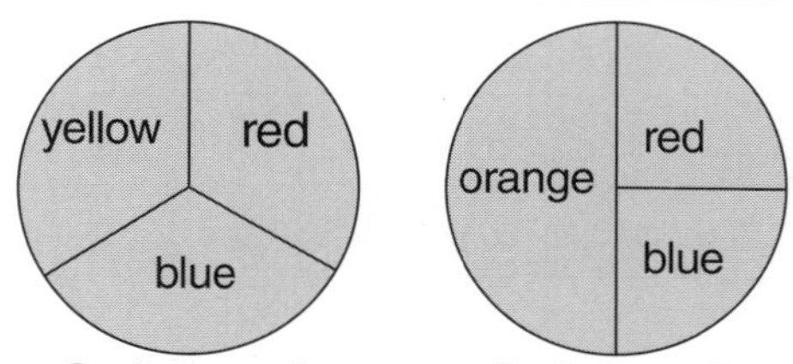

Spinner A **Spinner B**

12. A family went on a trip. They drove 180 miles. After $\frac{2}{3}$ of that distance, they stopped to eat. How many miles did they still have to drive after they ate?

____

NAME: ______________________

DIRECTIONS Solve each problem.

1. 329 – 78 = ______

2. 10 x 23 = ______

3. 10)340

4. List all the factors of 30.

____

5. $1\frac{1}{2} + \frac{1}{2}$ = ______

6. $(12 - 2 \times 3)^2$ = ______

7. ☐ of 160 = 16

8. Find *p*. $p - 5 = -8$

p = ______

9. How many pints are in a gallon?

____

10. How many faces are on the prism?

____

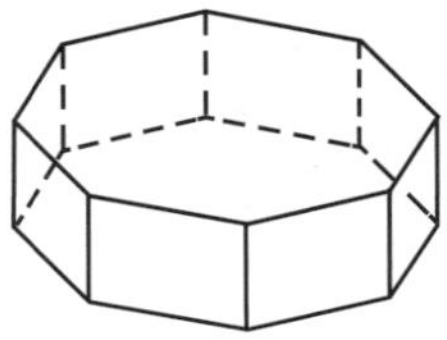

11. Two red cubes, two green cylinders, and three yellow rectangular prisms were put into a bag. What is the probability that you will pull out a yellow block?

____

12. If I write the numbers 1 through 43, how many digits do I write?

____

SCORE

1. Ⓨ Ⓝ
2. Ⓨ Ⓝ
3. Ⓨ Ⓝ
4. Ⓨ Ⓝ
5. Ⓨ Ⓝ
6. Ⓨ Ⓝ
7. Ⓨ Ⓝ
8. Ⓨ Ⓝ
9. Ⓨ Ⓝ
10. Ⓨ Ⓝ
11. Ⓨ Ⓝ
12. Ⓨ Ⓝ

___ / 12
Total

DAY 68

NAME: ____________________

DIRECTIONS Solve each problem.

SCORE

1. Ⓨ Ⓝ
2. Ⓨ Ⓝ
3. Ⓨ Ⓝ
4. Ⓨ Ⓝ
5. Ⓨ Ⓝ
6. Ⓨ Ⓝ
7. Ⓨ Ⓝ
8. Ⓨ Ⓝ
9. Ⓨ Ⓝ
10. Ⓨ Ⓝ
11. Ⓨ Ⓝ
12. Ⓨ Ⓝ

___ / 12 Total

1. Double 16.

____

2. What is the product of 34 and 6?

____

3. (–45) ÷ (–15) = ______

4. What is the number before 230,000?

____

5. 25% of 80 is ______.

6. 8 – 15 + 20 = ______

7. $\square \cdot 1 = \frac{27}{5}$

8. Find *x*. $4x = -28$

$x =$ ______

9. How many meters are in 956 centimeters?

____

10. How many vertices are there in a quadrilateral?

____

11. What is the outlier in this data set?

14, 82, 78, 89, 73, 91

____

12. I am part of a whole. I am twice the value of one-eighth. I am a percentage. What am I?

____

NAME: ______________________

DIRECTIONS Solve each problem.

1.

$$\begin{array}{r} 194 \\ -\ 63 \\ \hline \end{array}$$

2. 147 x 10 = ______

3. 369 ÷ 3 = ______

4. List the first three multiples of 5.

____

5. Write 6 ones + 6 tenths + 9 hundredths as a decimal.

____

6. 5 (10 – 8) = ______

7. 5.6 + ☐ = 8.5

8. Find *j*. *j* + 8= 21

j = ______

9. Calculate the perimeter of a rectangle that is 6 m by 7 m.

____

10. Are all quadrilaterals rectangles?

____

11.

Cookies Baked

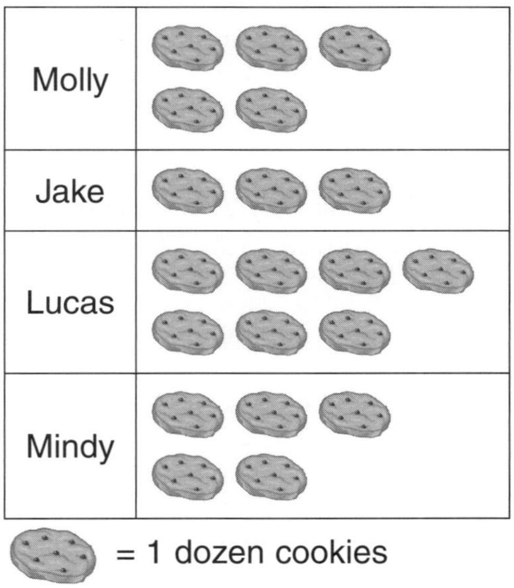

One quarter of Mindy's cookies were chocolate chip. How many were not chocolate chip?

____

12. Eight people were at a party. If each person shook hands with every other person, how many handshakes were there?

____

SCORE

1. Ⓨ Ⓝ
2. Ⓨ Ⓝ
3. Ⓨ Ⓝ
4. Ⓨ Ⓝ
5. Ⓨ Ⓝ
6. Ⓨ Ⓝ
7. Ⓨ Ⓝ
8. Ⓨ Ⓝ
9. Ⓨ Ⓝ
10. Ⓨ Ⓝ
11. Ⓨ Ⓝ
12. Ⓨ Ⓝ

___ / 12
Total

DAY 70

NAME: ____________________

DIRECTIONS Solve each problem.

SCORE
1. Ⓨ Ⓝ
2. Ⓨ Ⓝ
3. Ⓨ Ⓝ
4. Ⓨ Ⓝ
5. Ⓨ Ⓝ
6. Ⓨ Ⓝ
7. Ⓨ Ⓝ
8. Ⓨ Ⓝ
9. Ⓨ Ⓝ
10. Ⓨ Ⓝ
11. Ⓨ Ⓝ
12. Ⓨ Ⓝ
___ / 12 Total

1. 80 + (–90) = ______

2. $\begin{array}{r} 34 \\ \times\ 4 \\ \hline \end{array}$

3. How many groups of six are in 126?

____

4. How many digits are in the number 369,472?

____

5. $\frac{5}{8} + (-\frac{3}{8}) =$ ______

6. Write the next number in the sequence. 108, 208, 308,

____

7. 25% of ☐ is 70.

8. Write the expression for 10 less than *r*.

____

9. Write 11:49 A.M. in a 24-hour time format.

____

10. Use a protractor to measure the angle.

____

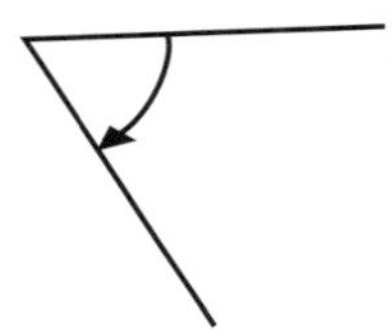

11. A single 6-sided die is used. What is the probability of rolling a number greater than 5?

____

12. A sweater that normally costs $25.00 is on sale for 10% off. What will the discount be? What will the cost of the sweater be?

Discount: ______________

Cost: ______________

NAME: ____________________

DIRECTIONS Solve each problem.

1. 76 – 48 = ______

2. 15 • 7 = ______

3. 137 ÷ 4 = ______

4. How many hundreds are in the number 367,594?

____

5. $2\frac{1}{5} + 3\frac{2}{5} =$ ______

6. 12 ÷ 4 + 5 • 3 = ______

7. $\frac{3}{4} = \frac{\square}{8}$

8. Find u if $u^2 = 49$.

$u =$ ______

9. How many liters are in 9,500 milliliters?

____

10. Name the shape that is located at (E,5).

____

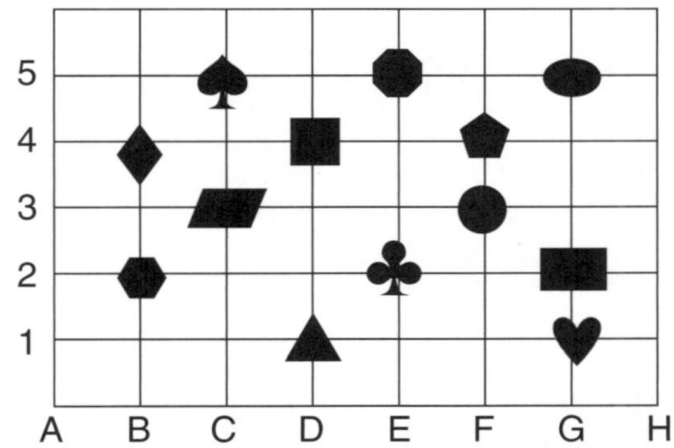

11. Create a bar graph of the data below.

Sara saved $15.00. Ang saved one-third of what Sara saved. Ben saved $10.00 more than Sara. Tina saved twice as much as Ang.

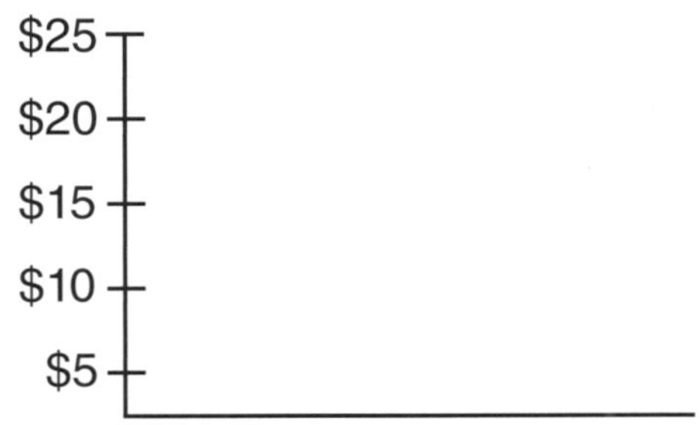

12. Use the graph above. If Tina spends half of her money, how much will she have left?

____

SCORE

1. Ⓨ Ⓝ
2. Ⓨ Ⓝ
3. Ⓨ Ⓝ
4. Ⓨ Ⓝ
5. Ⓨ Ⓝ
6. Ⓨ Ⓝ
7. Ⓨ Ⓝ
8. Ⓨ Ⓝ
9. Ⓨ Ⓝ
10. Ⓨ Ⓝ
11. Ⓨ Ⓝ
12. Ⓨ Ⓝ

___ / 12

Total

NAME: ______________________________

DIRECTIONS Solve each problem.

SCORE

1. Ⓨ Ⓝ
2. Ⓨ Ⓝ
3. Ⓨ Ⓝ
4. Ⓨ Ⓝ
5. Ⓨ Ⓝ
6. Ⓨ Ⓝ
7. Ⓨ Ⓝ
8. Ⓨ Ⓝ
9. Ⓨ Ⓝ
10. Ⓨ Ⓝ
11. Ⓨ Ⓝ
12. Ⓨ Ⓝ

___ / 12
Total

1. $75 + 68 =$ ______

2. $-10 \times 15 =$ ______

3. $7\overline{)276}$

4. Write 86,391 in expanded notation.

____

____

5. How many tenths are in $2\frac{2}{10}$?

____

6. $9 + (-50) + 70 =$ ______

7. Solve for *g*. $\frac{1}{3}g = 12$

$g =$ ______

8. $\frac{4}{5}$ of ☐ $= 24$

9. How many grams are in 2.525 kilograms?

____

10. Name the two quadrilaterals with four equal sides.

____

____

11. What is the probability you will spin a word that has two letters that are the same in it?

____

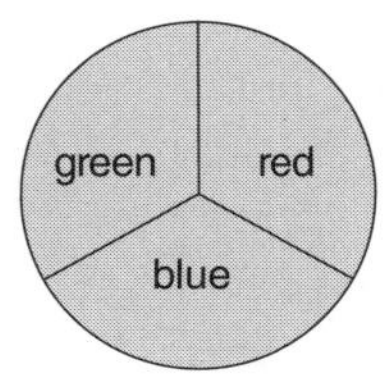

12. Mario wants to ride his bike further each day. He rides 3 miles on the first day, 6 miles on the second day, and 9 miles on the third day. If he follows this pattern, how many miles will he ride on the ninth day?

____

____

NAME: ______________________

DIRECTIONS Solve each problem.

1. Write the difference when 68 is subtracted from 92.

____

2.
$$\begin{array}{r} 10 \\ \times\ 10 \\ \hline \end{array}$$

3. $264 \div (-4) =$ ______

4. Round 367,240 to the nearest hundred.

____

5. Write $3\frac{1}{3}$ as an improper fraction.

____

6. $18 \div 6 - 4 =$ ______

7. 20% of ☐ is 16.

8. Find *k*.
$k \div 42 = 4$

$k =$ ______

9. Show 24 minutes after 2 on the digital clock.

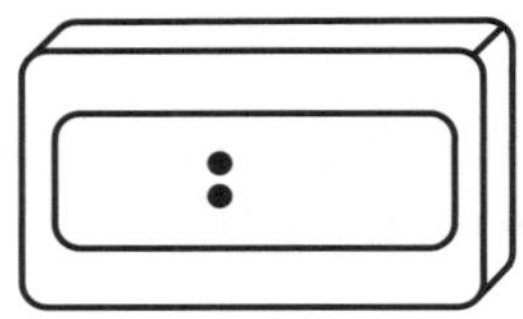

10. Name the solid shape.

____

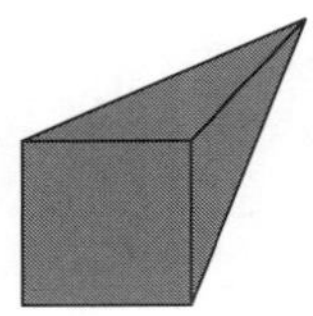

11. If you toss a 6-sided die, what is the probability you will get an even number?

____

12. How many matches would be needed to form 40 large triangles in the pattern below?

____

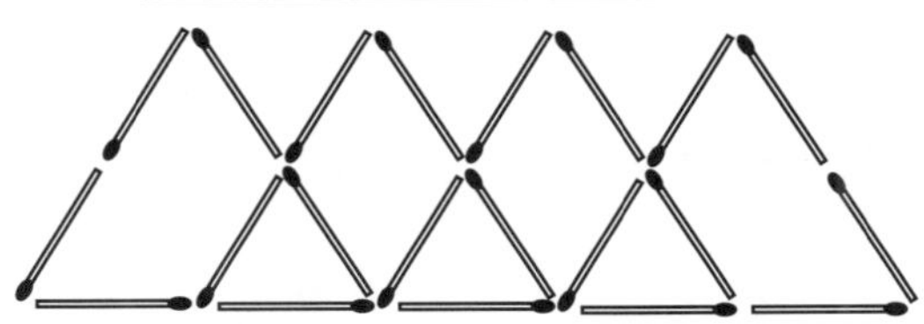

SCORE

1. Ⓨ Ⓝ
2. Ⓨ Ⓝ
3. Ⓨ Ⓝ
4. Ⓨ Ⓝ
5. Ⓨ Ⓝ
6. Ⓨ Ⓝ
7. Ⓨ Ⓝ
8. Ⓨ Ⓝ
9. Ⓨ Ⓝ
10. Ⓨ Ⓝ
11. Ⓨ Ⓝ
12. Ⓨ Ⓝ

___ / 12 Total

NAME: ______________________________

DIRECTIONS Solve each problem.

SCORE

1. Ⓨ Ⓝ
2. Ⓨ Ⓝ
3. Ⓨ Ⓝ
4. Ⓨ Ⓝ
5. Ⓨ Ⓝ
6. Ⓨ Ⓝ
7. Ⓨ Ⓝ
8. Ⓨ Ⓝ
9. Ⓨ Ⓝ
10. Ⓨ Ⓝ
11. Ⓨ Ⓝ
12. Ⓨ Ⓝ

___ / 12 Total

1.

$$\begin{array}{r} 35 \\ 16 \\ +\ 43 \\ \hline \end{array}$$

2. 10 • 20 = ______

3. What is the quotient when 237 is divided by 6?

____

4. Is 2,437 an even or an odd number?

____

5. 10% of 60 is ______.

6. Write the next number in the pattern.

–5, –10, –15, ______

7. 60,000 + ______________

+ 400 + 30 + 2 = 67,432

8. Find x. $x - 6.7 = 2.1$

x = ______

9. How many centimeters are in 9.5 meters?

____

10. Complete the chart for the shape.

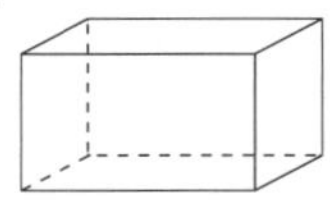

Name the figure.	
How many surfaces?	
How many vertices?	
Does it stack or roll?	
Is it a plane shape or a solid shape?	

11. **Boys and Girls in Class**

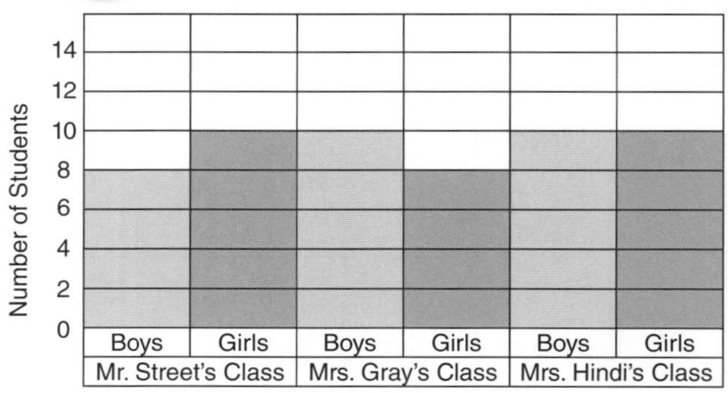

What is the total number of students in all three classes?

____

12. Use three of the numerals 3, 4, 5, 12, or 15 to complete the number sentence. Use any numeral once and only once.

(______ – ______) x ______ = 24

NAME: ____________________

DIRECTIONS Solve each problem.

1. $-6 + 2 =$ ______

2. $102 \times 4 =$ ______

3. $6 \overline{)432}$

4. What is the even number after 699?

____

5. $\frac{8}{9} - \frac{4}{9} =$ ______

6. $11 + 38 + (-12) =$ ______

7. $6 + 6 + 6 + 6 = 4 \times \square$

8. Write the expression for the quotient when *a* is divided by *b*.

____

9. Calculate the area of a rectangle that is 8 m by 9 m.

____

10. Is 75° an acute or an obtuse angle?

____

11. What is the median of this set of data?
61, 70, 63, 65, 71, 82

____

12. Complete the magic square so each row, column, and diagonal adds up to the same number. Use each number 3–11 only once.

	3	8
	7	
6		

SCORE

1. Ⓨ Ⓝ
2. Ⓨ Ⓝ
3. Ⓨ Ⓝ
4. Ⓨ Ⓝ
5. Ⓨ Ⓝ
6. Ⓨ Ⓝ
7. Ⓨ Ⓝ
8. Ⓨ Ⓝ
9. Ⓨ Ⓝ
10. Ⓨ Ⓝ
11. Ⓨ Ⓝ
12. Ⓨ Ⓝ

___ / 12
Total

DAY 76

NAME: ____________________

DIRECTIONS Solve each problem.

SCORE

1. Ⓨ Ⓝ
2. Ⓨ Ⓝ
3. Ⓨ Ⓝ
4. Ⓨ Ⓝ
5. Ⓨ Ⓝ
6. Ⓨ Ⓝ
7. Ⓨ Ⓝ
8. Ⓨ Ⓝ
9. Ⓨ Ⓝ
10. Ⓨ Ⓝ
11. Ⓨ Ⓝ
12. Ⓨ Ⓝ

___ / 12 Total

1. Double 28. ______

2.

$$\begin{array}{r} 25 \\ \times\ 5 \\ \hline \end{array}$$

3. Divide 273 by 4.

____

4. Is a negative number less than zero?

____

5. Write $\frac{16}{5}$ as a mixed number.

____

6. $-3\ (5 + 7) =$ ______

7. $100 \div \square = 10$

8. Solve for m if $\frac{3}{5}m = 9$.

$m =$ ______

9. Write 8:47 A.M. in a 24-hour time format.

____

10. Draw a side view of the cube.

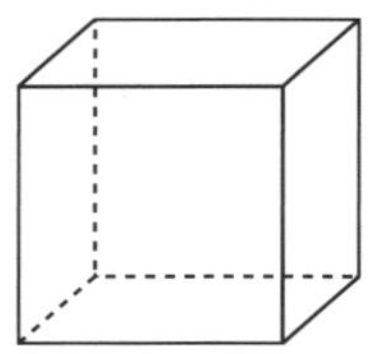

11. What is the probability the spinner will land on anything but football?

____

12. Complete the factor wheel to show all the factors of the number 20.

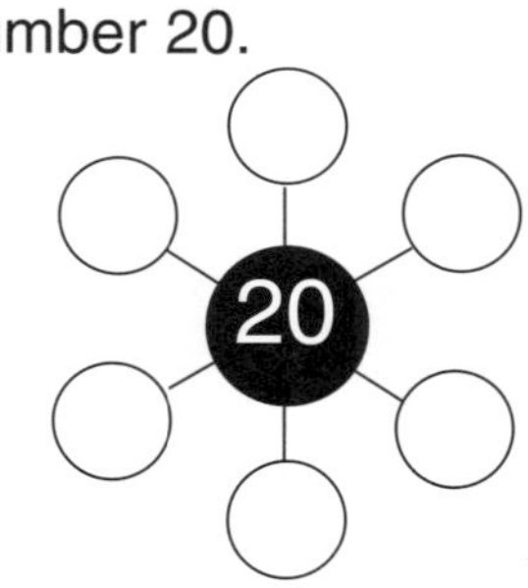

NAME: ____________________

DIRECTIONS Solve each problem.

1. Calculate 38 less than 92.

____

2. $872 \cdot 10 =$ ______

3. $7\overline{)281}$

4. Is 3 a factor of 37?

____

5. Write the improper fraction for $4\frac{1}{3}$.

____

6. Complete the input/output chart. Look for a pattern and write the rule.

Input	78	68	58	48	38	28
Output	53	43	33			

____

____

7. Find *h*. $h - 12 = -6$

$h =$ ______

8. Solve for *b*. $\frac{3}{4}b = \frac{9}{4}$

$b =$ ______

9. What time is it one half-hour after 3:42 A.M.?

____

10. How many edges does a cube have?

____

11. **Color of Vehicles Sighted**

Blue	卌 ||
Green	|||
Red	||||
White	卌 ||||
Black	卌 ||

Which color vehicles were seen with the same frequency?

____

12. The cost of the Ferris wheel is $\frac{1}{3}$ of the cost of the roller coaster. The roller coaster costs $6.00. How much does it cost to ride the Ferris wheel?

____

SCORE

1. Ⓨ Ⓝ
2. Ⓨ Ⓝ
3. Ⓨ Ⓝ
4. Ⓨ Ⓝ
5. Ⓨ Ⓝ
6. Ⓨ Ⓝ
7. Ⓨ Ⓝ
8. Ⓨ Ⓝ
9. Ⓨ Ⓝ
10. Ⓨ Ⓝ
11. Ⓨ Ⓝ
12. Ⓨ Ⓝ

___ / 12 Total

NAME: ____________________

DIRECTIONS Solve each problem.

SCORE

1. Ⓨ Ⓝ
2. Ⓨ Ⓝ
3. Ⓨ Ⓝ
4. Ⓨ Ⓝ
5. Ⓨ Ⓝ
6. Ⓨ Ⓝ
7. Ⓨ Ⓝ
8. Ⓨ Ⓝ
9. Ⓨ Ⓝ
10. Ⓨ Ⓝ
11. Ⓨ Ⓝ
12. Ⓨ Ⓝ

___ / 12 Total

1. Calculate 52 and 29 more.

____

2. 372 x 10 = ______

3. Divide 437 by 9.

____

4. Circle the prime number(s).

63 71 81 91

5. Is $\frac{10}{12}$ less than, greater than, or equal to $\frac{5}{6}$?

____

6. 2 x 5 – 4 x 3 = ______

7. $2\frac{2}{3} = \frac{\square}{3}$

8. Find *f*. $34f = 204$

$f =$ ______

9. Calculate the area of a square with 12 cm sides.

____

10. How many lines of symmetry does a rectangle have?

____

11. Inside a bag of candy there are 16 lollipops, 12 pieces of chocolate, and 7 pieces of licorice. If you reach into the bag and grab a piece of candy, what is the probability that it will not be a lollipop?

____

12. A burger restaurant serves twice as many cheeseburgers as hamburgers. It also sells $\frac{1}{3}$ as many double hamburgers as regular hamburgers. If the restaurant sells 120 cheeseburgers, how many double hamburgers does it sell?

____

NAME: ____________________

DIRECTIONS Solve each problem.

1. Calculate 25 less than 81.

____

2. $392 \cdot 15 =$ ______

3. $527 \div 6 =$ ______

4. Is 394 evenly divisible by 4?

____

5. $\frac{2}{3} \times \frac{4}{5} =$ ______

6. $5^2 - 6^2 =$ ______

7. $86 - \square = 32$

8. Solve for p. $\frac{1}{5}p = 10$

$p =$ ______

9. How many millimeters are in 7 centimeters?

____

10. At what angle do perpendicular lines meet?

____

11. In a game, the probability of the spinner landing on a 2 is $\frac{1}{3}$. How many times would you expect to land on a 2 if you spin the spinner 12 times?

____

12. Paul bought a pet and supplies at a pet store. He spent $14.95 to buy his hamster. He also bought a cage for $25.95. The food for the hamster cost $2.00 for a week's supply. If he bought a four-week supply of food, what was his total bill at the pet store?

____

SCORE

1. Ⓨ Ⓝ
2. Ⓨ Ⓝ
3. Ⓨ Ⓝ
4. Ⓨ Ⓝ
5. Ⓨ Ⓝ
6. Ⓨ Ⓝ
7. Ⓨ Ⓝ
8. Ⓨ Ⓝ
9. Ⓨ Ⓝ
10. Ⓨ Ⓝ
11. Ⓨ Ⓝ
12. Ⓨ Ⓝ

___ / 12 Total

DAY 80

NAME: ____________________

DIRECTIONS Solve each problem.

SCORE

1. Ⓨ Ⓝ
2. Ⓨ Ⓝ
3. Ⓨ Ⓝ
4. Ⓨ Ⓝ
5. Ⓨ Ⓝ
6. Ⓨ Ⓝ
7. Ⓨ Ⓝ
8. Ⓨ Ⓝ
9. Ⓨ Ⓝ
10. Ⓨ Ⓝ
11. Ⓨ Ⓝ
12. Ⓨ Ⓝ

___ / 12 Total

1. Add 94 to 687.

____

2. 35 x (–6) = ______

3. $8\overline{)291}$

4. Write the smallest possible four-digit number using the digits 5, 9, 3, and 8.

____

5. Write $\frac{3}{10}$ as a percentage.

____

6. Write the next number in the sequence. 2,065; 2,165; 2,265;

____

7. $\frac{1}{10}$ of ☐ is 8.

8. Write the expression for two less than *x*.

____

9. Calculate the area of the shape.

____

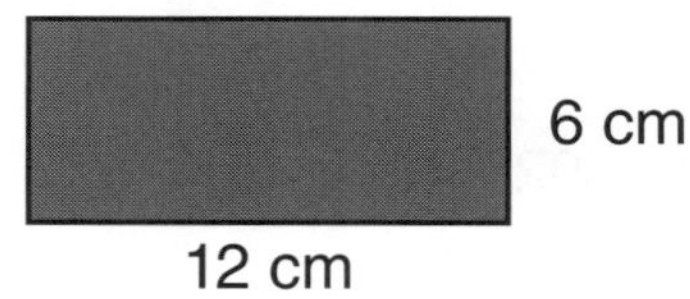

10. Is the angle *acute*, *obtuse*, or *reflex*?

____

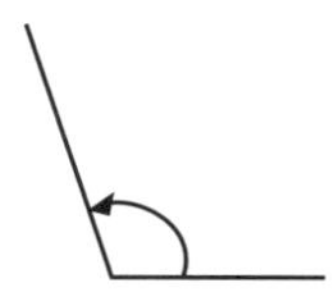

11.

	Regular Price	Discount
Pants	\$32	25%
Shirts	\$24	30%
Shoes	\$45	35%
Socks	\$4	10%

What will the discounted price of the socks be?

____

12. Hannah wants to save $\frac{1}{3}$ of her allowance each week to buy a new dress that costs \$45.00. If her allowance is \$6.00 each week, how many weeks will she have to save to buy the dress?

____

NAME: ______________________________

DIRECTIONS Solve each problem.

1. Write the difference when 97 is subtracted from 721.

____

2.
$$\begin{array}{r} 52 \\ \times\ 3 \\ \hline \end{array}$$

3. $573 \div 9 =$ ______

4. What is the value of the digit 9 in the number 937,241?

____

5. Write $\frac{13}{5}$ as a mixed number.

____

6. $1 + 2 \bullet 3 - 4 =$ ______

7. $21 + 3 = \square \times 8$

8. Find *w*. $w^2 = 144$

$w =$ ______

9. What is the elapsed time between 8:53 A.M. and 9:46 A.M.?

____

10. Which line is parallel to line H?

____

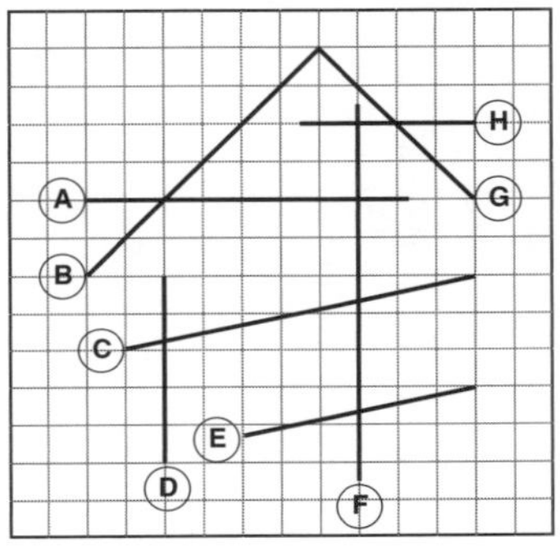

11. Record the data in the pictograph.

Mark read 30 books. Eric read 50 books.

 = 10 books

12. If it costs $30.00 for adults and $25.00 for children to get into the amusement park, how much would it cost for two parents and three kids to get into the amusement park?

____

SCORE

1. Ⓨ Ⓝ
2. Ⓨ Ⓝ
3. Ⓨ Ⓝ
4. Ⓨ Ⓝ
5. Ⓨ Ⓝ
6. Ⓨ Ⓝ
7. Ⓨ Ⓝ
8. Ⓨ Ⓝ
9. Ⓨ Ⓝ
10. Ⓨ Ⓝ
11. Ⓨ Ⓝ
12. Ⓨ Ⓝ

___ / 12 Total

DAY 82

NAME: ____________________

DIRECTIONS Solve each problem.

SCORE

1. Ⓨ Ⓝ
2. Ⓨ Ⓝ
3. Ⓨ Ⓝ
4. Ⓨ Ⓝ
5. Ⓨ Ⓝ
6. Ⓨ Ⓝ
7. Ⓨ Ⓝ
8. Ⓨ Ⓝ
9. Ⓨ Ⓝ
10. Ⓨ Ⓝ
11. Ⓨ Ⓝ
12. Ⓨ Ⓝ

___ / 12 Total

1. Double 27. ______

2. 316 • 10 = ______

3. $7\overline{)529}$

4. 9,000 + 700 + 30 + 6 =

____

5. Write $\frac{23}{10}$ as a mixed number.

____

6. Complete the table. Then write the conversion rule for grams to kilograms.

Gram	3,000		4,500		6,000
Kilogram	3	3.75		5.25	

____

____

7. $\frac{3}{4} = \frac{\square}{8}$

8. Solve fo z. $\frac{z}{3} = -7$

z = ______

9. How many grams are in 3.5 kilograms?

____

10. Circle the acute angle.

48° 169° 295°

11. What is the probability you will spin a word with the letter *r* in it?

____

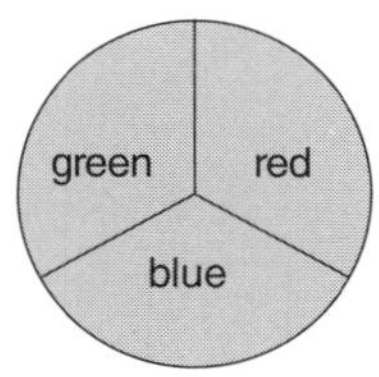

12. A new pair of shoes costs $50.00. If there is a 25% off sale, what is the sale price of the shoes?

____

DAY 83

NAME: ______________________________

DIRECTIONS Solve each problem.

1.
$$\begin{array}{r} 86 \\ -\ 47 \\ \hline \end{array}$$

2. 72 x 100 = ______

3. What is the quotient when 824 is divided by 7?

____

4. Round 45,678 to the nearest thousand.

____

5. $\frac{1}{8} - \frac{4}{8} =$ ______

6. $6^2 + 3 \times 5 =$ ______

7. $0.75 = \frac{\square}{4}$

8. Find *q*. $\frac{50}{q} = 25$

$q =$ ______

9. How many minutes are from 5:32 P.M. to 6:19 P.M.?

____

10. Draw the cross-section for the solid.

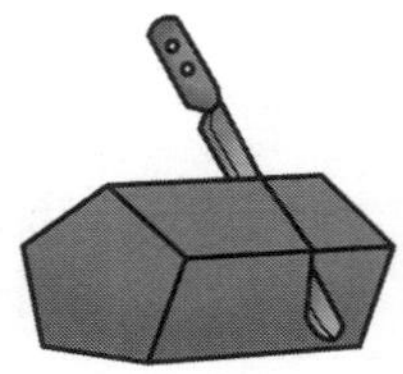

11.

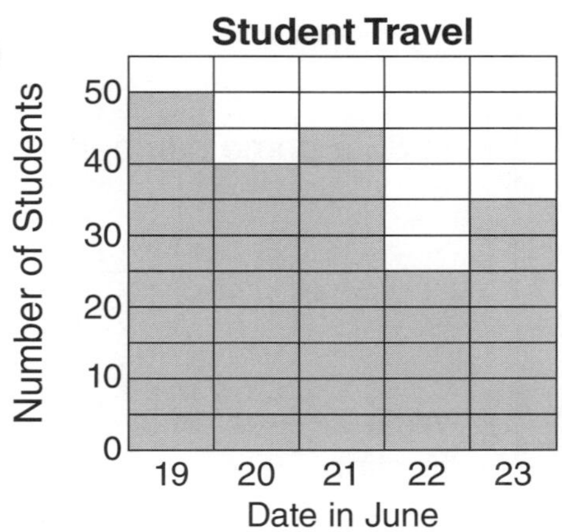

On which date did 50 students travel?

____

12. Jerry rents a movie once a month. It costs $3.00 to rent a movie. How much does Jerry spend in 1 year on rentals?

____

SCORE

1. Ⓨ Ⓝ
2. Ⓨ Ⓝ
3. Ⓨ Ⓝ
4. Ⓨ Ⓝ
5. Ⓨ Ⓝ
6. Ⓨ Ⓝ
7. Ⓨ Ⓝ
8. Ⓨ Ⓝ
9. Ⓨ Ⓝ
10. Ⓨ Ⓝ
11. Ⓨ Ⓝ
12. Ⓨ Ⓝ

___ / 12

Total

DAY 84

NAME: ____________________

DIRECTIONS Solve each problem.

SCORE

1. Ⓨ Ⓝ
2. Ⓨ Ⓝ
3. Ⓨ Ⓝ
4. Ⓨ Ⓝ
5. Ⓨ Ⓝ
6. Ⓨ Ⓝ
7. Ⓨ Ⓝ
8. Ⓨ Ⓝ
9. Ⓨ Ⓝ
10. Ⓨ Ⓝ
11. Ⓨ Ⓝ
12. Ⓨ Ⓝ

___ / 12
Total

1. 25 – 30 = ______

2.
$$\begin{array}{r} 463 \\ \times\ 10 \\ \hline \end{array}$$

3. 381 ÷ 6 = ______

4. Is 35 a prime number?

____

5. Write $2\frac{6}{10}$ as an improper fraction.

____

6. 17 – 7 x 2 = ______

7. $0.20 = \frac{\square}{10}$

8. Find *e*. *e* – 17 = 37

e = ______

9. How many total days are in May and June?

____

10. What is the term for a pair of angles that have a sum of 180°?

____

11. Imagine that you write each letter of the word *EXCELLENT* on a different card and then shuffle the cards. You turn the deck of cards facedown on a table and turn over the top card. What is the probability that you will turn over a consonant?

____

12. Kelly is making necklaces for her friends. She has 450 beads. If 30 beads are used in each necklace, how many necklaces can she make?

____

NAME: ______________________________

DIRECTIONS Solve each problem.

1. 749 – 68 = ______

2. 126 • 10 = ______

3. $4\overline{)261}$

4. What is the ordinal number for twelve?

____

5. $\frac{3}{10}$ of 30 is ______.

6. 36 ÷ 6 + 3 = ______

7. 950 ÷ 50 = 19 x ☐

8. Write the expression for twice a number *y* increased by 4.

____

9. How many liters are in 9,500 milliliters?

____

10. Is an obtuse angle less than 90°?

____

11. What is the mode for this set of data?

95, 78, 80, 95, 76, 81

____

12. Eight boxes each hold the same number of machine parts. Only one answer below shows the total number of parts for all eight boxes. Circle the answer.

A. 135 B. 138 C. 136 D. 133

SCORE

1. Ⓨ Ⓝ
2. Ⓨ Ⓝ
3. Ⓨ Ⓝ
4. Ⓨ Ⓝ
5. Ⓨ Ⓝ
6. Ⓨ Ⓝ
7. Ⓨ Ⓝ
8. Ⓨ Ⓝ
9. Ⓨ Ⓝ
10. Ⓨ Ⓝ
11. Ⓨ Ⓝ
12. Ⓨ Ⓝ

___ / 12 Total

NAME: ____________________

DIRECTIONS Solve each problem.

SCORE

1. Ⓨ Ⓝ
2. Ⓨ Ⓝ
3. Ⓨ Ⓝ
4. Ⓨ Ⓝ
5. Ⓨ Ⓝ
6. Ⓨ Ⓝ
7. Ⓨ Ⓝ
8. Ⓨ Ⓝ
9. Ⓨ Ⓝ
10. Ⓨ Ⓝ
11. Ⓨ Ⓝ
12. Ⓨ Ⓝ

___ / 12 Total

1. 92 + 46 = ______

2. −30 x (−40) = ______

3. $6\overline{)343}$

4. True or false? 64,281 > 64,218

____

5. Write 9 ones + 5 tenths + 3 hundredths as a decimal.

____

6. 36 ÷ (6 + 3) = ______

7. 8.4 + ☐ = 15.6

8. Find *h*. 17*h* = 34

h = ______

9. How many kilometers are in 6,250 meters?

____

10. Draw a picture showing what the rectangular prism looks like from the top.

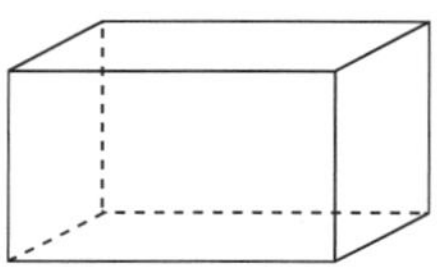

11. Which spinner would give you the best chance of landing on red?

____

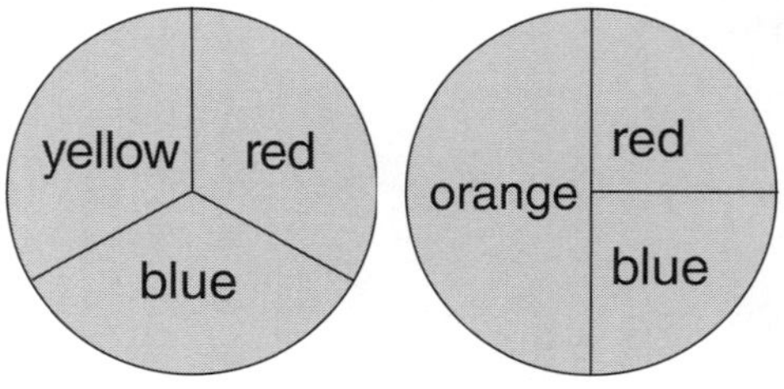

Spinner A **Spinner B**

12. For every apple Lisa buys at the store, she buys three bananas. If Lisa buys 7 apples at the store, how many bananas will she buy?

____

NAME: ____________________________

DIRECTIONS Solve each problem.

1. Calculate the difference for 76 less than 943.

____

2. $\begin{array}{r} 124 \\ \times \; 10 \\ \hline \end{array}$

3. $537 \div 8 =$ ______

4. List all the factors of 35.

____

5. $\frac{3}{14} \times \frac{7}{10} =$ ______

6. $17 - 7 \times 2^2 =$ ______

7. $\square \times 5 = 75 \div 3$

8. Solve for r. $\frac{r}{12} = 11$

$r =$ ______

9. How many meters are in 956 centimeters?

____

10. How many vertices are on the solid?

____

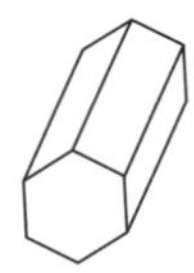

11. Two red cubes, two green cylinders, and three yellow rectangular prisms were put into a bag. What is the probability that you will pull out a green block?

____

12. The ratio of boys to girls is 2 to 3. If there are 20 boys, how many girls are there?

____

SCORE

1. Ⓨ Ⓝ
2. Ⓨ Ⓝ
3. Ⓨ Ⓝ
4. Ⓨ Ⓝ
5. Ⓨ Ⓝ
6. Ⓨ Ⓝ
7. Ⓨ Ⓝ
8. Ⓨ Ⓝ
9. Ⓨ Ⓝ
10. Ⓨ Ⓝ
11. Ⓨ Ⓝ
12. Ⓨ Ⓝ

___ / 12
Total

DAY 88

NAME: ______________________

DIRECTIONS Solve each problem.

SCORE

1. Ⓨ Ⓝ
2. Ⓨ Ⓝ
3. Ⓨ Ⓝ
4. Ⓨ Ⓝ
5. Ⓨ Ⓝ
6. Ⓨ Ⓝ
7. Ⓨ Ⓝ
8. Ⓨ Ⓝ
9. Ⓨ Ⓝ
10. Ⓨ Ⓝ
11. Ⓨ Ⓝ
12. Ⓨ Ⓝ

___ / 12 Total

1. Calculate the sum of 627 and 94.

____

2.

$$\begin{array}{r} 18 \\ \times\ 5 \\ \hline \end{array}$$

3. $-14 \div (-2) =$ ______

4. Is 16 a square number?

____

5. Write 75% as a decimal.

____

6. $(3 \times 8) \div (54 \div 9) =$ ______

7. $9{,}000 + 700 + \square + 6 = 9{,}736$

8. Solve for v. $\frac{1}{8}v = 20$

$v =$ ______

9. What is the volume of the prism?

____

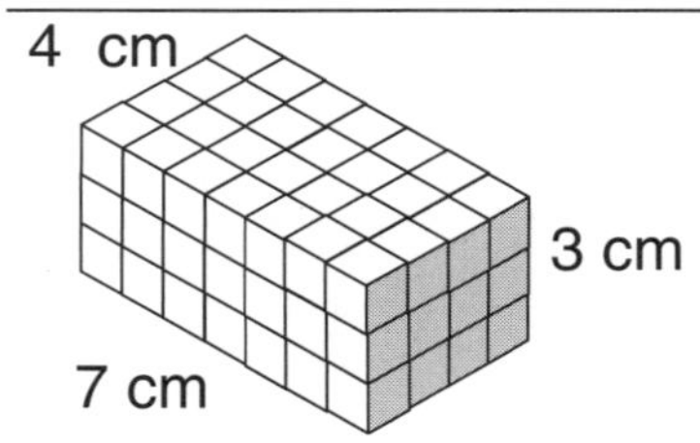

10. Is a pentagon a quadrilateral?

____

11.

Box A	Box B
A	A
Z	A
Z	Z
Z	T
T	T
T	S
S	M
S	G
S	G

If you randomly choose a letter from one of these columns, which column offers a better probability for choosing a *G*?

____

12. A factory can pack 25 cans in one box. How many boxes do they need for 200 cans?

____

NAME: ____________________

DIRECTIONS Solve each problem.

1.

$$\begin{array}{r} 21 \\ 32 \\ +\ 27 \\ \hline \end{array}$$

2. $43 \cdot 10 =$ ______

3. $4\overline{)237}$

4. List the first four multiples of 6.

____

5. $8 \times \frac{3}{4} =$ ______

6. Complete the input/output chart. Look for a pattern and write the rule.

Input	1	2	3	4	5	6
Output	1	4	9			

____

____

7. $3\frac{2}{3} = \frac{\square}{3}$

8. Find *g*. $g - 29 = 17$

$g =$ ______

9. How many centimeters are in 58 millimeters?

____

10. Do parallel lines ever meet?

____

11. **Cookies Baked**

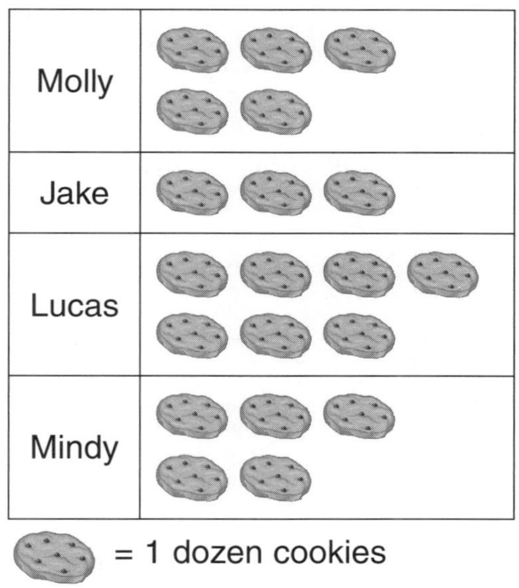

If Jake sells his cookies for $0.30 each, how much money will he earn?

____

12. Lani left her house at 8:15 A.M. She rode her bicycle for 50 minutes, visited with a friend for $1\frac{1}{2}$ hours, and then rode her bicycle back home for 50 minutes. What time did she arrive back home?

____

SCORE

1. Ⓨ Ⓝ
2. Ⓨ Ⓝ
3. Ⓨ Ⓝ
4. Ⓨ Ⓝ
5. Ⓨ Ⓝ
6. Ⓨ Ⓝ
7. Ⓨ Ⓝ
8. Ⓨ Ⓝ
9. Ⓨ Ⓝ
10. Ⓨ Ⓝ
11. Ⓨ Ⓝ
12. Ⓨ Ⓝ

___ / 12 **Total**

DAY 90

NAME: ____________________

DIRECTIONS Solve each problem.

SCORE

1. Ⓨ Ⓝ
2. Ⓨ Ⓝ
3. Ⓨ Ⓝ
4. Ⓨ Ⓝ
5. Ⓨ Ⓝ
6. Ⓨ Ⓝ
7. Ⓨ Ⓝ
8. Ⓨ Ⓝ
9. Ⓨ Ⓝ
10. Ⓨ Ⓝ
11. Ⓨ Ⓝ
12. Ⓨ Ⓝ

___ / 12 Total

1. $50 - (-8) =$ ______

2.

$$\begin{array}{r} 100 \\ \times\ \ 10 \\ \hline \end{array}$$

3. $629 \div 6 =$ ______

4. How many digits are in 165?

____

5. $\frac{3}{8} + \frac{5}{8} =$ ______

6. Write the next number in the sequence. 45, 54, 63, 72,

____

7. $2.9 + 5.8 = 13.2 - \square$

8. Find *x*. $22 - x = 15$

$x =$ ______

9. Calculate the perimeter of the shape.

____

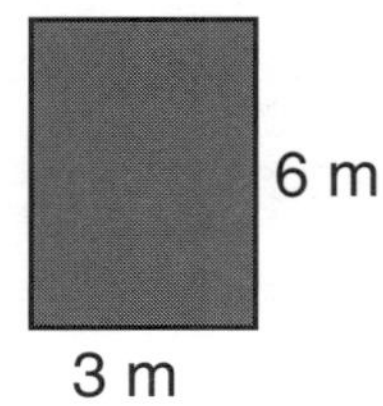

10. Is 106° less than or greater than a right angle?

____

11. A box of a dozen donuts contains 5 chocolate donuts, 4 sprinkled donuts, 2 lemon donuts, and 1 raspberry-filled donut. What is the probability that you will reach in and not grab a sprinkled donut?

____

12. A palindrome is a number that is the same backwards and forwards, for example 242. The addition problems below are also palindromes. Complete the chart with palindromes.

Addition	Palindrome
423 + 324	747
	929
314 + 413	
	383

NAME: ____________________

DIRECTIONS Solve each problem.

1. 96 – 67 = ______

2. –46 x 5 = ______

3. How many groups of 6 are in 24?

____

4. How many ten thousands are in 158,407?

____

5. $\frac{7}{8} - \frac{3}{8} =$ ______

6. –5 x 3 + 7 x 2 + 10 = ______

7. ☐ x 7 = 63

8. Find *a*. 5*a* = –35

a = ______

9. How many minutes are there from 12 minutes to 7:00 until 23 minutes past 7:00?

____

10. What is the area of a rectangle that measures 3 cm by 10 cm?

____

11. On which day were there 1,400 vehicles?

____

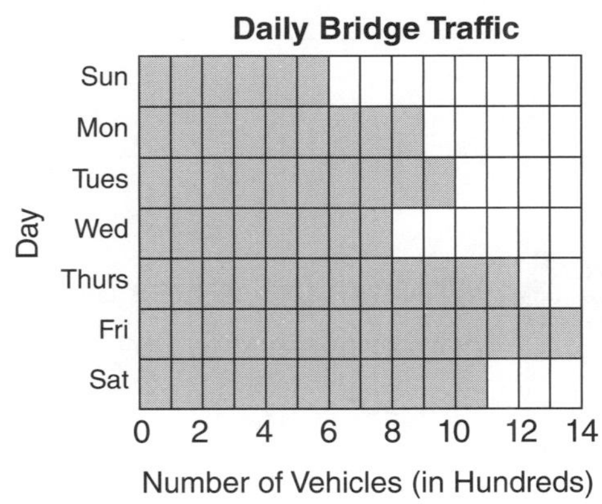

12. Maria can make 4 bows out of a yard of ribbon. How many yards of ribbon does she need to make 20 bows?

____

SCORE

1. Ⓨ Ⓝ
2. Ⓨ Ⓝ
3. Ⓨ Ⓝ
4. Ⓨ Ⓝ
5. Ⓨ Ⓝ
6. Ⓨ Ⓝ
7. Ⓨ Ⓝ
8. Ⓨ Ⓝ
9. Ⓨ Ⓝ
10. Ⓨ Ⓝ
11. Ⓨ Ⓝ
12. Ⓨ Ⓝ

___ / 12 Total

NAME: ____________________

DIRECTIONS Solve each problem.

SCORE

1. Ⓨ Ⓝ
2. Ⓨ Ⓝ
3. Ⓨ Ⓝ
4. Ⓨ Ⓝ
5. Ⓨ Ⓝ
6. Ⓨ Ⓝ
7. Ⓨ Ⓝ
8. Ⓨ Ⓝ
9. Ⓨ Ⓝ
10. Ⓨ Ⓝ
11. Ⓨ Ⓝ
12. Ⓨ Ⓝ

___ / 12 Total

1. $8 + 8 + 8 + 8 =$ ______

2. $45 \times 10 =$ ______

3. $8 \overline{)231}$

4. Write the expanded notation for the number 56,729.

____

____

5. Which of the values below is not equivalent to the other two? 0.3, 30%, $\frac{3}{100}$

____

6. $-5 \times (3 + 7) + (2 \times 10) =$ ______

7. $\frac{2}{3} = \frac{\square}{6}$

8. Find *k*. $-3k = 30$

$k =$ ______

9. How many centimeters are in 5 meters?

____

10. How many right angles are inside a square?

____

11. Draw a spinner that has a 25% probability of landing on green and a 75% probability of landing on yellow.

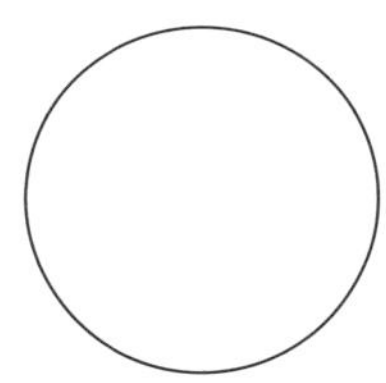

12. Compare a hexagonal pyramid to a hexagonal prism.

	Faces	Edges	Vertices
Hexagonal Pyramid			
Hexagonal Prism			

NAME: ______________________________

DIRECTIONS Solve each problem.

1. $74 - 39 =$ ______

2.
$$\begin{array}{r} 94 \\ \times\ 10 \\ \hline \end{array}$$

3. Divide 72 by –8.

____

4. Round 4,529 to the nearest hundred.

____

5. How many eighths are in $1\frac{1}{8}$?

____

6. $(5 + 2)^2 - 3^2 =$ ______

7. $14 + \square = 40 - 5$

8. Write the expression for *d* less than 12.

____

9. How many kilograms are in 4,000 grams?

____

10. How many axes of symmetry does the shape have?

____

11.

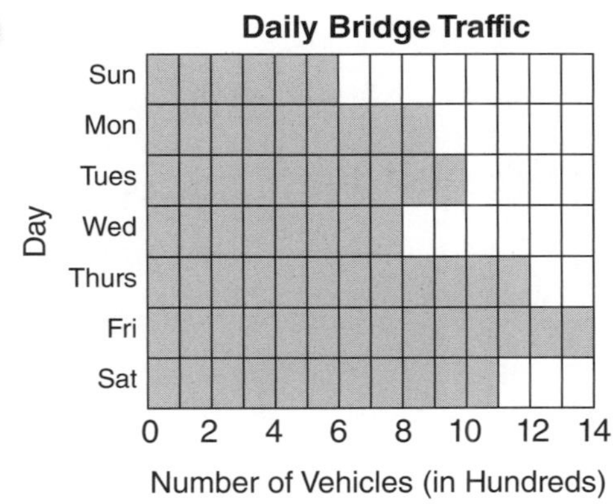

If there is a $3.00 toll to cross the bridge, how much money was collected on Monday?

____

12. Kent can swim 100 m in 50 seconds. How long will it take him to swim 300 m?

____

SCORE

1. Ⓨ Ⓝ
2. Ⓨ Ⓝ
3. Ⓨ Ⓝ
4. Ⓨ Ⓝ
5. Ⓨ Ⓝ
6. Ⓨ Ⓝ
7. Ⓨ Ⓝ
8. Ⓨ Ⓝ
9. Ⓨ Ⓝ
10. Ⓨ Ⓝ
11. Ⓨ Ⓝ
12. Ⓨ Ⓝ

___ / 12
Total

DAY 94

NAME: ______________________________

DIRECTIONS Solve each problem.

SCORE

1. Ⓨ Ⓝ
2. Ⓨ Ⓝ
3. Ⓨ Ⓝ
4. Ⓨ Ⓝ
5. Ⓨ Ⓝ
6. Ⓨ Ⓝ
7. Ⓨ Ⓝ
8. Ⓨ Ⓝ
9. Ⓨ Ⓝ
10. Ⓨ Ⓝ
11. Ⓨ Ⓝ
12. Ⓨ Ⓝ

___ / 12 Total

1. $\begin{array}{r} 326 \\ -\ 43 \\ \hline \end{array}$

2. $10 \times 20 =$ _______

3. $451 \div 6 =$ _______

4. $11^2 =$ _______

5. $\frac{2}{5}$ of 40 is _______.

6. $(5 - 2)^2 - 3^2 =$ _______

7. $\frac{1}{5}$ of ☐ is 4.

8. Find x.
$x + 10 = -6$

$x =$ _______

9. How many milliliters are in 6.5 liters?

____

10. Complete the chart for the shape.

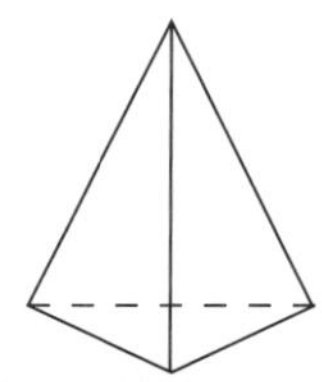

Name the figure.	
How many surfaces?	
How many vertices?	
Does it stack or roll?	
Is it a plane shape or a solid shape?	

11. The numbers 20 through 30 were written on individual cards and placed in a bag. If you take one card from the bag, what is the probability that it will be a multiple of 4?

____

12. A train left Main Street at 2:30 P.M. It arrived at the next stop at 3:02 P.M. How long did the train take to reach the stop?

____

NAME: ______________________________

DIRECTIONS Solve each problem.

1. Calculate the sum of 34, 48, and 67.

____

2. $5 \cdot 32 =$ ______

3. Calculate the quotient when 720 is divided by 8.

____

4. What number is 20 more than 3,645?

____

5. Write $\frac{12}{5}$ as a mixed number.

____

6. $12 \div 4 + 2 \times 8 =$ ______

7. $46 - \square = 23 + 7$

8. Find n. $\frac{3}{4}n = 12$

$n =$ ______

9. Calculate the area of the shaded triangle.

____

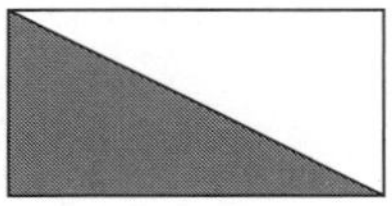

10. How many degrees does a straight angle measure?

____

11. What is the mean of this set of data?
\$3.60, \$3.90, \$4.50, \$5.40

____

12. Complete the subtraction table.

–	64	68		76	81	
		49				
29			44			
39						46
	15					

SCORE

1. Ⓨ Ⓝ
2. Ⓨ Ⓝ
3. Ⓨ Ⓝ
4. Ⓨ Ⓝ
5. Ⓨ Ⓝ
6. Ⓨ Ⓝ
7. Ⓨ Ⓝ
8. Ⓨ Ⓝ
9. Ⓨ Ⓝ
10. Ⓨ Ⓝ
11. Ⓨ Ⓝ
12. Ⓨ Ⓝ

___ / 12 Total

DAY
96

NAME: ______________________

DIRECTIONS Solve each problem.

SCORE

1. Ⓨ Ⓝ
2. Ⓨ Ⓝ
3. Ⓨ Ⓝ
4. Ⓨ Ⓝ
5. Ⓨ Ⓝ
6. Ⓨ Ⓝ
7. Ⓨ Ⓝ
8. Ⓨ Ⓝ
9. Ⓨ Ⓝ
10. Ⓨ Ⓝ
11. Ⓨ Ⓝ
12. Ⓨ Ⓝ

___ / 12
Total

1. $-10 - (-6) =$ ______

2. $17 \times 100 =$ ______

3. How many groups of eight are in 32?

____

4. Is –9 a negative or positive number?

____

5. 25% of 125 is ________.

6. $12 \div (4 + 2) \times 8 =$ ______

7. ☐ $\times 8 = 64$

8. Find h. $h - 5 = -34$

$h =$ ______

9. How many grams are in $\frac{1}{4}$ kilograms?

____

10. Draw a top view of the square pyramid.

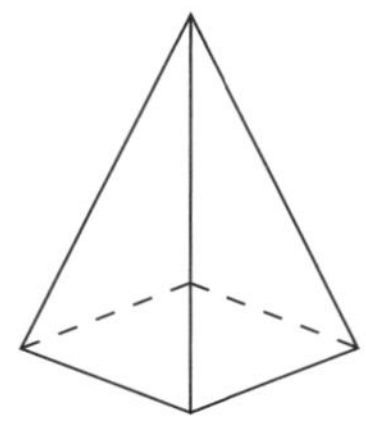

11. What is the probability the spinner will land on a sport that begins with the letter *s*?

____

12. Use three of the numerals 3, 4, 5, 12, or 15 to complete the number sentence. Do not use any numeral more than once.

______ ÷ ______ + ______ = 10

NAME: ____________________

DIRECTIONS Solve each problem.

1. 135 + 48 = ______

2.
```
  63
x  5
----
```

3. 450 ÷ 9 = ______

4. Is 9 a factor of 63?

____

5. $\frac{3}{4}$ of 16 is ______.

6. (12 ÷ 4 + 2) x 8 = ______

7. $\frac{1}{3}$ of ☐ is 8.

8. Find w when $w^2 = 9$.

w = ______

9. Write 19:21 in a 12-hour time format.

____

10. How many faces are on the solid?

____

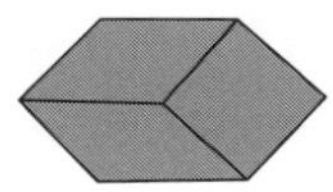

11. **Color of Vehicles Sighted**

Blue	𝍸 ||
Green	|||
Red	||||
White	𝍸 ||||
Black	𝍸 ||

Half of the red vehicles were trucks. How many red vehicles were not trucks?

____

12. Circle the factors of the given product.

Possible Factors									Product
5	4	7	16	2	9	15	13	12	92

SCORE

1. Ⓨ Ⓝ
2. Ⓨ Ⓝ
3. Ⓨ Ⓝ
4. Ⓨ Ⓝ
5. Ⓨ Ⓝ
6. Ⓨ Ⓝ
7. Ⓨ Ⓝ
8. Ⓨ Ⓝ
9. Ⓨ Ⓝ
10. Ⓨ Ⓝ
11. Ⓨ Ⓝ
12. Ⓨ Ⓝ

___ / 12 Total

DAY

98

NAME: ______________________________

DIRECTIONS Solve each problem.

SCORE

1. Ⓨ Ⓝ
2. Ⓨ Ⓝ
3. Ⓨ Ⓝ
4. Ⓨ Ⓝ
5. Ⓨ Ⓝ
6. Ⓨ Ⓝ
7. Ⓨ Ⓝ
8. Ⓨ Ⓝ
9. Ⓨ Ⓝ
10. Ⓨ Ⓝ
11. Ⓨ Ⓝ
12. Ⓨ Ⓝ

___ / 12 Total

1.

$$\begin{array}{r} 142 \\ -\ \ 67 \\ \hline \end{array}$$

2. $-36 \times (-5) =$ ______

3. $128 \div 4 =$ ______

4. What is 100 more than 356,937?

____

5. Does $\frac{4}{5} = \frac{8}{10}$? ______

6. $24 \div 8 - 4 + 6 \times 2 =$ ______

7. $1\frac{7}{8} = \frac{\square}{8}$

8. Write the expression for the quotient of 17 and *b* if *b* is the divisor.

____

9. What is the time one-half hour after 11:56 A.M.?

____

10. Circle the regular polygons.

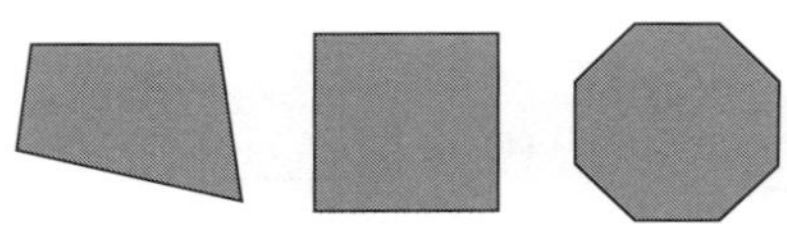

11. Inside a bag of candy there are 16 lollipops, 12 pieces of chocolate, and 7 pieces of licorice. If you reach into the bag and grab a piece of candy, what is the probability that it will not be a piece of chocolate?

____

12. Jose has softball practice every weeknight for 45 minutes. How many hours and minutes does he practice in one week?

____

NAME: ____________________

DIRECTIONS Solve each problem.

1. Calculate the difference when 98 is subtracted from 523.

____

2. 80 x 30 = ______

3. 5 $\overline{)243}$

4. Is 364 a multiple of 7?

____

5. How many halves are in $3\frac{1}{2}$?

____

6. 24 ÷ (8 – 4) + 6 x 2 = ______

7. 25 – ☐ = –50

8. Find *j*. *j* – 21= –8

j = ______

9. Calculate the perimeter of a regular hexagon with 5 cm sides.

____

10. True or false? Perpendicular lines always meet at a right angle.

____

11. **Points Scored**

	Game 1	Game 2	Game 3
Sara	14	15	14
Allison	19	13	11
Phillip	21	19	20
Sonia	16	13	15

If Phillip scored one 3-point shot in Game 1 and did not shoot any free throws, how many 2-point shots did he score?

____

12. At a conference, one car was provided for every 4 people. How many cars were needed if there were 76 people?

____

SCORE

1. Ⓨ Ⓝ
2. Ⓨ Ⓝ
3. Ⓨ Ⓝ
4. Ⓨ Ⓝ
5. Ⓨ Ⓝ
6. Ⓨ Ⓝ
7. Ⓨ Ⓝ
8. Ⓨ Ⓝ
9. Ⓨ Ⓝ
10. Ⓨ Ⓝ
11. Ⓨ Ⓝ
12. Ⓨ Ⓝ

___ / 12 Total

DAY 100

NAME: ______________________________

DIRECTIONS Solve each problem.

SCORE

1. Ⓨ Ⓝ
2. Ⓨ Ⓝ
3. Ⓨ Ⓝ
4. Ⓨ Ⓝ
5. Ⓨ Ⓝ
6. Ⓨ Ⓝ
7. Ⓨ Ⓝ
8. Ⓨ Ⓝ
9. Ⓨ Ⓝ
10. Ⓨ Ⓝ
11. Ⓨ Ⓝ
12. Ⓨ Ⓝ

___ / 12
Total

1.

$$\begin{array}{r} 35 \\ 29 \\ +\ 45 \\ \hline \end{array}$$

2.

$$\begin{array}{r} 14 \\ \times\ 6 \\ \hline \end{array}$$

3. What is the remainder when 125 is divided by 8?

____

4. Write the smallest possible number using 4, 6, 5, 9, and 3.

____

5. Arrange the numbers in ascending order. 6.8, 6.3, 3.5

____

6. Write the next number in the sequence.

32, 40, 48, 56, _____

7. 67 – ☐ = 35

8. Find q. $\frac{q}{-7} = -8$

q = ______

9. 8 quarts = ______ gallons

10. Use a protractor to measure the angle.

____

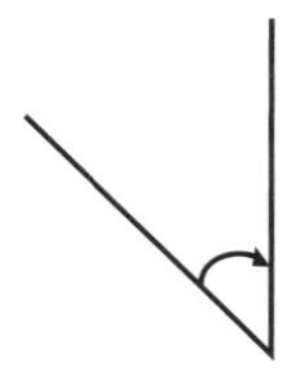

11.

	Regular Price	Discount
Pants	$32	25%
Shirts	$24	30%
Shoes	$45	35%
Socks	$4	10%

Which is the most expensive item after the discount?

____

12. In magic squares, each row, column, and diagonal adds up to the same number. Complete the magic square using the numbers 1–16.

1		13	
			7
	5		9
15	10	3	6

NAME: ____________________

DIRECTIONS Solve each problem.

1. 100 – 67 = ______

2. 40 x 6 = ______

3. 350 ÷ 7 = ______

4. What is the value of the digit 6 in the number 3,675?

____

5. 13.8 – 6.9 = ______

6. Complete the table. Then write the conversion rule for millimeters to centimeters.

Millimeter	50		120	
Centimeter	5	8.5		15.5

____

____

7. 56 ÷7 = 32 – ☐

8. Distribute. $2(x + 1) =$

____

9. What is the volume of the prism?

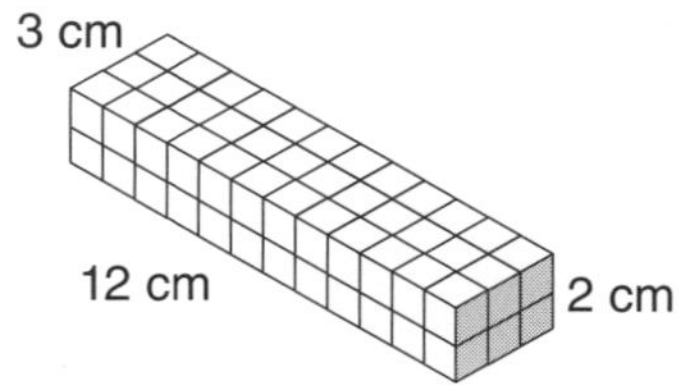

____

10. Name the shape that is located at (D,1).

____

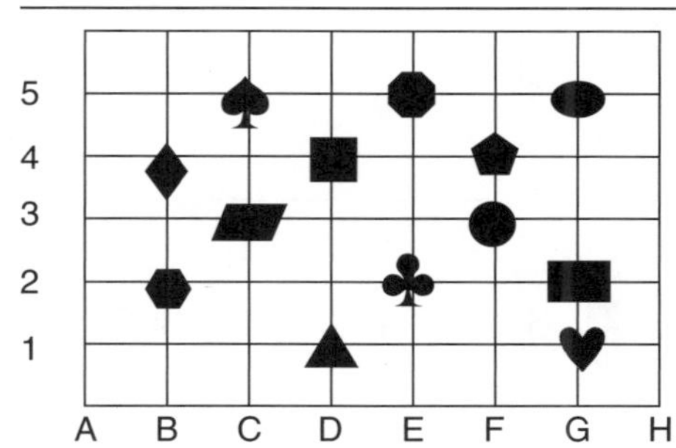

11. Record the data on the circle graph.

Twenty-four people were surveyed. Twelve drive cars. Six drive trucks. Three drive motorcycles. The rest drive mini vans.

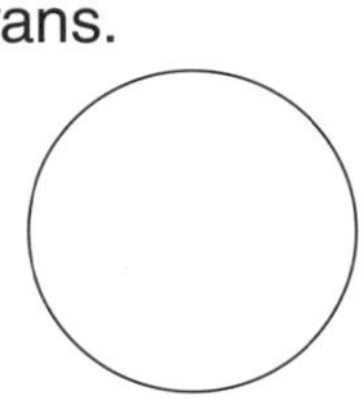

12. A ladder is 8 feet tall. How many inches is it?

____

SCORE

1. Ⓨ Ⓝ
2. Ⓨ Ⓝ
3. Ⓨ Ⓝ
4. Ⓨ Ⓝ
5. Ⓨ Ⓝ
6. Ⓨ Ⓝ
7. Ⓨ Ⓝ
8. Ⓨ Ⓝ
9. Ⓨ Ⓝ
10. Ⓨ Ⓝ
11. Ⓨ Ⓝ
12. Ⓨ Ⓝ

___ / 12
Total

NAME: ______________________________

DIRECTIONS Solve each problem.

SCORE

1. Ⓨ Ⓝ
2. Ⓨ Ⓝ
3. Ⓨ Ⓝ
4. Ⓨ Ⓝ
5. Ⓨ Ⓝ
6. Ⓨ Ⓝ
7. Ⓨ Ⓝ
8. Ⓨ Ⓝ
9. Ⓨ Ⓝ
10. Ⓨ Ⓝ
11. Ⓨ Ⓝ
12. Ⓨ Ⓝ

___ / 12
Total

1. Calculate the sum of 385 and 97.

____

2. 37 x 5 = ______

3. How many groups of nine are in 45?

____

4. 60,000 + 8,000 + 300 + 90 + 1 =

____

5. Write $\frac{6}{100}$ as a percentage.

____

6. Insert parentheses to make the following true.

3 + 5 x 2 = 16

7. ☐ + 27 = 72

8. Find *y*.
$7y = 84$

y = ______

9. 4 pints = ______ quarts

10. Here are five views of the same cube.

Draw the shape that is opposite the .

11. Draw a spinner that has a one in three chance of landing on red and a two-thirds chance of landing on yellow.

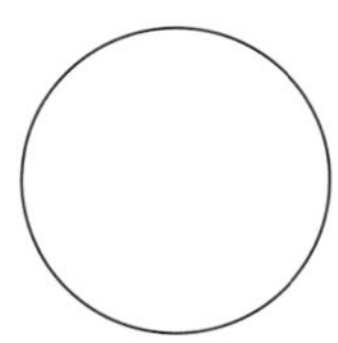

12. Twelve colored pencils vary in length from 10.5 cm to 12.7 cm. Circle the amount below that could be the total of their lengths.

120.5 cm   125.6 cm

134.9 cm   153.7 cm

NAME: ____________________

DIRECTIONS Solve each problem.

1. Subtract 186 from 372.

____

2. 30 • 70 = ______

3. 573 ÷ 8 = ______

4. Round 3,579 to the nearest thousand.

____

5. $5 \times \frac{2}{3} =$ ______

6. 24 ÷ 8 – (4 + 6) x 2 = ______

7. 4 + 7 = 121 ÷ ☐

8. Distribute.

4(5 + x) = ____________________

9. Calculate the perimeter of the shape.

____

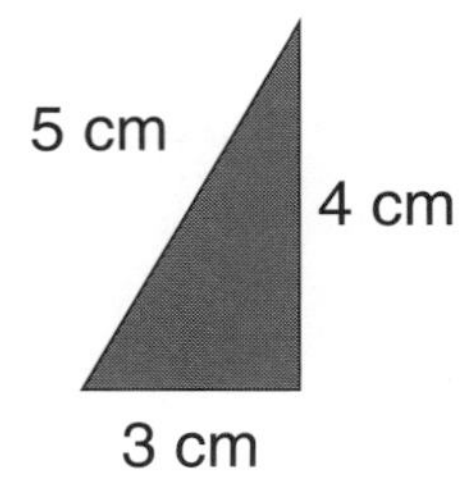

10. Name the solid shape.

____

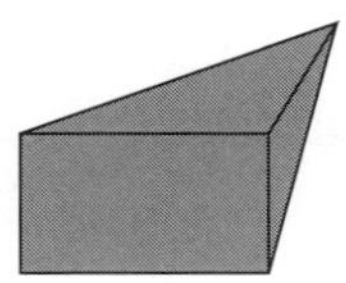

11. Steve, Mark, Melissa, Joe, and Mary are in a group. They randomly line up at the door. What is the probability that the name of the first person in line begins with *M*?

____

12. In a bouquet, there are an equal number of tulips and roses. There are twice as many daisies as there are tulips or roses. If there are 24 daisies in the bouquet, what is the total number of flowers in the bouquet?

____

SCORE

1. Ⓨ Ⓝ
2. Ⓨ Ⓝ
3. Ⓨ Ⓝ
4. Ⓨ Ⓝ
5. Ⓨ Ⓝ
6. Ⓨ Ⓝ
7. Ⓨ Ⓝ
8. Ⓨ Ⓝ
9. Ⓨ Ⓝ
10. Ⓨ Ⓝ
11. Ⓨ Ⓝ
12. Ⓨ Ⓝ

___ / 12 Total

DAY 104

NAME: ____________________

DIRECTIONS Solve each problem.

SCORE

1. Ⓨ Ⓝ
2. Ⓨ Ⓝ
3. Ⓨ Ⓝ
4. Ⓨ Ⓝ
5. Ⓨ Ⓝ
6. Ⓨ Ⓝ
7. Ⓨ Ⓝ
8. Ⓨ Ⓝ
9. Ⓨ Ⓝ
10. Ⓨ Ⓝ
11. Ⓨ Ⓝ
12. Ⓨ Ⓝ

___ / 12

Total

1. 23 + 42 + 13 = ______

2. 5 x 49 = ______

3. $4\overline{)285}$

4. Is 23,473 an even or an odd number?

____

5. 0 + 5 tenths + 8 hundredths =

____

6. 8 – 7 + 6 – 5 + 4 = ______

7. Find *d*. 3*d* = 12

d = ______

8. Write the expression for seven more than *t*.

____

9. What is the average speed if 225 miles are covered in 5 hours?

____

10. Complete the chart for the shape.

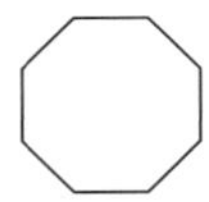

Name the figure.	
How many sides?	
How many angles?	
Does it have symmetry?	
Is it a plane shape or a solid shape?	

11. Imagine that you write each letter of the word *EXCELLENT* on a different card. You shuffle the cards, turn the deck of cards facedown on a table, and turn over the top card. What is the probability that you will turn over a letter made up of only straight lines?

____

12. Rhianna saves 25% of her allowance. She spends 50% of her allowance. She gives the rest to charity. If she gives $2 to charity each week, how much allowance does she get?

____

DAY 105

NAME: ____________________

DIRECTIONS Solve each problem.

1. $-8 - (-20) =$ ______

2. $5 \times 18 =$ ______

3. $360 \div 6 =$ ______

4. Write the ordinal number for thirty-nine.

____

5. $\frac{1}{2} + \frac{2}{6} =$ ______

6. $8 - (7 + 6 - 5) + 4 =$ ______

7. $323 - \square = 125 + 176$

8. Find y. $15y = 60$

$y =$ ______

9. 18 inches = ______ yards

10. How many degrees are in a right angle?

____

11. What is the median of this set of data?

105, 90, 82, 99, 93

____

12. If this pattern is continued until there are 50 rhombuses, how many matches will form the perimeter of the whole pattern?

____

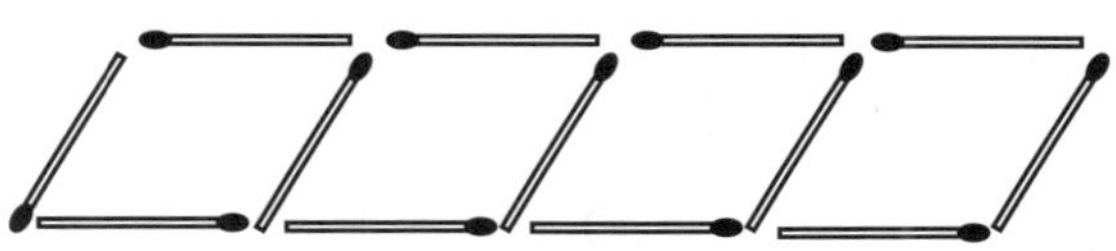

SCORE

1. Ⓨ Ⓝ
2. Ⓨ Ⓝ
3. Ⓨ Ⓝ
4. Ⓨ Ⓝ
5. Ⓨ Ⓝ
6. Ⓨ Ⓝ
7. Ⓨ Ⓝ
8. Ⓨ Ⓝ
9. Ⓨ Ⓝ
10. Ⓨ Ⓝ
11. Ⓨ Ⓝ
12. Ⓨ Ⓝ

___ / 12 Total

NAME: ______________________

DIRECTIONS Solve each problem.

SCORE

1. Ⓨ Ⓝ
2. Ⓨ Ⓝ
3. Ⓨ Ⓝ
4. Ⓨ Ⓝ
5. Ⓨ Ⓝ
6. Ⓨ Ⓝ
7. Ⓨ Ⓝ
8. Ⓨ Ⓝ
9. Ⓨ Ⓝ
10. Ⓨ Ⓝ
11. Ⓨ Ⓝ
12. Ⓨ Ⓝ

___ / 12
Total

1. 9 + 9 + 9 + 9 + 9 = ______

2.
$$\begin{array}{r} 52 \\ \times\ 10 \\ \hline \end{array}$$

3. Find the quotient when 134 is divided by 9.

____

4. Is 9,521 less than, greater than, or equal to 9,251?

____

5. How many eighths are in $1\frac{3}{8}$?

____

6. 2 + 3 x 2 = ______

7. 6,000 + 500 + ☐ + 9 = 6,549

8. Distribute.

5(*p* – 2) = ______________

9. Is 36 cm^2 the area of a 6 cm square?

____

10. What polygon forms the base of a hexagonal pyramid?

____

11. Which spinner would give you the best chance of spinning red or blue?

____

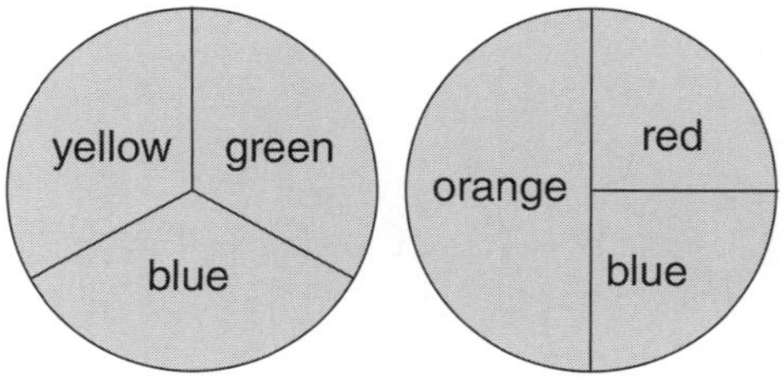

Spinner A **Spinner B**

12. Complete the chart to show your understanding of fractions, decimals, and percents.

Fraction	Decimal	Percent
$\frac{16}{20}$		

NAME: ____________________

DIRECTIONS Solve each problem.

1. $61 - 39 =$ ______

2. $-10 \times (-83) =$ ______

3. $4\overline{)434}$

4. List all of the factors of 40.

____

5. Write $\frac{9}{10}$ as a percentage.

____

6. $18 - 6 \times 3 + 2 =$ ______

7. 50% of ☐ is 50.

8. Find *b*. $\frac{b}{6} = 22$

$b =$ ______

9. Calculate the area of a square with 7.5 cm sides.

____

10. How many edges does a cone have?

____

11. Two red cubes, two green cylinders, and three yellow rectangular prisms were placed in a bag. If you reach into the bag and pull out an object, what is the probability that it will be a cylinder?

____

12. Complete the factor wheel to show all the factors of the number 32.

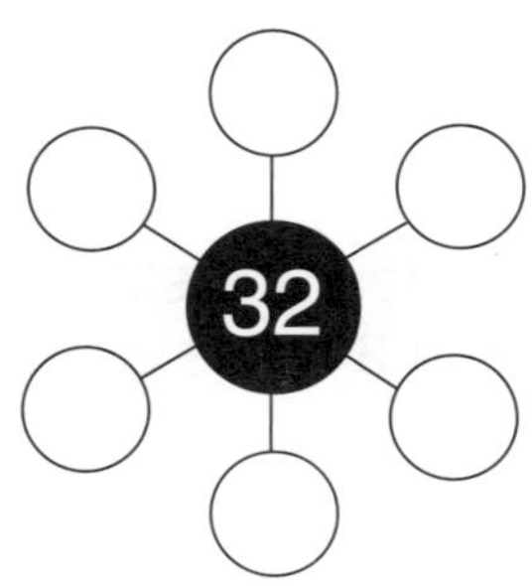

SCORE

1. Ⓨ Ⓝ
2. Ⓨ Ⓝ
3. Ⓨ Ⓝ
4. Ⓨ Ⓝ
5. Ⓨ Ⓝ
6. Ⓨ Ⓝ
7. Ⓨ Ⓝ
8. Ⓨ Ⓝ
9. Ⓨ Ⓝ
10. Ⓨ Ⓝ
11. Ⓨ Ⓝ
12. Ⓨ Ⓝ

___ / 12
Total

DAY
108

NAME: ____________________

DIRECTIONS Solve each problem.

SCORE

1. Ⓨ Ⓝ
2. Ⓨ Ⓝ
3. Ⓨ Ⓝ
4. Ⓨ Ⓝ
5. Ⓨ Ⓝ
6. Ⓨ Ⓝ
7. Ⓨ Ⓝ
8. Ⓨ Ⓝ
9. Ⓨ Ⓝ
10. Ⓨ Ⓝ
11. Ⓨ Ⓝ
12. Ⓨ Ⓝ

___ / 12
Total

1.
$$\begin{array}{r} 43 \\ 38 \\ +\ 16 \\ \hline \end{array}$$

2. Multiply 63 and 10.

____

3. $4\overline{)280}$

4. List the prime numbers between 2 and 10.

____

5. 4 x 2.5 = ______

6. 3 x 6 – 3 x 5 = ______

7. ☐ x 48 = 96

8. Find *m*.
20*m* = 100

m = ______

9. Calculate the distance a car can travel in 3 hours at 55 mph.

____

10. Name the polygon with 8 sides.

____

11.

Box A	Box B
A	A
Z	A
Z	Z
Z	T
T	T
T	S
S	M
S	Z
S	G

If you randomly choose a letter from one of these columns, from which column would you have a better probability of choosing a letter made up of only straight lines?

____

12. Round each item in the bill to the nearest nickel. Then calculate the total and find the change from $20.00.

____

$2.64
$3.45
$1.24
$2.14
$0.79
$0.66
$1.35

NAME: ______________________________

DIRECTIONS Solve each problem.

1. 400 + (–78) = ______

2. 5 x 46 = ______

3. What is the quotient when 614 is divided by 7?

____

4. List the first three multiples of 4.

____

5. 10% of 50 is ______.

6. $5 \times 2^2 =$ ______

7. $2\frac{1}{3} = \frac{\square}{3}$

8. Write the expression for the sum of one-half and *s*.

____

9. How many millimeters are in 3.5 centimeters?

____

10. What is the diameter of a circle with a radius of 3.45 cm?

____

11. In a game, the probability of spinning a 5 or 6 is $\frac{2}{3}$. How many times would you expect to land on a number other than 5 or 6 if you spin the spinner 15 times?

____

12. Arrange each number 1 through 9 in the circles so that the sum of the numbers in a straight line across the center of the circle is 18.

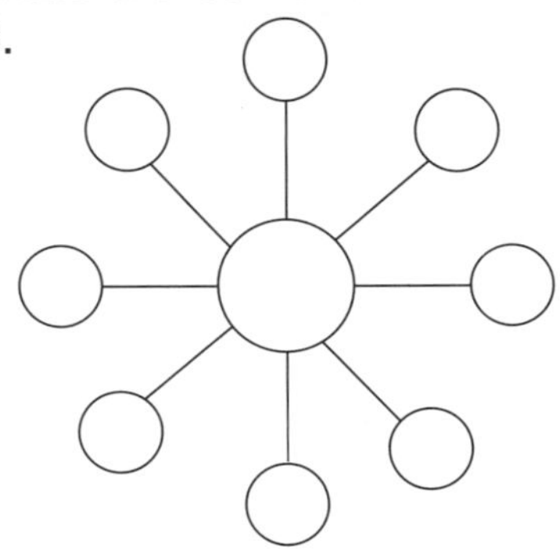

SCORE

1. Ⓨ Ⓝ
2. Ⓨ Ⓝ
3. Ⓨ Ⓝ
4. Ⓨ Ⓝ
5. Ⓨ Ⓝ
6. Ⓨ Ⓝ
7. Ⓨ Ⓝ
8. Ⓨ Ⓝ
9. Ⓨ Ⓝ
10. Ⓨ Ⓝ
11. Ⓨ Ⓝ
12. Ⓨ Ⓝ

___ / 12 Total

DAY 110

NAME: ______________________

DIRECTIONS Solve each problem.

SCORE

1. Ⓨ Ⓝ
2. Ⓨ Ⓝ
3. Ⓨ Ⓝ
4. Ⓨ Ⓝ
5. Ⓨ Ⓝ
6. Ⓨ Ⓝ
7. Ⓨ Ⓝ
8. Ⓨ Ⓝ
9. Ⓨ Ⓝ
10. Ⓨ Ⓝ
11. Ⓨ Ⓝ
12. Ⓨ Ⓝ

___ / 12 Total

1. 38 + 29 + 32 = ______

2.

$$\begin{array}{r} 43 \\ \times\ 10 \\ \hline \end{array}$$

3. Calculate 130 divided by 6.

____

4. How many digits are in the number 7,469,023?

____

5. Write $1\frac{4}{5}$ as an improper fraction.

____

6. Write the next number in the sequence. 105, 155, 205, ______

7. 14.5 + ☐ = 20.2

8. Find *c*. $c - 17.5 = 20$

c = ______

9. Calculate the area of the triangle.

____

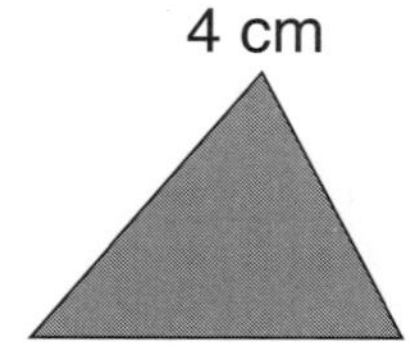

10. Is 123° greater than, less than, or equal to a right angle?

____

11. Below are the math test scores for 10 sixth graders. What is the median score?

75, 67, 90, 80, 90, 60, 95, 82, 78, 100

____

12. Write the number that is made up of these place values:

5 ten thousands

9 tens

8 hundreds

2 ones

7 thousands

____

NAME: ____________________

DIRECTIONS Solve each problem.

1. 200 – 94 = ______

2. 10 • 61 = ______

3. $5\overline{)23}$

4. What is the value of the digit 2 in the number 425,611?

____

5. True or false? 0.75 > 0.60

____

6. $(5 \times 2)^2$ = ______

7. 81 – 25 = ☐ + 3

8. Find *r*. $r + 5.6 = 10.8$

r = ______

9. How many milliliters are in $3\frac{1}{2}$ liters?

____

10. Name the shape that is located at (C,3).

____

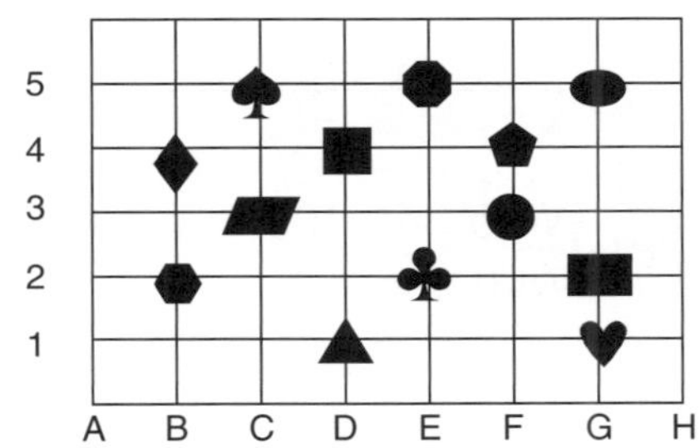

11. Record the data in the horizontal bar graph. California had 8 inches of rain. Oregon had 10 inches of rain. Washington had 14 inches of rain.

Annual Rainfall

State	0	2	4	6	8	10	12	14
California								
Oregon								
Washington								

Inches of Rain

12. Your chances of winning a prize in a raffle are $\frac{1}{50}$. If 1,000 tickets are sold, how many people will win prizes if each person can only win one prize?

____

SCORE

1. Ⓨ Ⓝ
2. Ⓨ Ⓝ
3. Ⓨ Ⓝ
4. Ⓨ Ⓝ
5. Ⓨ Ⓝ
6. Ⓨ Ⓝ
7. Ⓨ Ⓝ
8. Ⓨ Ⓝ
9. Ⓨ Ⓝ
10. Ⓨ Ⓝ
11. Ⓨ Ⓝ
12. Ⓨ Ⓝ

___ / 12 Total

DAY
112

NAME: ______________________________

DIRECTIONS Solve each problem.

SCORE

1. Ⓨ Ⓝ
2. Ⓨ Ⓝ
3. Ⓨ Ⓝ
4. Ⓨ Ⓝ
5. Ⓨ Ⓝ
6. Ⓨ Ⓝ
7. Ⓨ Ⓝ
8. Ⓨ Ⓝ
9. Ⓨ Ⓝ
10. Ⓨ Ⓝ
11. Ⓨ Ⓝ
12. Ⓨ Ⓝ

___ / 12
Total

1.
$$\begin{array}{r} 371 \\ +\ 45 \\ \hline \end{array}$$

2. 35 x 10 = ______

3. What is the quotient when 423 is divided by 8?

____

4. Write 348,109 in expanded notation.

____

5. Circle the value below that is not equivalent to the other two values.

0.6 60% $\frac{6}{100}$

6. Complete the table. Look for a pattern and write the rule.

Number of Hexagons	1	2	3	4	5
Number of Sides	6				

____

____

7. ☐ + 4.8 = 10

8. Solve for h if $25h = 500$.

h = ______

9. $\frac{3}{4}$ gallon = ______ quarts

10. Are all of the inside angles equal in a regular pentagon?

____

11. Draw a spinner that has a one-third probability of landing on blue and a two-thirds probability of landing on orange.

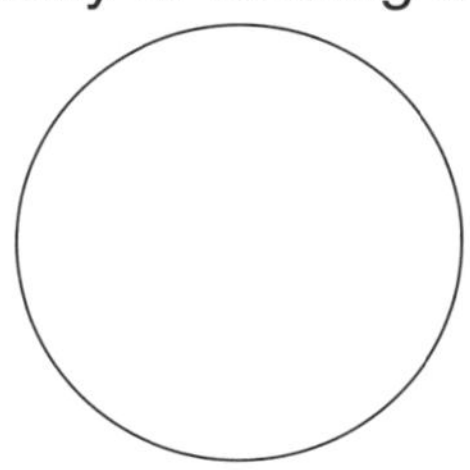

12. Karrie has a collection of 36 music CDs. If 15 of the CDs have country music, 19 of the CDs have pop songs, and the rest have classical music, how many CDs have classical music?

____

DAY 113

NAME: ____________________

DIRECTIONS Solve each problem.

1.
$$\begin{array}{r} 283 \\ -\ 197 \\ \hline \end{array}$$

2. Calculate the product of 5 and 51.

____

3. $7\overline{)252}$

4. Is 98,456 closer to 98,450 or 98,460?

____

5. Write the improper fraction for $3\frac{3}{5}$.

____

6. 25 x 3 + 4 x 12 = ______

7. 38 + ☐ = 92

8. Find *b*. $\frac{b}{7} = 18$

b = ______

9. Calculate the perimeter of a square that measures 5.5 m on its sides.

____

10. Draw the cross-section for the solid.

11. If you roll a 6-sided die, what is the probability that you will get a number greater than 5?

____

12. Harold bought 5 dozen cookies to share with his classmates. If there are 20 students in the class, how many cookies does each student get?

____

SCORE

1. Ⓨ Ⓝ
2. Ⓨ Ⓝ
3. Ⓨ Ⓝ
4. Ⓨ Ⓝ
5. Ⓨ Ⓝ
6. Ⓨ Ⓝ
7. Ⓨ Ⓝ
8. Ⓨ Ⓝ
9. Ⓨ Ⓝ
10. Ⓨ Ⓝ
11. Ⓨ Ⓝ
12. Ⓨ Ⓝ

___ / 12 Total

DAY
114

NAME: ____________________

DIRECTIONS Solve each problem.

SCORE

1. Ⓨ Ⓝ
2. Ⓨ Ⓝ
3. Ⓨ Ⓝ
4. Ⓨ Ⓝ
5. Ⓨ Ⓝ
6. Ⓨ Ⓝ
7. Ⓨ Ⓝ
8. Ⓨ Ⓝ
9. Ⓨ Ⓝ
10. Ⓨ Ⓝ
11. Ⓨ Ⓝ
12. Ⓨ Ⓝ

___ / 12 Total

1. 35 + 27 + 38 = ______

2.

$$\begin{array}{r} 40 \\ \times\ 60 \\ \hline \end{array}$$

3. How many groups of eight are in 64?

____

4. 2 cubed = ______

5. Does $\frac{8}{12} = \frac{3}{4}$? ______

6. 25 x (3 + 4) x 12 = ______

7. 92 – 38 = 20 + ☐

8. Find *b*. 12.9 + *b* = 20

b = ______

9. Find the average speed if 183 km is traveled in 3 hours.

____

10. Complete the chart for the shape.

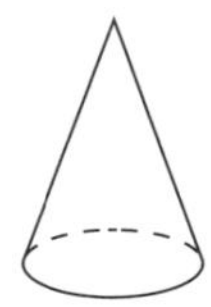

Name the figure.	
How many surfaces?	
How many vertices?	
Does it stack or roll?	
Is it a plane shape or a solid shape?	

11. The numbers 20 through 30 were written on individual cards and placed in a bag. If you take one card from the bag, what is the probability that it will *not* have the digit 2 on it?

____

12. Noel's age in 8 years will be three times as old as it was 2 years ago. How old is Noel now?

____

NAME: ______________________

DIRECTIONS Solve each problem.

1. Find the sum of 38 and 46.

____

2. $-5 \cdot 65 =$ ______

3. $462 \div 10 =$ ______

4. What is the next prime number after 7?

____

5. Is $\frac{4}{10} + \frac{6}{100}$ equal to 0.045?

____

6. $15 + 7 \times 5 - 4 =$ ______

7. 10% of ☐ is 9.

8. Find *m*. $25 - m = 25.5$

$m =$ ______

9. What is the area of a square with 7-cm sides?

____

10. Use a protractor to measure the angle. Then identify it as either *acute*, *reflex*, *obtuse*, or *straight*.

Angle	
Size	
Name	

11. Misty's mom told her she can participate in two sports this fall. She can choose from soccer, basketball, swimming, and tennis. List all the possible combinations of sports she can choose.

____

____

____

____

12. Some classrooms have 35 chairs while others have only 30. The total number of chairs in 10 classrooms is 330. How many classrooms have 35 chairs?

____

SCORE

1. Ⓨ Ⓝ
2. Ⓨ Ⓝ
3. Ⓨ Ⓝ
4. Ⓨ Ⓝ
5. Ⓨ Ⓝ
6. Ⓨ Ⓝ
7. Ⓨ Ⓝ
8. Ⓨ Ⓝ
9. Ⓨ Ⓝ
10. Ⓨ Ⓝ
11. Ⓨ Ⓝ
12. Ⓨ Ⓝ

___ / 12 Total

DAY 116

NAME: ______________________________

DIRECTIONS Solve each problem.

SCORE

1. Ⓨ Ⓝ
2. Ⓨ Ⓝ
3. Ⓨ Ⓝ
4. Ⓨ Ⓝ
5. Ⓨ Ⓝ
6. Ⓨ Ⓝ
7. Ⓨ Ⓝ
8. Ⓨ Ⓝ
9. Ⓨ Ⓝ
10. Ⓨ Ⓝ
11. Ⓨ Ⓝ
12. Ⓨ Ⓝ

___ / 12 Total

1. 400 – 67 = ______

2. 10 x 73 = ______

3. What is half of 78? ______

4. What number is 6 less than 1?

____

5. $\frac{3}{5}$ of 21 is ______.

6. 15 + 7 x (5 – 4) = ______

7. 7 x ☐ = 63

8. Find *p*. $14p = 42$

$p =$ ______

9. Calculate the volume of a rectangular prism with sides that measure 5 m, 4 m, and 3 m.

____

10. What shape is found on the base of a square pyramid?

____

11.

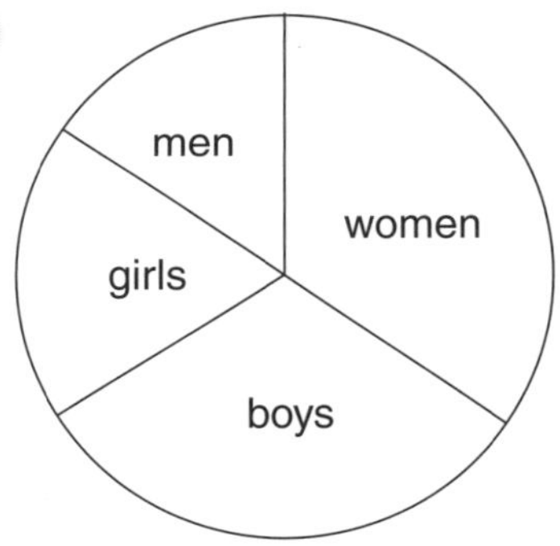

Were there fewer men or women?

____

12. Complete the multiplication table.

×		4	7	5		
			70			
20					160	
	270					
40						240

DAY 117

NAME: ____________________

DIRECTIONS Solve each problem.

1.
```
  268
+  53
-----
```

2. 7 x 30 = ______

3. 6)‾46

4. List the factors of 35.

____

5. Write $3 + \frac{5}{10} + \frac{6}{100} + \frac{8}{1000}$ as a decimal.

____

6. (15 + 7) x 5 – 4 = ______

7. 749 – ☐ = 68

8. Find *v*. $8v = 4{,}000$

v = ______

9. How many grams are in $1\frac{1}{2}$ kg?

____

10. How many vertices does this solid have?

____

11.

Color of Vehicles

Blue	𝍸 ||
Green	|||
Red	||||
White	𝍸 ||||
Black	𝍸 ||

What is the range of this set of data?

____

12. Harrison wants to share the candy he got for Halloween with his friends. He gives away $\frac{1}{2}$ of his candy to his friends at school, $\frac{1}{4}$ to his friends in the neighborhood, and the rest to his scout pack. If he gives 26 pieces away at his scout meeting, how many pieces of candy did he start with?

____

SCORE

1. Ⓨ Ⓝ
2. Ⓨ Ⓝ
3. Ⓨ Ⓝ
4. Ⓨ Ⓝ
5. Ⓨ Ⓝ
6. Ⓨ Ⓝ
7. Ⓨ Ⓝ
8. Ⓨ Ⓝ
9. Ⓨ Ⓝ
10. Ⓨ Ⓝ
11. Ⓨ Ⓝ
12. Ⓨ Ⓝ

___ / 12 **Total**

NAME: ____________________

DIRECTIONS Solve each problem.

SCORE

1. Ⓨ Ⓝ
2. Ⓨ Ⓝ
3. Ⓨ Ⓝ
4. Ⓨ Ⓝ
5. Ⓨ Ⓝ
6. Ⓨ Ⓝ
7. Ⓨ Ⓝ
8. Ⓨ Ⓝ
9. Ⓨ Ⓝ
10. Ⓨ Ⓝ
11. Ⓨ Ⓝ
12. Ⓨ Ⓝ

___ / 12 Total

1. Subtract 89 from 264.

____

2.

$$\begin{array}{r} 10 \\ \times\ 39 \\ \hline \end{array}$$

3. $53 \div 9 =$ ______

4. Write the number right before 3,000,000.

____

5. Simplify $\frac{8}{12}$.

____

6. $(15 + 7) \times (5 - 4) =$ ______

7. $67 \times \square = 335$

8. Solve for x when $\frac{x}{12} = 600$.

$x =$ ______

9. Calculate the distance a boat can travel in 4 hours at 130 $\frac{\text{km}}{\text{h}}$.

____

10. True or false? The sides of a regular polygon are equal.

____

11. Inside a bag of candy there are 16 lollipops, 12 pieces of chocolate, and 7 pieces of licorice. If you reach in the bag and grab a piece of candy, what is the probability that it will not be licorice?

____

12. Use three of the numerals 3, 4, 5, 12, or 15 to complete the number sentence. Do not use any numeral more than once.

(______ – ______) x ______ = 9

NAME: ____________________

DIRECTIONS Solve each problem.

1. $24 + 25 + 26 =$ ______

2. $5 \times (-67) =$ ______

3. $9\overline{)261}$

4. Is 504 a multiple of 9?

____

5. $\frac{7}{10} - \frac{2}{5} =$ ______

6. $5^2 - 3 \times 4 =$ ______

7. $79 - 46 = 15 \square 18$

8. Distribute.

$7(x - 9) =$ ______________

9. What is the volume of a container (in centimeters^3) that holds 750 milliliters?

____

10. Do parallel lines always stay the same distance apart?

____

11.

Points Scored

	Game 1	Game 2	Game 3
Sara	14	15	14
Allison	19	13	11
Phillip	21	19	20
Sonia	16	13	15

What was the average number of points Allison scored in all three games?

____

12. Peter used small cubes to form this stack. How many cubes are in the stack?

____

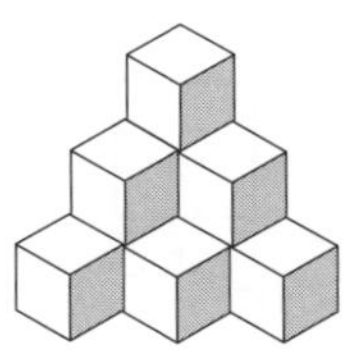

SCORE

1. Ⓨ Ⓝ
2. Ⓨ Ⓝ
3. Ⓨ Ⓝ
4. Ⓨ Ⓝ
5. Ⓨ Ⓝ
6. Ⓨ Ⓝ
7. Ⓨ Ⓝ
8. Ⓨ Ⓝ
9. Ⓨ Ⓝ
10. Ⓨ Ⓝ
11. Ⓨ Ⓝ
12. Ⓨ Ⓝ

___ / 12 Total

DAY 120

NAME: ______________________________

DIRECTIONS Solve each problem.

SCORE

1. Ⓨ Ⓝ
2. Ⓨ Ⓝ
3. Ⓨ Ⓝ
4. Ⓨ Ⓝ
5. Ⓨ Ⓝ
6. Ⓨ Ⓝ
7. Ⓨ Ⓝ
8. Ⓨ Ⓝ
9. Ⓨ Ⓝ
10. Ⓨ Ⓝ
11. Ⓨ Ⓝ
12. Ⓨ Ⓝ

___ / 12 Total

1. Take 46 away from 84.

____

2.

$$\begin{array}{r} 73 \\ \times\ 10 \\ \hline \end{array}$$

3. Calculate 197 ÷ 20.

____

4. Write the largest possible number using the digits 6, 4, 8, 2, and 7.

____

5. Circle the value that is not equivalent to the other two.

$\frac{6}{10}$ 6% 0.6

6. Write the next number in the sequence.

1,107; 1,057; 1,007; ________

7. $1\frac{3}{4} = \frac{\square}{4}$

8. Solve for y when $\frac{48}{y} = 12$.

$y =$ ______

9. How many grams are in 4.7 kilograms?

____

10. Is a right angle greater than, less than, or equal to 75°?

____

11.

	Regular Price	Discount
Pants	$32	25%
Shirts	$24	30%
Shoes	$45	35%
Socks	$4	10%

If you purchase a pair of shoes at the discounted price, how much money will you save?

____

12. The Simons recycle bottles and cans. They recycle four times as many cans as bottles. If they recycle 156 cans, how many bottles do they recycle?

____

NAME: ____________________

DIRECTIONS Solve each problem.

1. Find the sum of 257 and 64.

____

2. $10 \cdot 24 =$ ______

3. $9\overline{)738}$

4. What is the place value of 7 in the number 174,569?

____

5. Write the improper fraction for $1\frac{2}{3}$.

____

6. Complete the table. Then write the conversion rule for centimeters to meters.

Centimeter	300	500		900	
Meter	3		7		11

____

____

7. Find a. $a + 2 = 10$

$a =$ ______

8. Find d. $28d = 56$

$d =$ ______

9. How many liters are in 5,275 milliliters?

____

10. Which line segment is perpendicular to lines A and H?

____

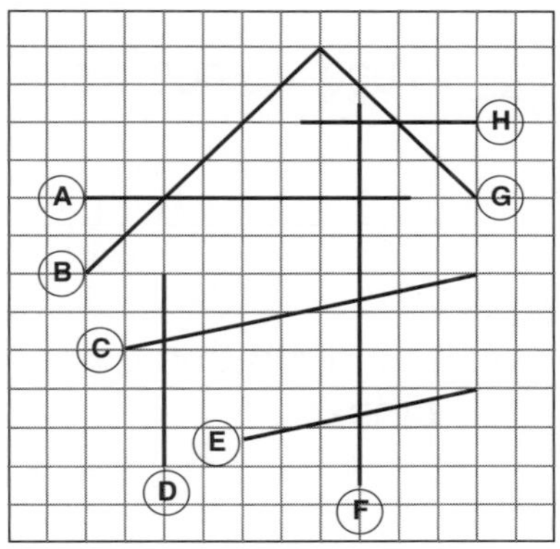

11. Reina counted the number of tickets sold for the school play for 10 nights. What is the range?
20, 26, 19, 24, 19, 28, 22, 18, 24, 24

____

12. Mai's pencil is 24 cm long. She sharpens it, and it loses $\frac{1}{8}$ of its length. How long is her pencil now?

____

SCORE

1. Ⓨ Ⓝ
2. Ⓨ Ⓝ
3. Ⓨ Ⓝ
4. Ⓨ Ⓝ
5. Ⓨ Ⓝ
6. Ⓨ Ⓝ
7. Ⓨ Ⓝ
8. Ⓨ Ⓝ
9. Ⓨ Ⓝ
10. Ⓨ Ⓝ
11. Ⓨ Ⓝ
12. Ⓨ Ⓝ

___ / 12 Total

DAY
122

NAME: ____________________

DIRECTIONS Solve each problem.

SCORE

1. Ⓨ Ⓝ
2. Ⓨ Ⓝ
3. Ⓨ Ⓝ
4. Ⓨ Ⓝ
5. Ⓨ Ⓝ
6. Ⓨ Ⓝ
7. Ⓨ Ⓝ
8. Ⓨ Ⓝ
9. Ⓨ Ⓝ
10. Ⓨ Ⓝ
11. Ⓨ Ⓝ
12. Ⓨ Ⓝ

___ / 12 Total

1. 188 – 294 = ______

2. 4 x 600 = ______

3. What is half of 92? ______

4. 40,000 + 9,000 + 60 + 8 =

____

5. Round 4.8 to the nearest whole number.

____

6. $(5^2 - 3) \times 4$ = ______

7. 0.10 of ☐ is 9.

8. Find *e*. $2.5e = 100$

e = ______

9. What time is two hours before 22:17?

____

10. What is the name of a triangle with exactly two equal angles?

____

11. Draw a spinner that has a 25% probability of landing on green, a 25% probability of landing on orange, and a 50% probability of landing on blue.

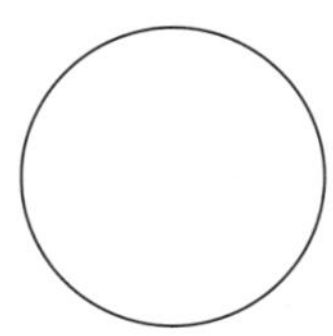

12. Circle the factors of the given product.

Possible Factors									Product
6	5	9	4	2	17	3	16	15	105

NAME: ______________________________

DIRECTIONS Solve each problem.

1. Calculate the sum of 45 and 39.

____

2.
```
   43
x   5
-----
```

3. 149 ÷ 5 = ______

4. Round 12,685 to the nearest thousand.

____

5. Write $4 + \frac{5}{100} + \frac{3}{1000}$ as a decimal.

____

6. 8 + 9 x 3 – 1 = ______

7. 194 ☐ 63 = 131

8. Find *k*. *k* + 73 = 125

k = ______

9. How many meters are in 8.475 kilometers?

____

10. How many axes of symmetry does the shape have?

____

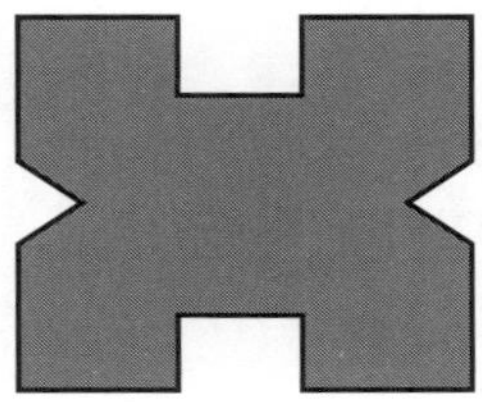

11. Steve, Mark, Melissa, Joe, and Mary are in a group. They randomly line up at the door. What is the probability that a person whose name begins with *S* lines up first?

____

12. Mark had twice as much money as Karen. When Mark gave Karen $10.00, they both had the same amount. How much did Karen have originally?

____

SCORE

1. Ⓨ Ⓝ
2. Ⓨ Ⓝ
3. Ⓨ Ⓝ
4. Ⓨ Ⓝ
5. Ⓨ Ⓝ
6. Ⓨ Ⓝ
7. Ⓨ Ⓝ
8. Ⓨ Ⓝ
9. Ⓨ Ⓝ
10. Ⓨ Ⓝ
11. Ⓨ Ⓝ
12. Ⓨ Ⓝ

___ / 12 Total

DAY
124

NAME: ____________________________

DIRECTIONS Solve each problem.

SCORE

1. Ⓨ Ⓝ
2. Ⓨ Ⓝ
3. Ⓨ Ⓝ
4. Ⓨ Ⓝ
5. Ⓨ Ⓝ
6. Ⓨ Ⓝ
7. Ⓨ Ⓝ
8. Ⓨ Ⓝ
9. Ⓨ Ⓝ
10. Ⓨ Ⓝ
11. Ⓨ Ⓝ
12. Ⓨ Ⓝ

___ / 12
Total

1. $\begin{array}{r} 328 \\ -\ 169 \\ \hline \end{array}$

2. 4 x 40 = ______

3. $7\overline{)95}$

4. How do you know that 9 is a square number?

____

5. $\frac{3}{5} - \frac{2}{10} =$ ______

6. 305 ÷ 5 = 60 + ☐

7. $\square^2 = 25$

8. 7 x ☐ = 30 – 9

9. Calculate the average hourly speed when 180 miles are traveled in 4 hours.

____

10. Complete the chart for the shape.

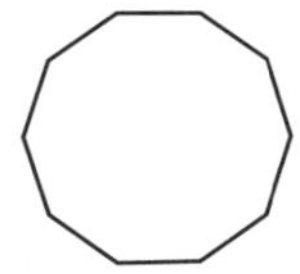

Name the figure.	
How many sides?	
How many angles?	
Does it have symmetry?	
Is it a plane shape or a solid shape?	

11. **Time Spent on Homework**

Day	Minutes
Monday	52
Tuesday	45
Wednesday	30
Thursday	45
Friday	0

One-half of the time on Wednesday was spent reading. How many minutes were spent reading on Wednesday?

____

12. William has a binder with 32 pages in it. Each page holds 4 baseball cards. If the book is $\frac{3}{4}$ full, how many baseball cards are in the binder?

____

NAME: ____________________________

DIRECTIONS Solve each problem.

1. Add 37, 46, and 54.

____

2. Find the product of 6 and 50.

____

3. 9 ⟌171

4. What is the ordinal number for twenty?

____

5. Round 5.1 to the nearest whole number.

____

6. Insert parenthesis to make the following true.

8 + 9 x 3 – 1 = 50

7. 369 ÷ ☐ = 123

8. Find *q*. $q - 89 = 121$

q = ______

9. What is the volume of a solid that is 3 m long, 2 m wide, and 4 m tall?

____

10. Name the triangle.

____

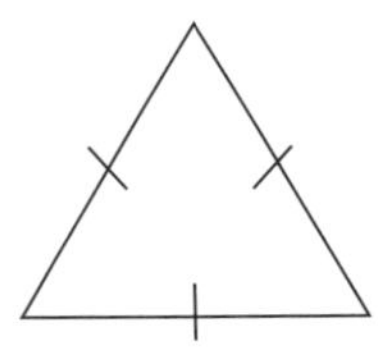

11. List all possible outcomes you can get when you flip two coins.

____

____

12. Mindy saves more than $12.70 each week. In five weeks, could she save $61.50, $63.00, $62.90, or $64.20?

____

SCORE

1. Ⓨ Ⓝ
2. Ⓨ Ⓝ
3. Ⓨ Ⓝ
4. Ⓨ Ⓝ
5. Ⓨ Ⓝ
6. Ⓨ Ⓝ
7. Ⓨ Ⓝ
8. Ⓨ Ⓝ
9. Ⓨ Ⓝ
10. Ⓨ Ⓝ
11. Ⓨ Ⓝ
12. Ⓨ Ⓝ

___ / 12 Total

DAY
126

NAME: ______________________

DIRECTIONS Solve each problem.

SCORE

1. Ⓨ Ⓝ
2. Ⓨ Ⓝ
3. Ⓨ Ⓝ
4. Ⓨ Ⓝ
5. Ⓨ Ⓝ
6. Ⓨ Ⓝ
7. Ⓨ Ⓝ
8. Ⓨ Ⓝ
9. Ⓨ Ⓝ
10. Ⓨ Ⓝ
11. Ⓨ Ⓝ
12. Ⓨ Ⓝ

___ / 12
Total

1. Subtract 69 from 237.

____

2. 30 x 8 = ______

3. $5\overline{)414}$

4. Is 35,647 greater than, less than, or equal to 35,764?

____

5. Write 12.95 as a mixed number.

____

6. Insert parentheses to make the following equation true.

8 + 9 x 3 – 1 = 26

7. 4 + 16 = 4 x ☐

8. Find *r*. 19*r* = 190

r = ______

9. Calculate the area of the shaded triangle.

____

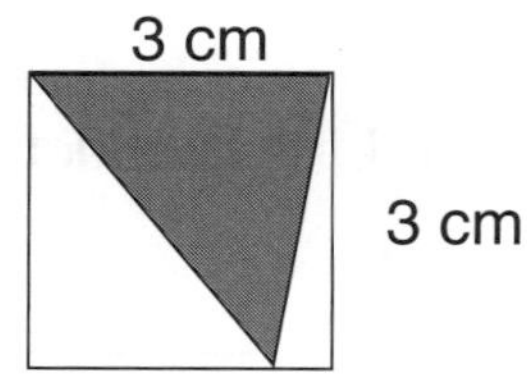

10. What is the shape of the base on a pentagonal pyramid?

____

11. Which spinner would give you the best chance of landing on a word with 6 letters?

____

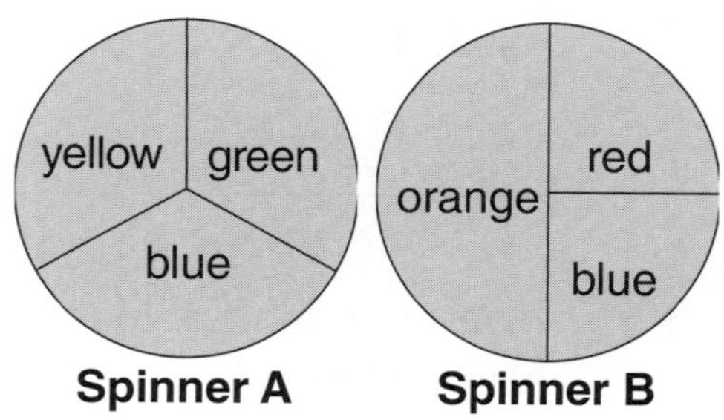

12. How many feet are in a hundred yard dash?

____

NAME: ______________________________

DIRECTIONS Solve each problem.

SCORE

1.
$$\begin{array}{r} 90 \\ +\ 50 \\ \hline \end{array}$$

2. 5 x 17 = ______

3. Divide 728 into 8 equal groups.

____

4. List all of the factors of 56.

____

5. $\frac{5}{12}$ of 144 is ______.

6. 7 x 8 – 4 x 3 = ______

7. .9 = ☐ %

8. Find z. $\frac{z}{21} = 7$

z = ______

9. Write 6:58 P.M. in a 24-hour time format.

____

10. How many faces are on the solid?

____

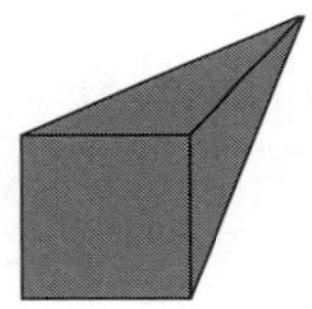

11. Two red cubes, two green cylinders, and three yellow rectangular prisms were placed into a bag. If you reach into the bag and pull out an object, what is the probability that it will not be a red block?

____

12. A collection of chickens and pigs has a total of 70 legs and 26 heads. How many chickens are there?

____

1. Ⓨ Ⓝ
2. Ⓨ Ⓝ
3. Ⓨ Ⓝ
4. Ⓨ Ⓝ
5. Ⓨ Ⓝ
6. Ⓨ Ⓝ
7. Ⓨ Ⓝ
8. Ⓨ Ⓝ
9. Ⓨ Ⓝ
10. Ⓨ Ⓝ
11. Ⓨ Ⓝ
12. Ⓨ Ⓝ

___ / 12 **Total**

DAY
128

NAME: ____________________

DIRECTIONS Solve each problem.

SCORE

1. Ⓨ Ⓝ
2. Ⓨ Ⓝ
3. Ⓨ Ⓝ
4. Ⓨ Ⓝ
5. Ⓨ Ⓝ
6. Ⓨ Ⓝ
7. Ⓨ Ⓝ
8. Ⓨ Ⓝ
9. Ⓨ Ⓝ
10. Ⓨ Ⓝ
11. Ⓨ Ⓝ
12. Ⓨ Ⓝ

___ / 12 **Total**

1. 93 – 48 = ______

2. Calculate the product of 78 and 6.

____

3. $6\overline{)283}$

4. Which is greater: 3^3 or 5^2?

____

5. Round 3.6 to the nearest whole number.

____

6. Insert parentheses to make the following true.

7 x 8 – 4 x 3 = 84

7. ☐ x 10 = 8,720

8. Find *w*. $w^2 = 64$

w = ______

9. Calculate the distance a car can travel in 2 hours at 55 mph.

____

10. What is the sum of the angles in a quadrilateral?

____

11. What are the outliers in this data set?

518, 722, 560, 543, 251, 523

____

12. Paula, Fiona, and Veronica are playing a guessing game. Fiona's guess is 1,381 more than Paula's number. Paula's number is 1,523 less than Veronica's number. Veronica's number is 3,243. What is Fiona's number?

____

NAME: ____________________

DIRECTIONS Solve each problem.

1. Double 39.

____

2.
$$\begin{array}{r} 40 \\ \times\ 20 \\ \hline \end{array}$$

3. What is the quotient when 791 is divided by 9?

____

4. List the first five multiples of 8.

____

5. Write 2.38 as a mixed number.

____

6. $64 \div 4 \times 2 \div 8 =$ ______

7. $36 \div 6 = 2 \times \square$

8. Distribute.

$12(8 - n) =$ ________________

9. What is the volume of a container (in cm^3) that holds 350 mL?

____

10. Do parallel lines meet at 90°?

____

11.

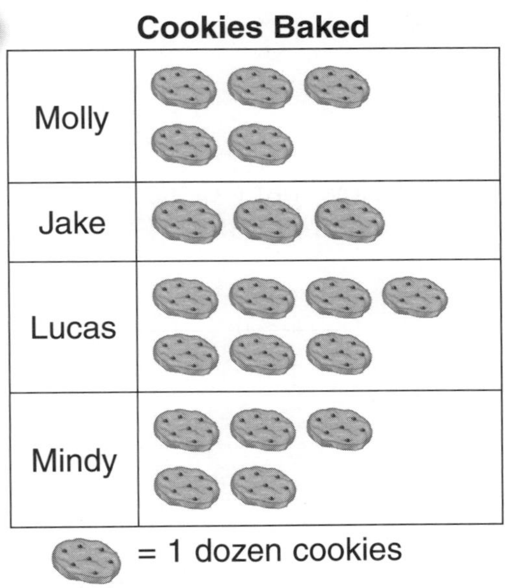

How many more cookies did Lucas bake than Mindy?

____

12. Compare an octagonal pyramid with an octagonal prism.

	Faces	Edges	Vertices
Octagonal Pyramid			
Octagonal Prism			

SCORE

1. Ⓨ Ⓝ
2. Ⓨ Ⓝ
3. Ⓨ Ⓝ
4. Ⓨ Ⓝ
5. Ⓨ Ⓝ
6. Ⓨ Ⓝ
7. Ⓨ Ⓝ
8. Ⓨ Ⓝ
9. Ⓨ Ⓝ
10. Ⓨ Ⓝ
11. Ⓨ Ⓝ
12. Ⓨ Ⓝ

___ / 12 Total

DAY 130

NAME: ____________________

DIRECTIONS Solve each product.

SCORE

1. Ⓨ Ⓝ
2. Ⓨ Ⓝ
3. Ⓨ Ⓝ
4. Ⓨ Ⓝ
5. Ⓨ Ⓝ
6. Ⓨ Ⓝ
7. Ⓨ Ⓝ
8. Ⓨ Ⓝ
9. Ⓨ Ⓝ
10. Ⓨ Ⓝ
11. Ⓨ Ⓝ
12. Ⓨ Ⓝ

___ / 12 Total

1. Subtract 89 from 274.

____

2. 5 • 29 = ______

3. $6\overline{)285}$

4. How many digits are in the number 385,604?

____

5. $\frac{3}{5} + \frac{1}{10} =$ ______

6. Write the next number in the sequence. 2,175; 2,125; 2,075;

____

7. 7,000 + ☐ + 60 + 5 = 7,965

8. Write the expression for the product of 17 and *s*.

____

9. How many grams are in $\frac{1}{4}$ kilogram?

____

10. Use a protractor to measure the angle.

____

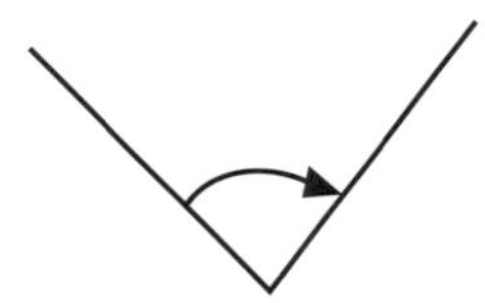

11. What is the mode of this set of data?

18, 25, 31, 31, 44, 68, 76

____

12. In magic squares, each row, column, and diagonal adds up to the same number. Complete the magic square using the numbers 2–17.

13		10	
14	3		
	12	6	
2	15	5	16

DAY 131

NAME: ____________________

DIRECTIONS Solve each problem.

1. Calculate the sum of 28, 39, and 57.

____

2. 91 x 5 = ______

3. 463 ÷ 5 = ______

4. What is the value of the digit 4 in 34,600?

____

5. $\frac{7}{12} + \frac{1}{6} =$ ______

6. 64 ÷ (4 x 2) ÷ 8 = ______

7. 147 ÷ 7 = 3 x ☐

8. Find *h*. *h* x 7 = 77

h = ______

9. What is the time two hours after 11:01 P.M.?

____

10. What shape is located at (B,4)?

____

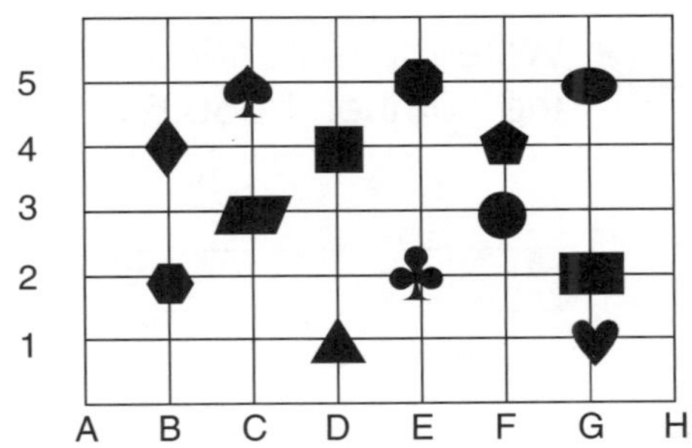

11. Record the data in the chart.

The Kims drink 3 gallons of milk each week and 1 gallon of juice. The Bergs drink 2 gallons of juice and 4 gallons of milk. Both families drink 4 gallons of water each week.

12. Caleb has a marble collection with 132 marbles. Half of the marbles are cat's-eyes, 25% are mixed colors, and the rest are solid black. How many marbles are solid black?

____

SCORE

1. Ⓨ Ⓝ
2. Ⓨ Ⓝ
3. Ⓨ Ⓝ
4. Ⓨ Ⓝ
5. Ⓨ Ⓝ
6. Ⓨ Ⓝ
7. Ⓨ Ⓝ
8. Ⓨ Ⓝ
9. Ⓨ Ⓝ
10. Ⓨ Ⓝ
11. Ⓨ Ⓝ
12. Ⓨ Ⓝ

___ / 12 Total

DAY 132

NAME: ________________________

DIRECTIONS Solve each problem.

SCORE

1. Ⓨ Ⓝ
2. Ⓨ Ⓝ
3. Ⓨ Ⓝ
4. Ⓨ Ⓝ
5. Ⓨ Ⓝ
6. Ⓨ Ⓝ
7. Ⓨ Ⓝ
8. Ⓨ Ⓝ
9. Ⓨ Ⓝ
10. Ⓨ Ⓝ
11. Ⓨ Ⓝ
12. Ⓨ Ⓝ

___ / 12 Total

1. 97 – 285 = ______

2.
$$\begin{array}{r} 16 \\ \times\ 20 \\ \hline \end{array}$$

3. 267 ÷ 7 = ______

4. Write the expanded notation for the number 1,350,607.

____

____

5. Write $2\frac{5}{8}$ as an improper fraction.

____

6. Complete the table. Look for a pattern and write the rule.

Number of Decagons	1	2	3	4	5
Number of Sides	10				

____

____

7. Distribute

5(*b* + 4) =

____

8. Find *n*. $\frac{100}{n} = 5$

n = ______

9. 1.5 gallons = ______ quarts

10. To make this pattern, has Tile A been *reflected*, *translated*, or *rotated*?

____

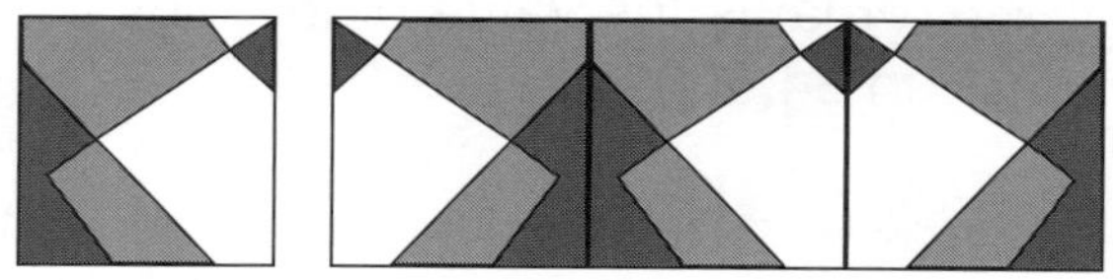

Tile A

11. Draw a spinner that has an equal chance of landing on a 1, 2, or 3.

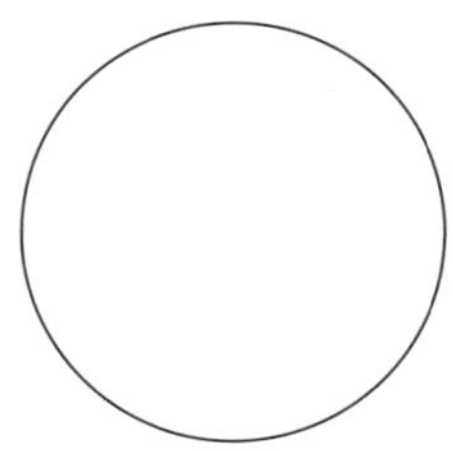

12. Rick practices piano every day for 35 minutes. How many hours and minutes does he practice in a 30-day month?

____

NAME: ____________________

DIRECTIONS Solve each problem.

1. Add 170 and 47.

____

2. 5 x 30 = ______

3. 5)285

4. Is 45,368 closer to 45,000 or 46,000?

____

5. Write 0.84 as a percentage.

____

6. 64 ÷ (4 x 2 ÷ 8) = ______

7. 196 – 47 = ☐ + 52

8. Find *y*. $86 - y = 45$

y = ______

9. Calculate the perimeter of a square with 3.5-m sides.

____

10. Name the solid shape.

____

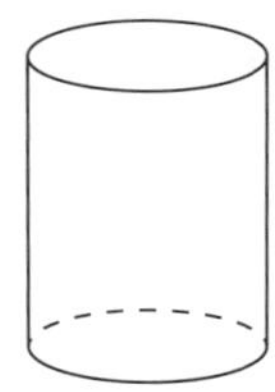

11. If you roll a 6-sided die, what is the probability you will get a number less than 4?

____

12. Carole bought a dress on sale for $27. The original cost of the dress was $36. What percent was she given off the original price?

____

SCORE

1. Ⓨ Ⓝ
2. Ⓨ Ⓝ
3. Ⓨ Ⓝ
4. Ⓨ Ⓝ
5. Ⓨ Ⓝ
6. Ⓨ Ⓝ
7. Ⓨ Ⓝ
8. Ⓨ Ⓝ
9. Ⓨ Ⓝ
10. Ⓨ Ⓝ
11. Ⓨ Ⓝ
12. Ⓨ Ⓝ

___ / 12
Total

DAY
134

NAME: ______________________________

DIRECTIONS Solve each problem.

SCORE

1. Ⓨ Ⓝ
2. Ⓨ Ⓝ
3. Ⓨ Ⓝ
4. Ⓨ Ⓝ
5. Ⓨ Ⓝ
6. Ⓨ Ⓝ
7. Ⓨ Ⓝ
8. Ⓨ Ⓝ
9. Ⓨ Ⓝ
10. Ⓨ Ⓝ
11. Ⓨ Ⓝ
12. Ⓨ Ⓝ

___ / 12
Total

1. 16 + 27 + 34 = ______

2. Multiply 5 and 30.

____

3. $6 \overline{)346}$

4. Calculate the square root of 49.

____

5. Round 5.25 to the nearest whole number.

____

6. 12 – 20 x 5 = ______

7. 234 + ☐ = 299

8. Distribute.

$4(x - 21) =$ ______________

9. Find the average speed when 200 km are traveled in 4 hours.

____

10. Complete the chart for the shape.

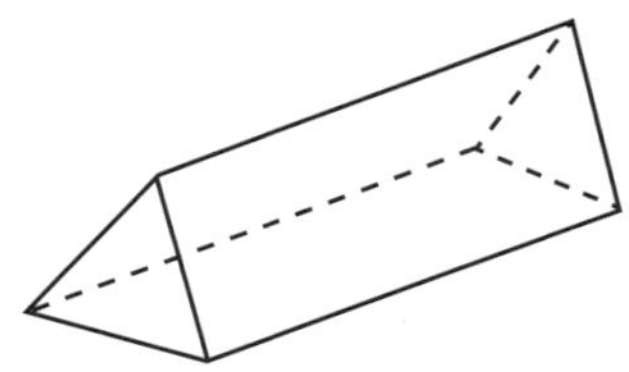

Name the figure.	
How many surfaces?	
How many vertices?	
Does it stack or roll?	
Is it a plane shape or a solid shape?	

11. The numbers 20 through 30 were written on individual cards and placed in a bag. If you take one card from the bag, what is the probability that it will be a multiple of 5?

____

12. Which fraction added to $\frac{8}{15}$ will make 1 whole?

____

DAY 135

NAME: ______________________________

DIRECTIONS Solve each problem.

1. 84 – 56 = ______

2.
```
   50
x   6
-----
```

3. 567 ÷ 8 = ______

4. What is the number 100 after 3,875?

____

5. 60% of 30 is ______.

6. Write the next number in the sequence. 3,096; 3,146; 3,196;

____

7. $\frac{7}{10} = \square \%$

8. Find *v*. $v + 19.9 = 20$

v = ______

9. What is the volume of a cup (in cm^3) that holds 500 mL?

____

10. How many total degrees are in two right angles?

____

11. What is the median of this set of data?

523, 491, 501, 479, 512

____

12. Cookies cost $6.00 for a dozen. What is the cost for 8 cookies?

____

SCORE

1. Ⓨ Ⓝ
2. Ⓨ Ⓝ
3. Ⓨ Ⓝ
4. Ⓨ Ⓝ
5. Ⓨ Ⓝ
6. Ⓨ Ⓝ
7. Ⓨ Ⓝ
8. Ⓨ Ⓝ
9. Ⓨ Ⓝ
10. Ⓨ Ⓝ
11. Ⓨ Ⓝ
12. Ⓨ Ⓝ

___ / 12
Total

NAME: ____________________

DIRECTIONS Solve each problem.

SCORE

1. Ⓨ Ⓝ
2. Ⓨ Ⓝ
3. Ⓨ Ⓝ
4. Ⓨ Ⓝ
5. Ⓨ Ⓝ
6. Ⓨ Ⓝ
7. Ⓨ Ⓝ
8. Ⓨ Ⓝ
9. Ⓨ Ⓝ
10. Ⓨ Ⓝ
11. Ⓨ Ⓝ
12. Ⓨ Ⓝ

___ / 12 Total

1. Calculate the sum of 35, 48, and 47.

____

2. Multiply 60 by 40.

____

3. Divide 462 by 7.

____

4. Is 15 a negative or positive number?

____

5. Round 3.78 to the nearest whole number.

____

6. (12 – 20) x 5 = ______

7. Write $\frac{17}{4}$ as a mixed number.

____

8. Write the expression for the difference when 49 is subtracted from *g*.

____

9. Write 9:26 A.M. in a 24-hour time format.

____

10. Can the top view of a sphere be a circle?

____

11.

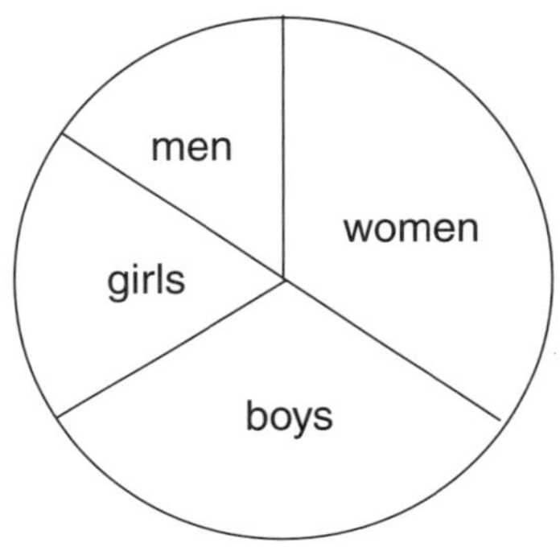

Was the total of men and women the same as the total of boys and girls?

____

12. Sam gets a $2.00 rebate for every $8.00 he spends on trading cards. If Sam spends $24.00 on trading cards, how much will he get in rebates?

____

NAME: ______________________________

DIRECTIONS Solve each problem.

1.
$$\begin{array}{r} 362 \\ -\ 68 \\ \hline \end{array}$$

2. $3 \times 40 =$ ______

3. $8\overline{)924}$

4. Write the factors of 27.

____

5. Write $2\frac{3}{4}$ as an improper fraction.

____

6. $18 \div 6 + 4^2 - 5 =$ ______

7. $943 - \square = 425$

8. Find q. $\frac{q}{32} = 6$

$q =$ ______

9. How many grams are in 3.9 kilograms?

____

10. How many edges does a rectangular prism have?

____

11. What is the probability of not picking a triangle?

____

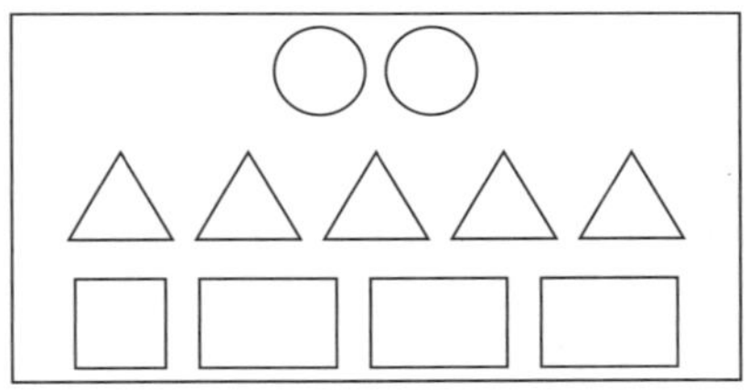

12. Complete the factor wheel to show all the factors of the number in the center.

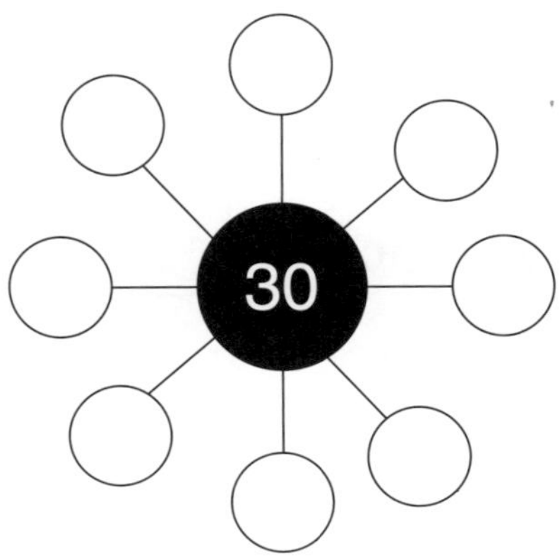

SCORE

1. Ⓨ Ⓝ
2. Ⓨ Ⓝ
3. Ⓨ Ⓝ
4. Ⓨ Ⓝ
5. Ⓨ Ⓝ
6. Ⓨ Ⓝ
7. Ⓨ Ⓝ
8. Ⓨ Ⓝ
9. Ⓨ Ⓝ
10. Ⓨ Ⓝ
11. Ⓨ Ⓝ
12. Ⓨ Ⓝ

___ / 12 Total

DAY 138

NAME: ____________________

DIRECTIONS Solve each problem.

SCORE

1. Ⓨ Ⓝ
2. Ⓨ Ⓝ
3. Ⓨ Ⓝ
4. Ⓨ Ⓝ
5. Ⓨ Ⓝ
6. Ⓨ Ⓝ
7. Ⓨ Ⓝ
8. Ⓨ Ⓝ
9. Ⓨ Ⓝ
10. Ⓨ Ⓝ
11. Ⓨ Ⓝ
12. Ⓨ Ⓝ

___ / 12 Total

1.

$$\begin{array}{r} 28 \\ 39 \\ +\ 47 \\ \hline \end{array}$$

2. 40 x 50 = ______

3. 432 ÷ 9 = ______

4. List all the composite numbers between 11 and 19.

____

5. Write $2\frac{2}{3}$ as an improper fraction.

____

6. 18 – 5 x 2 = ______

7. 350 ÷ 10 = 7 x ☐

8. Distribute.

$13(4 - h) =$ ____________

9. How many months are in two years?

____

10. How many sides does a pentagon have?

____

11. Inside a bag of candy there are 16 lollipops, 12 pieces of chocolate, and 7 pieces of licorice. If you reach in the bag and grab a piece of candy, what is the probability that it will be either a lollipop or a piece of chocolate?

____

12. A recipe calls for $\frac{1}{3}$ cup of butter. If you want to triple the recipe, how much butter do you need?

____

NAME: ______________________

DIRECTIONS Solve each problem.

1. Subtract 139 from 456.

____

2.
$$\begin{array}{r} 20 \\ \times\ 60 \\ \hline \end{array}$$

3. 461 ÷ 3 = ______

4. Is 683 evenly divisible by 7?

____

5. Write the numeral for three and fifty-eight hundredths.

____

6. (2 + 7) – 8 x 3 = ______

7. 10% of ☐ is 6.

8. Find *x*. $x + 7 = 21$

x = ______

9. How many kilometers are in 9,300 meters?

____

10. Calculate the radius of a circle with a diameter of 4.56 m.

____

11. In a game, the probability of spinning a *yes* is $\frac{1}{2}$. How many times would you expect to land on *yes* if you spin the spinner 100 times?

____

12. Luke invites 15 people to his party. $\frac{3}{5}$ of the people can come. How many people will come to the party?

____

SCORE

1. Ⓨ Ⓝ
2. Ⓨ Ⓝ
3. Ⓨ Ⓝ
4. Ⓨ Ⓝ
5. Ⓨ Ⓝ
6. Ⓨ Ⓝ
7. Ⓨ Ⓝ
8. Ⓨ Ⓝ
9. Ⓨ Ⓝ
10. Ⓨ Ⓝ
11. Ⓨ Ⓝ
12. Ⓨ Ⓝ

___ / 12
Total

NAME: ______________________________

DIRECTIONS Solve each problem.

SCORE

1. Ⓨ Ⓝ
2. Ⓨ Ⓝ
3. Ⓨ Ⓝ
4. Ⓨ Ⓝ
5. Ⓨ Ⓝ
6. Ⓨ Ⓝ
7. Ⓨ Ⓝ
8. Ⓨ Ⓝ
9. Ⓨ Ⓝ
10. Ⓨ Ⓝ
11. Ⓨ Ⓝ
12. Ⓨ Ⓝ

___ / 12 Total

1. 24 + 32 + 45 = ______

2. Multiply 120 by 300.

____

3. Calculate 528 ÷ 4.

____

4. Write the smallest possible number using 8, 1, 2, and 4.

____

5. Round 4.75 to the nearest whole number.

____

6. Write the next number in the sequence. 1,560; 1,660; 1,760;

____

7. $\frac{9}{10} - \square = \frac{4}{10}$

8. Find *y*. $17 - y = 9$

$y =$ ______

9. Record the line length.

____

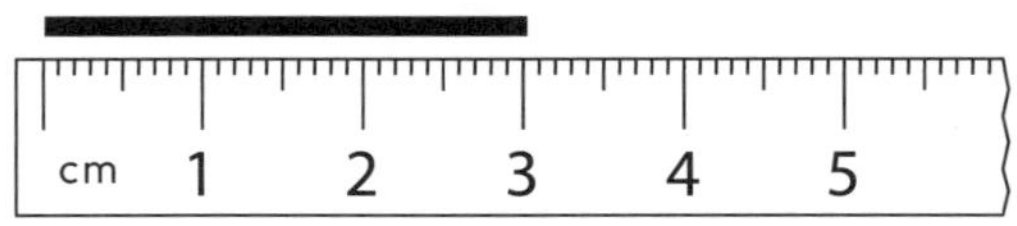

10. Is the angle *acute*, *obtuse*, or *reflex*?

____

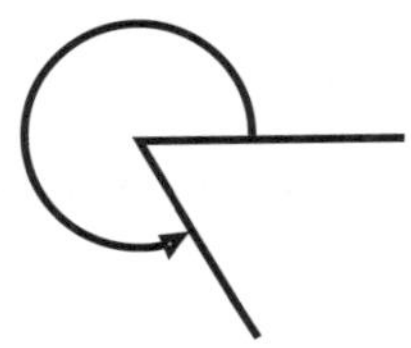

11. **Sale Prices of Clothes**

	Regular Price	Discount
Pants	$32	25%
Shirts	$24	30%
Shoes	$45	35%
Socks	$4	10%

What is the total of all four items before their discounts?

____

12. Use three of the numerals 3, 4, 5, 12, or 15 to complete the number sentence. Use any numeral once and only once.

______ ÷ ______ + ______ = 6

NAME: ______________________________

DIRECTIONS Solve each problem.

1. 100 – 69 = ______

2. Double 38.

____

3. 6 $\overline{)284}$

4. What is the place value of 5 in the number 3,562?

____

5. Write 55% as a decimal.

____

6. 3 + 5 x 8 – 2 x 10 = ______

7. 10% of ☐ is 12.

8. Find *b*. $\frac{b}{9} = 24$

b = ______

9. 2 quarts = ______ pints

10. Calculate the area of the shaded triangle.

____

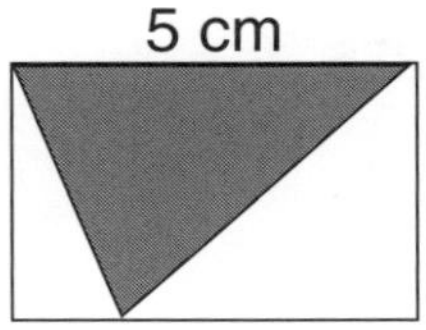

11.

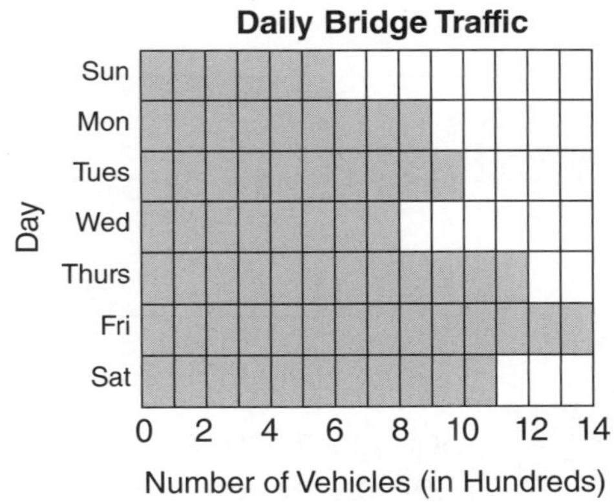

On which day were there 800 vehicles?

____

12. Which three-dimensional figure has 6 rectangular faces and 8 vertices?

____

SCORE

1. Ⓨ Ⓝ
2. Ⓨ Ⓝ
3. Ⓨ Ⓝ
4. Ⓨ Ⓝ
5. Ⓨ Ⓝ
6. Ⓨ Ⓝ
7. Ⓨ Ⓝ
8. Ⓨ Ⓝ
9. Ⓨ Ⓝ
10. Ⓨ Ⓝ
11. Ⓨ Ⓝ
12. Ⓨ Ⓝ

___ / 12 Total

DAY 142

NAME: ____________________

DIRECTIONS Solve each problem.

SCORE

1. Ⓨ Ⓝ
2. Ⓨ Ⓝ
3. Ⓨ Ⓝ
4. Ⓨ Ⓝ
5. Ⓨ Ⓝ
6. Ⓨ Ⓝ
7. Ⓨ Ⓝ
8. Ⓨ Ⓝ
9. Ⓨ Ⓝ
10. Ⓨ Ⓝ
11. Ⓨ Ⓝ
12. Ⓨ Ⓝ

___ / 12
Total

1.

$$\begin{array}{r} 180 \\ +\ \ 97 \\ \hline \end{array}$$

2. Calculate the product of 40 and 60.

____

3. $7\overline{)276}$

4. 80,000 + 7,000 + 400 + 60 + 1 =

____

5. Write $\frac{7}{10}$ as a percentage.

____

6. Complete the table. Then write the conversion rule for meters to kilometers.

Meter	4,000		6,500	
Kilometer		5.25		7.75

____

____

7. Distribute.
18(a + 2) = ____________________

8. Find c when c + 7.6 = 12.

c = ________

9. Find the area of a triangle with a base of 6 inches and a height of 11 inches

____

10. How many equal angles are there inside a regular hexagon?

____

11. Draw a spinner that has twice as much probability of landing on a 1 than a 2 or 3.

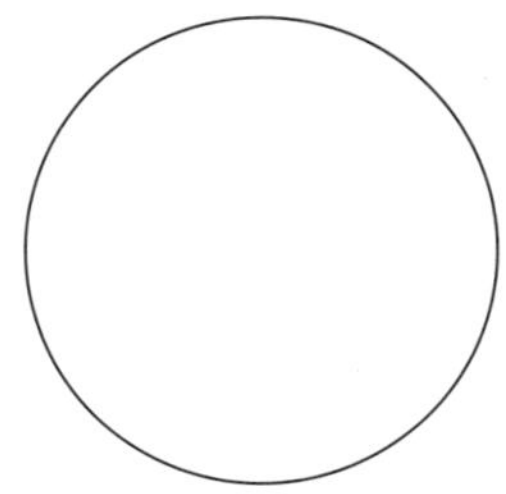

12. When Tracy works out, she likes to ride her bike twice as long as she runs. If she runs for 35 minutes, what is the total amount of time her workout will take?

____

NAME: ____________________

DIRECTIONS Solve each problem.

1. 325 – 39 = ______

2. 30 x 70 = ______

3. What is the quotient when 679 is divided by 9?

____

4. Round 67,104 to the nearest ten thousand.

____

5. Write $2\frac{5}{6}$ as an improper fraction.

____

6. Insert parentheses to make the equation true.

3 + 5 x 8 – 2 x 10 = 44

7. 18 + ☐ = 40

8. Find *m*. 15*m* = 120

m = ______

9. How many grams are in 3.25 kilograms?

____

10. What is one possible shape of the cross-section of a cone?

____

11. Steve, Mark, Melissa, Joe, and Mary are in a group. They randomly line up at the door. What is the probability that a person whose name has exactly three letters lines up first?

____

12. Complete the multiplication table.

×	20		40	50		70
6					360	
	180					
			280			
8		240				

SCORE

1. Ⓨ Ⓝ
2. Ⓨ Ⓝ
3. Ⓨ Ⓝ
4. Ⓨ Ⓝ
5. Ⓨ Ⓝ
6. Ⓨ Ⓝ
7. Ⓨ Ⓝ
8. Ⓨ Ⓝ
9. Ⓨ Ⓝ
10. Ⓨ Ⓝ
11. Ⓨ Ⓝ
12. Ⓨ Ⓝ

___ / 12 Total

DAY **144**

NAME: ______________________

DIRECTIONS Solve each problem.

SCORE

1. Ⓨ Ⓝ
2. Ⓨ Ⓝ
3. Ⓨ Ⓝ
4. Ⓨ Ⓝ
5. Ⓨ Ⓝ
6. Ⓨ Ⓝ
7. Ⓨ Ⓝ
8. Ⓨ Ⓝ
9. Ⓨ Ⓝ
10. Ⓨ Ⓝ
11. Ⓨ Ⓝ
12. Ⓨ Ⓝ

___ / 12 **Total**

1. 290 + 64 = ______

2. (–17) x (–20) = ______

3. $7\overline{)467}$

4. Is 42,358 an even number?

____

5. $\frac{7}{8} - \frac{3}{8}$ = ______

6. Insert parentheses to make the equation true.

3 + 5 x 8 – 2 x 10 = 303

7. ☐ – 58 = 106

8. Write the expression for 25 less than *x*.

____

9. 3 yards = ______ feet

10. Complete the chart for the shape.

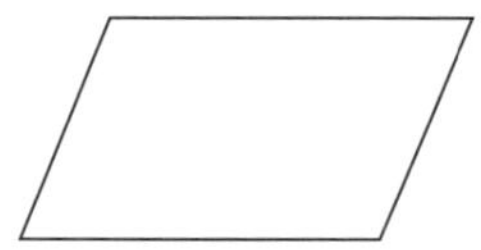

Name the figure.	
How many sides?	
How many angles?	
Does it have symmetry?	
Is it a plane shape or a solid shape?	

11. **Time Spent on Homework**

Day	Minutes
Monday	52
Tuesday	45
Wednesday	30
Thursday	45
Friday	0

What was the total number of hours and minutes spent on homework this week?

____

12. Each member of a class of 24 students drinks a pint of milk for lunch. How many total gallons of milk do the students drink?

____

NAME: ____________________

DIRECTIONS Solve each problem.

1.
$$\begin{array}{r} 236 \\ -\ 19 \\ \hline \end{array}$$

2. Multiply 145 by 20.

____

3. $546 \div 8 =$ ______

4. Write the ordinal number for fifty-one.

____

5. Find the sum of $1\frac{1}{6}$ and $\frac{1}{3}$.

____

6. Write the next number in the sequence. 3,064; 3,014; 2,964;

____

7. 30 x ☐ = 600

8. Find *f*. $12f = 108$

$f =$ ______

9. Calculate the volume of a rectangular prism that has side lengths of 6 cm, 4 cm, and 2 cm.

____

10. Is a 145° angle *obtuse*, *reflex,* or *straight*?

____

11. What is the mode of this set of data?

601, 611, 621, 611, 631

____

12. I am part of a whole. I am greater than one-tenth but less than 13%. My denominator is 8. What number am I?

____

SCORE

1. Ⓨ Ⓝ
2. Ⓨ Ⓝ
3. Ⓨ Ⓝ
4. Ⓨ Ⓝ
5. Ⓨ Ⓝ
6. Ⓨ Ⓝ
7. Ⓨ Ⓝ
8. Ⓨ Ⓝ
9. Ⓨ Ⓝ
10. Ⓨ Ⓝ
11. Ⓨ Ⓝ
12. Ⓨ Ⓝ

___ / 12 Total

DAY 146

NAME: ______________________

DIRECTIONS Solve each problem.

SCORE

1. Ⓨ Ⓝ
2. Ⓨ Ⓝ
3. Ⓨ Ⓝ
4. Ⓨ Ⓝ
5. Ⓨ Ⓝ
6. Ⓨ Ⓝ
7. Ⓨ Ⓝ
8. Ⓨ Ⓝ
9. Ⓨ Ⓝ
10. Ⓨ Ⓝ
11. Ⓨ Ⓝ
12. Ⓨ Ⓝ

___ / 12 Total

1.

$$\begin{array}{r} 243 \\ 168 \\ +\ 76 \\ \hline \end{array}$$

2. $10 \times 20 =$ ______

3. $5\overline{)149}$

4. Is 14,589 greater than 14,859?

____

5. Simplify $\frac{6}{10}$.

____

6. $(27 - 5 \times 3)^2 =$ ______

7. .75 of ☐ is 3.

8. Distribute.
$100(7 - p) =$

____

9. What is the area of a rectangle with a length of 8 m and a width of 7 m?

____

10. What is the shape of the base on a hexagonal pyramid?

____

11. Which spinner would give you a better chance of landing on a word with 4 letters?

____

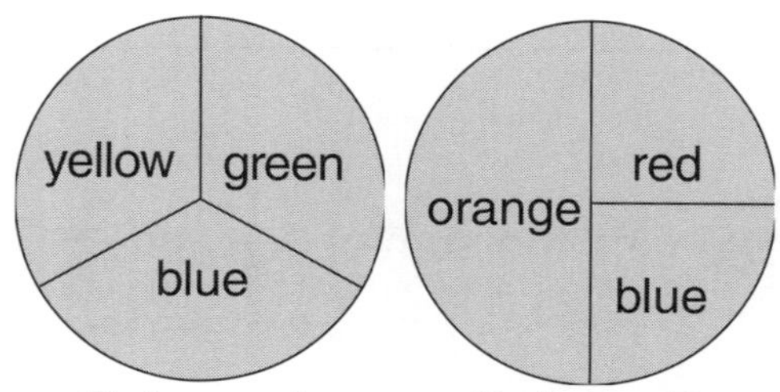

Spinner A **Spinner B**

12. Jack takes 4 steps every time his dad takes 3. How many steps will Jack take if his dad takes 12 steps?

____

NAME: ______________________________

DIRECTIONS Solve each problem.

1. Calculate the difference when 358 is subtracted from 841.

____

2. 6 • 300 = ______

3. $8 \overline{)77}$

4. List all the factors of 60.

____

____

5. Write $\frac{8}{3}$ as a mixed number.

____

6. $3^2 + 5 \times 2^2 =$ ______

7. $144 \div 12 = 3 \times \square$

8. Find *h*. $\frac{64}{h} = 16$

$h =$ ______

9. How many liters are in 7,500 milliliters?

____

10. How many vertices are on the square?

____

11. Two red blocks, two green blocks, and three yellow blocks were put into a bag. What is the probability that you will pull out a red or a green block?

____

12. Circle the factors of the given product.

Possible Factors									Product
8	2	6	3	5	4	12	10	21	124

SCORE

1. Ⓨ Ⓝ
2. Ⓨ Ⓝ
3. Ⓨ Ⓝ
4. Ⓨ Ⓝ
5. Ⓨ Ⓝ
6. Ⓨ Ⓝ
7. Ⓨ Ⓝ
8. Ⓨ Ⓝ
9. Ⓨ Ⓝ
10. Ⓨ Ⓝ
11. Ⓨ Ⓝ
12. Ⓨ Ⓝ

___ / 12 Total

DAY 148

NAME: ______________________

DIRECTIONS Solve each problem.

SCORE

1. Ⓨ Ⓝ
2. Ⓨ Ⓝ
3. Ⓨ Ⓝ
4. Ⓨ Ⓝ
5. Ⓨ Ⓝ
6. Ⓨ Ⓝ
7. Ⓨ Ⓝ
8. Ⓨ Ⓝ
9. Ⓨ Ⓝ
10. Ⓨ Ⓝ
11. Ⓨ Ⓝ
12. Ⓨ Ⓝ

___ / 12 Total

1. 268 + 54 = ______

2. $\begin{array}{r} 500 \\ \times \quad 3 \\ \hline \end{array}$

3. 164 ÷ 8 = ______

4. What is the next number after 156,789?

____

5. 50% of 90 is ______.

6. 15 ÷ (47 – 44) = ______

7. $2\frac{3}{5} = \frac{\square}{5}$

8. Distribute.
10(*b* + 7.8) =

____

9. Calculate the distance a boat can travel in 2 hours at 55 mph.

____

10. Are all hexagons regular polygons?

____

11.

Box A	Box B
A	A
Z	A
Z	Z
Z	T
T	T
T	S
S	M
S	G
S	G

If you randomly choose a letter from one of these columns, from which column would you have a better probability of choosing a vowel?

____

12. Write the number made up of these place values:

8 hundreds

4 tenths

3 ones

8 hundredths

7 tens

____

NAME: ______________________

DIRECTIONS Solve each problem.

1. 200 – 74 = ______

2. Calculate the product of 90 and 8.

____

3. 297 ÷ 6 = ______

4. List the first three multiples of 9.

____

5. 36% of 200 is ______.

6. 15 – 20 x 3 = ______

7. 40,000 + 9,000 + 400 + 70 + ☐ = 49,476

8. Find *r*. $r - 183 = 17$

$r =$ ______

9. What is the volume of a container (in cm^3) that holds 250 mL?

____

10. Can a triangle have perpendicular lines?

____

11. **Cookies Baked**

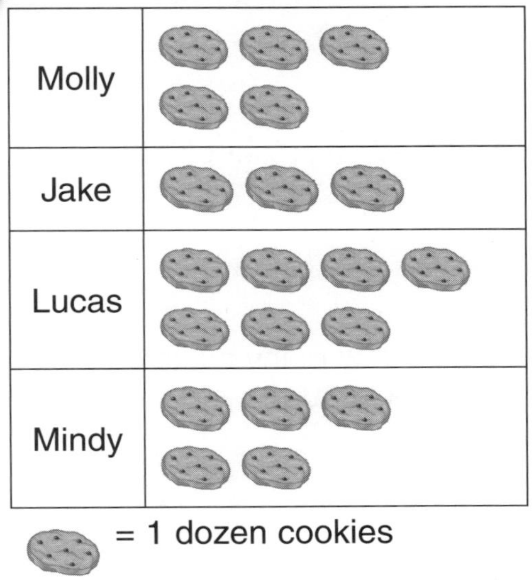

Jake will bake the same amount of cookies tomorrow. How many cookies will he bake in all?

____

12. Trevor had a collection with 126 trading cards in it. He finds a great deal at a store which increases his collection by $\frac{1}{3}$. Now how many trading cards does Trevor have?

____

SCORE

1. Ⓨ Ⓝ
2. Ⓨ Ⓝ
3. Ⓨ Ⓝ
4. Ⓨ Ⓝ
5. Ⓨ Ⓝ
6. Ⓨ Ⓝ
7. Ⓨ Ⓝ
8. Ⓨ Ⓝ
9. Ⓨ Ⓝ
10. Ⓨ Ⓝ
11. Ⓨ Ⓝ
12. Ⓨ Ⓝ

___ / 12 **Total**

DAY 150

NAME: ____________________

DIRECTIONS Solve each problem.

SCORE

1. Ⓨ Ⓝ
2. Ⓨ Ⓝ
3. Ⓨ Ⓝ
4. Ⓨ Ⓝ
5. Ⓨ Ⓝ
6. Ⓨ Ⓝ
7. Ⓨ Ⓝ
8. Ⓨ Ⓝ
9. Ⓨ Ⓝ
10. Ⓨ Ⓝ
11. Ⓨ Ⓝ
12. Ⓨ Ⓝ

___ / 12 Total

1.
$$\begin{array}{r} 25 \\ 26 \\ +\ 47 \\ \hline \end{array}$$

2. 20 x 30 = ______

3. What is half of 76? ______

4. How many digits are in 906,500?

____

5. Write 1.07 as a mixed number.

____

6. Write the next number in the sequence. 326, 276, 226,

____

7. 0.39 = ☐ %

8. Distribute.
$-2(x + 3) =$ ____________________

9. How many meters are in 3.8 kilometers?

____

10. Is the angle *acute*, *straight*, or *reflex*?

____

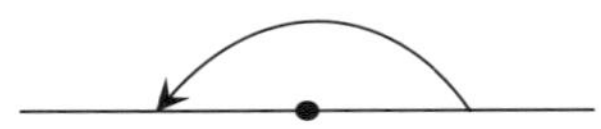

11. What is the median of this set of data?

78, 45, 32, 81, 18, 54, 23

____

12. Terri is allowed to play games on the computer 5 minutes for every 30 minutes she reads. If she reads for 6 hours one week, how many minutes can she play on the computer?

____

NAME: ____________________

DIRECTIONS Solve each problem.

1. 100 – 57 = ______

2. Calculate the product of 34 and 6.

____

3. 5 $\overline{)250}$

4. What is the value of the digit 8 in the number 169,378?

____

5. $\frac{2}{5} + \frac{7}{10} =$ ______

6. –10 + 3 x 7 = ______

7. 142 ☐ 67 = 75 + 0

8. Find *d*. 170 – *d* = 60

d = ______

9. What is the volume of the solid with a 4-cm square base that is 3 cm high?

____

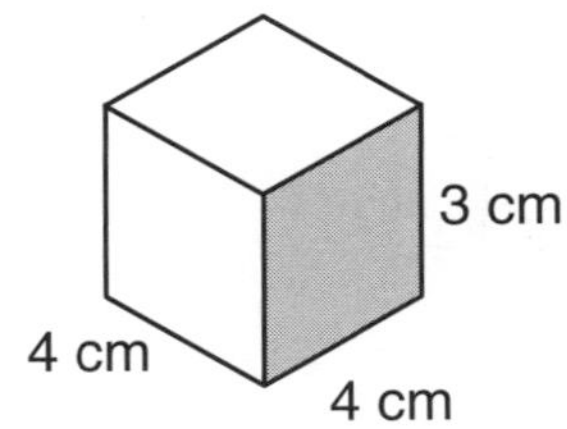

10. Which line is parallel to line C?

____

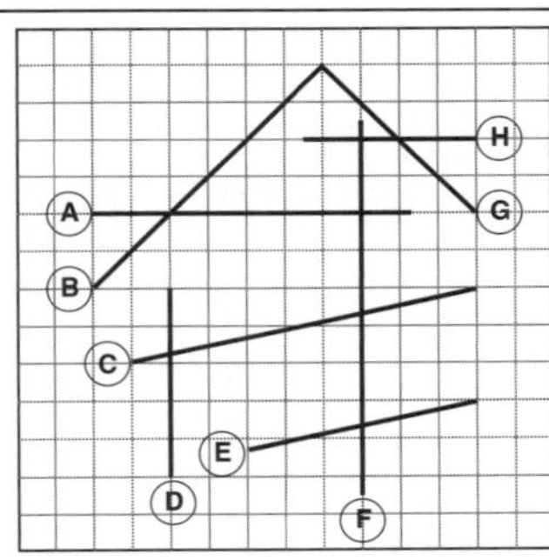

11. What is the mean of this set of data?
18, 25, 31, 31, 44, 68, 76

____

12. It takes a rollercoaster 3 minutes 45 seconds to run the track and 2 minutes 30 seconds to unload and load people in between runs. How many runs can the rollercoaster make in 1 hour?

____

SCORE

1. Ⓨ Ⓝ
2. Ⓨ Ⓝ
3. Ⓨ Ⓝ
4. Ⓨ Ⓝ
5. Ⓨ Ⓝ
6. Ⓨ Ⓝ
7. Ⓨ Ⓝ
8. Ⓨ Ⓝ
9. Ⓨ Ⓝ
10. Ⓨ Ⓝ
11. Ⓨ Ⓝ
12. Ⓨ Ⓝ

___ / 12 Total

NAME: ______________________

DIRECTIONS Solve each problem.

SCORE

1. Ⓨ Ⓝ
2. Ⓨ Ⓝ
3. Ⓨ Ⓝ
4. Ⓨ Ⓝ
5. Ⓨ Ⓝ
6. Ⓨ Ⓝ
7. Ⓨ Ⓝ
8. Ⓨ Ⓝ
9. Ⓨ Ⓝ
10. Ⓨ Ⓝ
11. Ⓨ Ⓝ
12. Ⓨ Ⓝ

___ / 12
Total

1. Add 65 to 258. _______

2. Calculate the product of 25 and 5.

____

3. $180 \div 3 =$ _______

4. Write the expanded notation for 461.

____

5. Round 4.39 to the nearest whole number.

____

6. Complete the input/output chart. Look for a pattern and write the rule.

Input	1	2	3	4	5
Output	5	10			

____

____

7. Find *x*. $20x = 600$

$x =$ _______

8. Write the expression for the quotient when *m* is divided by 34.

____

9. Write the time 10:47 A.M. in a 24-hour time format.

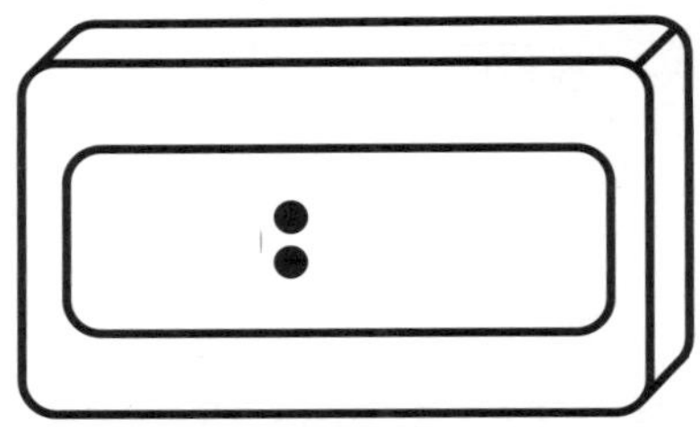

10. What is the sum of the inside angles of a rectangle?

____

11. Draw a spinner that has a 50% probability of landing on a 1, and an equal probability of landing on a 2 or 3.

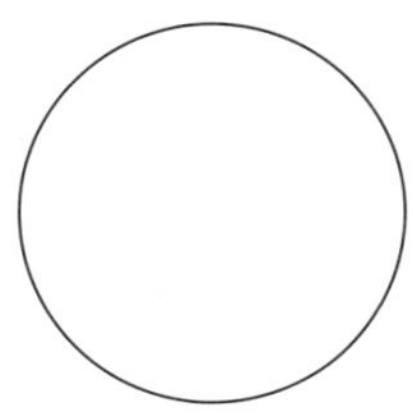

12. It costs $1.25 per mile in a taxi. How many miles did you travel if your change from $10.00 is $2.50?

____

DAY 153

NAME: ____________________

DIRECTIONS Solve each problem.

1. 582 – 97 = ______

2.

$$\begin{array}{r} 400 \\ \times \ \ 60 \\ \hline \end{array}$$

3. What is half of 58?

____

4. Round 358,962 to the nearest thousand.

____

5. 10% of 750 is ______.

6. –4 x 3 + 5 = ______

7. $3\frac{1}{4} = \frac{13}{\square}$

8. Distribute.

14(*t* – 10) = ______________

9. 108 inches = ______ feet

10. How many axes of symmetry does the shape have?

____

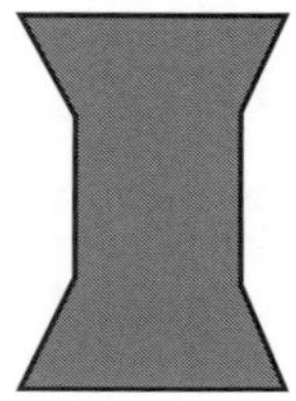

11.

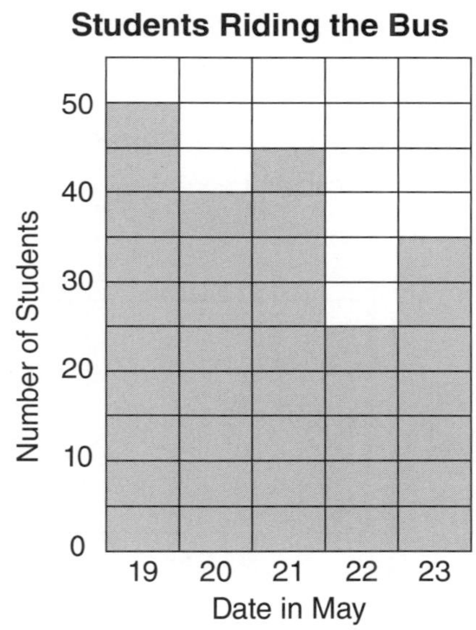

If the cost to ride the bus is $1.50, how much money did the bus company earn on the 19th?

____

12. You have $2.35. You want to buy gum that costs $.25 each. What is the greatest number of pieces of gum you can buy?

____

SCORE

1. Ⓨ Ⓝ
2. Ⓨ Ⓝ
3. Ⓨ Ⓝ
4. Ⓨ Ⓝ
5. Ⓨ Ⓝ
6. Ⓨ Ⓝ
7. Ⓨ Ⓝ
8. Ⓨ Ⓝ
9. Ⓨ Ⓝ
10. Ⓨ Ⓝ
11. Ⓨ Ⓝ
12. Ⓨ Ⓝ

___ / 12

Total

DAY 154

NAME: ____________________

DIRECTIONS Solve each problem.

SCORE

1. Ⓨ Ⓝ
2. Ⓨ Ⓝ
3. Ⓨ Ⓝ
4. Ⓨ Ⓝ
5. Ⓨ Ⓝ
6. Ⓨ Ⓝ
7. Ⓨ Ⓝ
8. Ⓨ Ⓝ
9. Ⓨ Ⓝ
10. Ⓨ Ⓝ
11. Ⓨ Ⓝ
12. Ⓨ Ⓝ

___ / 12 Total

1. $180 + 97 =$ ______

2. $50 \cdot 30 =$ ______

3. $6 \overline{)240}$

4. Is 242,277 an odd or an even number?

____

5. Simplify $\frac{6}{9}$.

____

6. $(17 + 5) \times 2 - 3 =$ ______

7. $\frac{3}{8} + \square = 1$

8. Find y. $\frac{y}{10} = 4.3$

$y =$ ______

9. Calculate the average speed when 180 km are traveled in 3 hours.

____

10. Complete the chart for the shape.

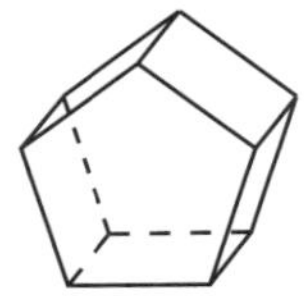

Name the figure.	
How many surfaces?	
How many vertices?	
Does it stack or roll?	
Is it a plane shape or a solid shape?	

11. The numbers 20 through 30 were written on individual cards and placed in a bag. If you pull one card from the bag, what is the probability that the number on it will be made up of only straight lines?

____

12. Complete the chart by rounding 1,673,424 to the specified place.

Ten	
Hundred	
Thousand	
Ten thousand	
Hundred Thousand	
Million	

NAME: ______________________________

DIRECTIONS Solve each problem.

1.
$$\begin{array}{r} 325 \\ -\ 39 \\ \hline \end{array}$$

2. Calculate the product of 45 and 5.

____

3. 492 ÷ 7 = ______

4. What number is 1,000 before 89,257?

____

5. Circle the value below that is not equivalent to the other two values.

0.5 50% $\frac{5}{100}$

6. Write the next number in the sequence. 1,025, 975, 925,

____

7. 72 ÷ 8 = 9 x ☐

8. Find *w*. $w^2 = 100$

$w =$ ______

9. What is the area of a square with 12-cm sides?

____

10. Name the triangle.

____

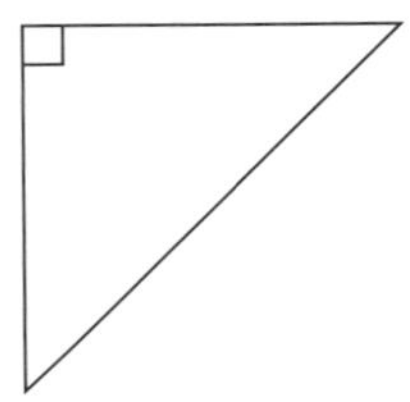

11. Michael has three chores he must do: unload the dishwasher, take out the trash, and feed the dog. List all the possible orders in which he can do his chores.

____

____

____

12. Tickets at a carnival cost $7.50 for 20 tickets or $20.00 for 50 tickets. Which is the better value?

____

SCORE

1. Ⓨ Ⓝ
2. Ⓨ Ⓝ
3. Ⓨ Ⓝ
4. Ⓨ Ⓝ
5. Ⓨ Ⓝ
6. Ⓨ Ⓝ
7. Ⓨ Ⓝ
8. Ⓨ Ⓝ
9. Ⓨ Ⓝ
10. Ⓨ Ⓝ
11. Ⓨ Ⓝ
12. Ⓨ Ⓝ

___ / 12 Total

DAY
156

NAME: ______________________________

DIRECTIONS Solve each problem.

SCORE

1. Ⓨ Ⓝ
2. Ⓨ Ⓝ
3. Ⓨ Ⓝ
4. Ⓨ Ⓝ
5. Ⓨ Ⓝ
6. Ⓨ Ⓝ
7. Ⓨ Ⓝ
8. Ⓨ Ⓝ
9. Ⓨ Ⓝ
10. Ⓨ Ⓝ
11. Ⓨ Ⓝ
12. Ⓨ Ⓝ

___ / 12
Total

1. Calculate the sum of 345, 271, and 196.

____

2. 64 x 6 = ______

3. $4\overline{)280}$

4. What number is 12 less than 3?

____

5. 20% of 250 is ______.

6. 17 + 5 x 2 – 3 = ______

7. 0.75 = ☐ %

8. Find *g*. $g - 108 = 23$

$g =$ ______

9. Write 9:26 P.M. in a 24-hour time format.

____

10. What is the shape of the base on a triangular prism?

____

11. What is the probability the spinner will land on a sport that involves water?

____

12. An extra-large pizza is cut into 18 slices at a party. There are 3 adults who eat 2 slices each. If a child eats half as many slices as an adult and the entire pizza is eaten, how many children are at the party?

____

NAME: ____________________

DIRECTIONS Solve each problem.

1. Calculate the difference between 461 and 49.

____

2.
$$\begin{array}{r} 40 \\ \times\ 60 \\ \hline \end{array}$$

3. $10\overline{)4{,}790}$

4. List the factors of 26.

____

5. Arrange in ascending order.
3.5, 3.8, 3.6

____

6. 3.4 + 1.5 x 2 = ______

7. $\frac{5}{10} = \frac{\square}{12}$

8. Write the expression for the sum of twice *x* and thirty-two.

____

9. How many minutes are in $1\frac{1}{2}$ hours?

____

10. How many faces does the solid have?

____

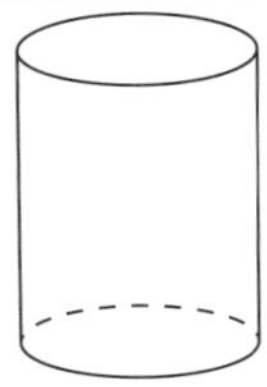

11. Look at the set of shapes. What is the probability of picking a shape with equal sides?

____

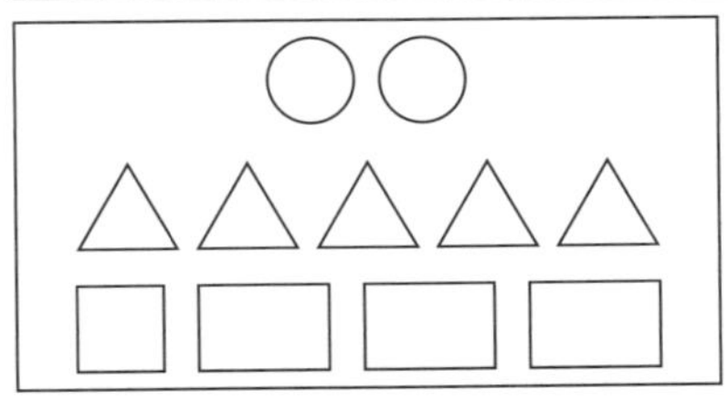

12. One eighth of the square is blue. One fourth of the square is green. Two of the sections are red. The rest is yellow. What fraction of the square is yellow?

____

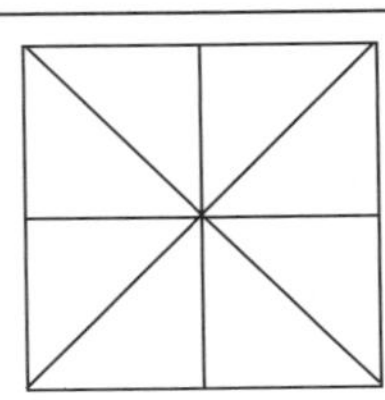

SCORE

1. Ⓨ Ⓝ
2. Ⓨ Ⓝ
3. Ⓨ Ⓝ
4. Ⓨ Ⓝ
5. Ⓨ Ⓝ
6. Ⓨ Ⓝ
7. Ⓨ Ⓝ
8. Ⓨ Ⓝ
9. Ⓨ Ⓝ
10. Ⓨ Ⓝ
11. Ⓨ Ⓝ
12. Ⓨ Ⓝ

___ / 12
Total

DAY
158

NAME: ____________________

DIRECTIONS Solve each problem.

SCORE
1. Ⓨ Ⓝ
2. Ⓨ Ⓝ
3. Ⓨ Ⓝ
4. Ⓨ Ⓝ
5. Ⓨ Ⓝ
6. Ⓨ Ⓝ
7. Ⓨ Ⓝ
8. Ⓨ Ⓝ
9. Ⓨ Ⓝ
10. Ⓨ Ⓝ
11. Ⓨ Ⓝ
12. Ⓨ Ⓝ
___ / 12 Total

1.

$$\begin{array}{r} 32 \\ 46 \\ +\ 28 \\ \hline \end{array}$$

2. 70 x 500 = ______

3. How many groups of four are in 120?

____

4. Calculate the cube root of 27.

____

5. $6 + \frac{5}{10} + \frac{6}{100} + \frac{4}{1000} =$

____

6. 14.7 + 2 x 1.2 – 8 = ______

7. 9.6 – ☐ = 5.8

8. Find *x*. $2x = 10$

$x =$ ______

9. Calculate the distance a train can travel in 5 hours at 50 kilometers per hour.

____

10. How many sides does a decagon have?

____

11. Inside a bag of candy there are 16 lollipops, 12 pieces of chocolate, and 7 pieces of licorice. If you reach in the bag and grab a piece of candy, what is the probability that it will be either a piece of chocolate or licorice?

____

12. Reanna worked 9 hours. She took a break after working $\frac{1}{3}$ of the time. How many hours did she still have to work when she came back from her break?

____

DAY 159

NAME: ______________________

DIRECTIONS Solve each problem.

1. $100 - 78 =$ ______

2. $6 \cdot 400 =$ ______

3. Is $148 \div 7$ greater than or less than $21\frac{2}{7}$?

____

4. Is 248 evenly divisible by 4?

____

5. Write 0.62 as a percentage.

____

6. $8.4 \times 7 - 3 \times 2.1 =$ ______

7. $\frac{2}{5} = \frac{\square}{15}$

8. Distribute.

$27(3 + u) =$ ______

9. What is the volume of a container (in cm^3) that holds 950 mL?

____

10. Do perpendicular lines ever meet?

____

11. In a game, the probability of the spinner landing on red or green is $\frac{4}{5}$. How many times would you expect to land on red or green if you spin the spinner 80 times?

____

12. At a conference, one car was provided for every 4 people. How many cars were needed if there were 91 people?

____

SCORE

1. Ⓨ Ⓝ
2. Ⓨ Ⓝ
3. Ⓨ Ⓝ
4. Ⓨ Ⓝ
5. Ⓨ Ⓝ
6. Ⓨ Ⓝ
7. Ⓨ Ⓝ
8. Ⓨ Ⓝ
9. Ⓨ Ⓝ
10. Ⓨ Ⓝ
11. Ⓨ Ⓝ
12. Ⓨ Ⓝ

___ / 12 Total

DAY
160

NAME: ______________________________

DIRECTIONS Solve each problem.

SCORE

1. Ⓨ Ⓝ
2. Ⓨ Ⓝ
3. Ⓨ Ⓝ
4. Ⓨ Ⓝ
5. Ⓨ Ⓝ
6. Ⓨ Ⓝ
7. Ⓨ Ⓝ
8. Ⓨ Ⓝ
9. Ⓨ Ⓝ
10. Ⓨ Ⓝ
11. Ⓨ Ⓝ
12. Ⓨ Ⓝ

___ / 12
Total

1. $148 + 35 =$ ______

2. $32 \times 200 =$ ______

3. Calculate $511 \div 6$.

____

4. Write the largest possible number using the digits 8, 4, 9, 2, and 5.

____

5. Is 25% greater than, less than, or equal to 0.3?

____

6. Write the next number in the sequence. 56, 64, 72,

____

7. $\frac{4}{5} = \frac{\square}{10}$

8. Find *a*. $2a = 1$

$a =$ ______

9. How many grams are in $1\frac{1}{2}$ kg + $\frac{3}{4}$ kg?

____

10. Use a protractor to measure the angle.

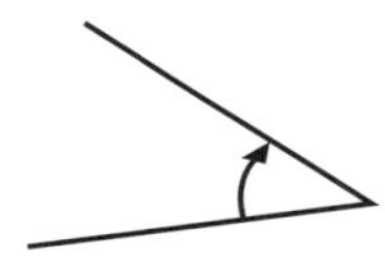

____

11. **Sale Prices of Clothes**

	Regular Price	Discount
Pants	$32	25%
Shirts	$24	30%
Shoes	$45	35%
Socks	$4	10%

What is the total of all four items after the discount?

____

12. Complete the magic square using the numbers 0–15.

5		6	
2	15		
9	4		
14	3	13	

NAME: ______________________________

DIRECTIONS Solve each problem.

1. 263 – 147 = ______

2.
$$\begin{array}{r} 100 \\ \times \ 43 \\ \hline \end{array}$$

3. How many groups of six are in 180?

____

4. What is the value of the digit 4 in the number 247,890?

____

5. Write 7.04 as a mixed number.

____

6. 2 x 3 ☐ 10 = 16

7. ☐ x 30 = 1,800

8. Find *k*. *k* + 45 = 371

k = ______

9. How many meters are in 624 centimeters?

____

10. What is the perimeter of a square with 15-m sides?

____

11.

Birds Seen

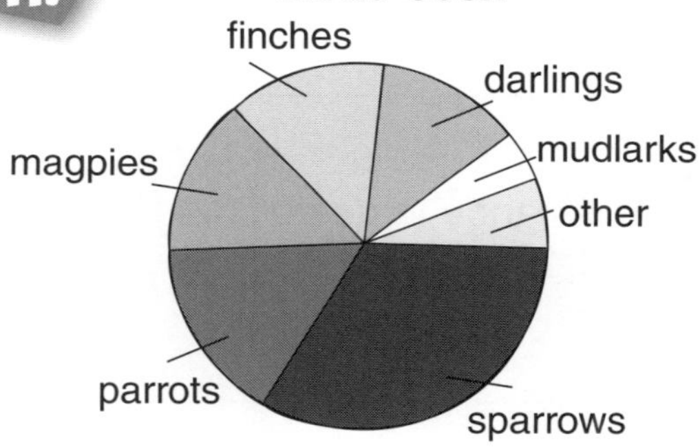

What fraction of the birds seen were either parrots or sparrows?

____

12. Round each item on the bill to the nearest nickel. Then find the change from $20.00 of the total rounded amount.

____

$0.87
$2.66
$3.90
$1.63
$2.53
$1.30

SCORE

1. Ⓨ Ⓝ
2. Ⓨ Ⓝ
3. Ⓨ Ⓝ
4. Ⓨ Ⓝ
5. Ⓨ Ⓝ
6. Ⓨ Ⓝ
7. Ⓨ Ⓝ
8. Ⓨ Ⓝ
9. Ⓨ Ⓝ
10. Ⓨ Ⓝ
11. Ⓨ Ⓝ
12. Ⓨ Ⓝ

___ / 12
Total

DAY
162

NAME: ____________________

DIRECTIONS Solve each problem.

SCORE

1. Ⓨ Ⓝ
2. Ⓨ Ⓝ
3. Ⓨ Ⓝ
4. Ⓨ Ⓝ
5. Ⓨ Ⓝ
6. Ⓨ Ⓝ
7. Ⓨ Ⓝ
8. Ⓨ Ⓝ
9. Ⓨ Ⓝ
10. Ⓨ Ⓝ
11. Ⓨ Ⓝ
12. Ⓨ Ⓝ

___ / 12
Total

1.
$$\begin{array}{r} 169 \\ +\ \ 78 \\ \hline \end{array}$$

2. 75 x 10 = ______

3. $6\overline{)120}$

4. 30,000 + 5,000 + 900 + 80 + 2 =

____

5. Arrange in descending order.
1.4, 1.6, 1.3

____

6. Complete the table. Then write the conversion rule for grams to kilograms.

Gram	9,000	8,500	8,000	
Kilogram				7.5

____

____

7. Distribute.

3(*x* + 9) = ____________

8. $w^2 = 1$ Solve for *w*.

w = ______

9. Find the area of a triangle with a base of 3 ft. and a height of 6 ft.

____

10. Here are five views of the same cube.

Draw the shape that is opposite from  on the cube.

11. Draw a spinner that has an equal probability of landing on green, red, yellow, or orange.

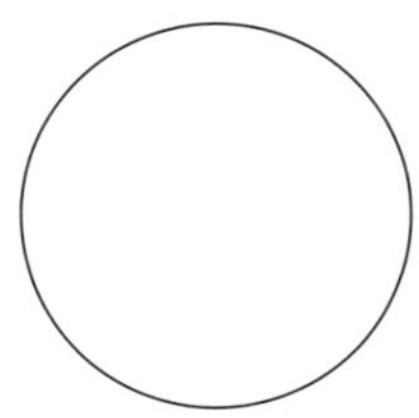

12. Kyle mows lawns on the weekend to earn some extra money. He can mow 5 lawns in 2 hours. If he earns $6.50 per lawn, how much does he earn per hour?

____

NAME: ____________________

DIRECTIONS Solve each problem.

SCORE

1. $\begin{array}{r} 234 \\ -\ 168 \\ \hline \end{array}$

2. 100 • 43 = ______

3. What is the quotient of 1,496 and 10?

____

4. Round 26,937 to the nearest thousand.

____

5. Simplify $\frac{4}{10}$.

____

6. (–3) + (–2) x (–5) = ______

7. 2.3 + 2.7 – ☐ = 1.8

8. Solve for r when $\frac{r}{3} = 16$.

$r =$ ________

9. Calculate the perimeter of a square with 3.5-cm sides.

____

10. Name the solid shape.

____

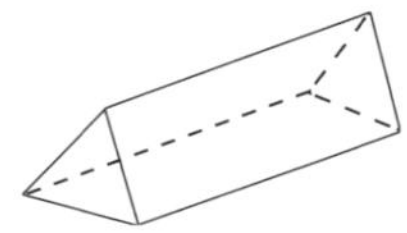

11.

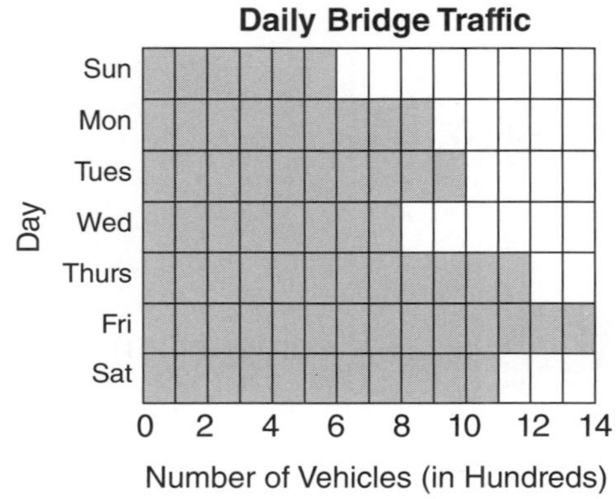

One-third of the vehicles that crossed the bridge on Thursday were trucks. How many trucks crossed the bridge on Thursday?

____

12. Complete the multiplication table.

×		30	40		60	
		300				
20				1,000		
						2,100
40	800					

1. Ⓨ Ⓝ
2. Ⓨ Ⓝ
3. Ⓨ Ⓝ
4. Ⓨ Ⓝ
5. Ⓨ Ⓝ
6. Ⓨ Ⓝ
7. Ⓨ Ⓝ
8. Ⓨ Ⓝ
9. Ⓨ Ⓝ
10. Ⓨ Ⓝ
11. Ⓨ Ⓝ
12. Ⓨ Ⓝ

___ / 12 Total

DAY
164

NAME: ______________________________

DIRECTIONS Solve each problem.

SCORE

1. Ⓨ Ⓝ
2. Ⓨ Ⓝ
3. Ⓨ Ⓝ
4. Ⓨ Ⓝ
5. Ⓨ Ⓝ
6. Ⓨ Ⓝ
7. Ⓨ Ⓝ
8. Ⓨ Ⓝ
9. Ⓨ Ⓝ
10. Ⓨ Ⓝ
11. Ⓨ Ⓝ
12. Ⓨ Ⓝ

___ / 12
Total

1. 1,430 + 300 = ______

2. 30 x 40 = ______

3. $5\overline{)192}$

4. Is 21 a composite number?

Circle: yes no

5. Round 6.37 to the nearest whole number.

____

6. (–2) x 3 + 4 • (–8) = ______

7. 6 x ☐ = 107 – 23

8. Write the expression for the product of nine hundred and *q*.

____

9. Calculate the perimeter of the shape.

____

10. What is the measure of each interior angle in an equilateral triangle?

____

11.

Time Spent on Homework

Day	Minutes
Monday	52
Tuesday	45
Wednesday	30
Thursday	45
Friday	0

One-third of the time on Thursday was spent studying for a spelling test. How many minutes were spent studying for the spelling test?

____

12. A bottle of cough syrup has 300 mL. If you take 5-mL spoonfuls 3 times a day, how many days will the cough syrup last?

____

NAME: ______________________________

DIRECTIONS Solve each problem.

1. Subtract 263 from 596.

____

2.
```
  100
x  43
```

3. 497 ÷ 7 = ______

4. What is the ordinal number for forty-seven?

____

5. Is $\frac{5}{10}$ greater than, less than, or equal to $\frac{6}{12}$? ______________

6. Write the next number in the sequence. 810, 900, 990,

____

7. Find *x*. $4x = 12$

$x =$ ______

8. Find *x*. $4x = 10$

$x =$ ______

9. What is the volume of a cube that measures 10 cm on each side?

____

10. Use a protracter to measure the angle. Then identify it as either *acute*, *reflex*, *obtuse*, or *straight*.

Angle	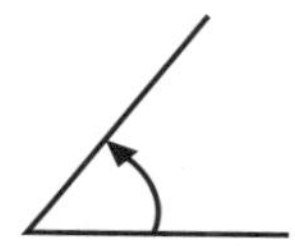
Size	
Name	

11. If you randomly pull out a crayon from a new box of eight different crayons, what is the probability you will pull out a red or blue

____

12. Uli drinks 50% more water than juice each day. If she drinks 2 cups of juice each day, how much water will she drink in a week?

____

SCORE

1. Ⓨ Ⓝ
2. Ⓨ Ⓝ
3. Ⓨ Ⓝ
4. Ⓨ Ⓝ
5. Ⓨ Ⓝ
6. Ⓨ Ⓝ
7. Ⓨ Ⓝ
8. Ⓨ Ⓝ
9. Ⓨ Ⓝ
10. Ⓨ Ⓝ
11. Ⓨ Ⓝ
12. Ⓨ Ⓝ

___ / 12
Total

DAY 166

NAME: ____________________

DIRECTIONS Solve each problem.

SCORE

1. Ⓨ Ⓝ
2. Ⓨ Ⓝ
3. Ⓨ Ⓝ
4. Ⓨ Ⓝ
5. Ⓨ Ⓝ
6. Ⓨ Ⓝ
7. Ⓨ Ⓝ
8. Ⓨ Ⓝ
9. Ⓨ Ⓝ
10. Ⓨ Ⓝ
11. Ⓨ Ⓝ
12. Ⓨ Ⓝ

___ / 12 Total

1.
$$\begin{array}{r} 156 \\ +\ \ 75 \\ \hline \end{array}$$

2. 71 x 100 = ______

3. $7\overline{)273}$

4. Is 46,304 greater than or less than 46,430?

____

5. $\frac{3}{4}$ of 84 is ______.

6. 4 x 5 ☐ 2 = 22

7. Distribute.

5(*x* + 2) = ____________________

8. Distribute.

–5(*x* + 2) = ____________________

9. How many millimeters are there in $5\frac{1}{2}$ cm?

____

10. Is the top view of a cone a circle?

Circle: yes no

11. Which spinner would give you the best chance of landing on a word that has the letter *l*?

____

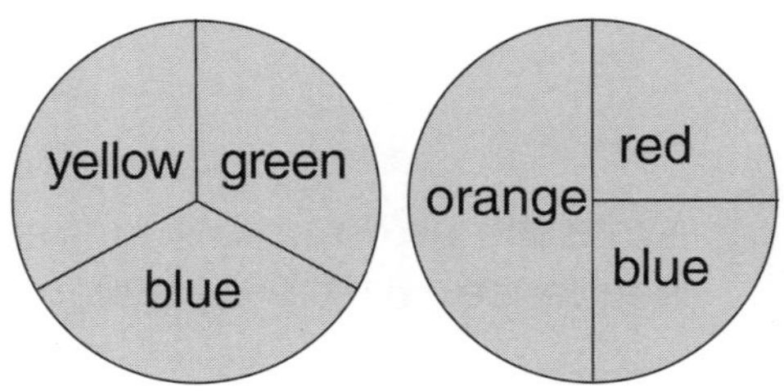

Spinner A Spinner B

12. Use three of the numerals 3, 4, 5, 12, or 15 to complete the number sentence. Do not use any numeral more than once.

(______ + ______) x ______ = 27

NAME: ____________________

DIRECTIONS Solve each problem.

1. Take 64 away from 192.

____

2. 60 • 400 = ______

3. Is 137 ÷ 4 greater than, less than, or equal to $34\frac{1}{4}$?

____

4. List all the factors of 40.

____

5. Simplify $\frac{12}{24}$.

____

6. 48 ÷ 4 + 8 – 6 x 2 = ______

7. Write the expression for the difference when eight is subtracted from *d*.

____

8. Write the expression for *d* less than eight.

____

9. How many cm^3 are in 950 mL of water?

____

10. How many edges does a rectangular pyramid have?

____

11. Two red cubes, two green cylinders, and three yellow rectangular prisms were put into a bag. If you reach in the bag and pull out an object, what is the probability that it will be a red or yellow object?

____

12. Complete the factor wheel to show all the factors of the number in the center.

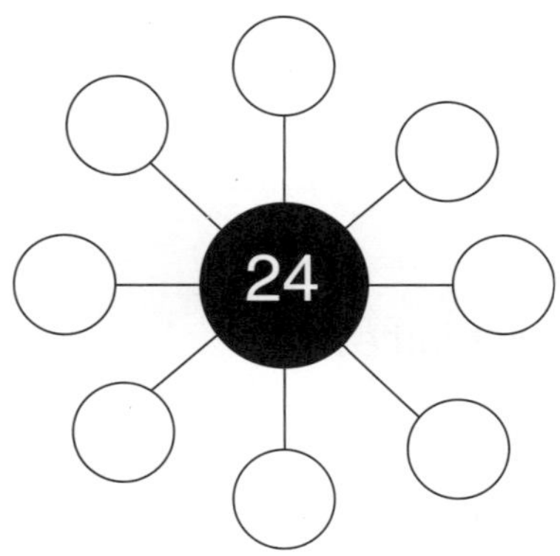

SCORE

1. Ⓨ Ⓝ
2. Ⓨ Ⓝ
3. Ⓨ Ⓝ
4. Ⓨ Ⓝ
5. Ⓨ Ⓝ
6. Ⓨ Ⓝ
7. Ⓨ Ⓝ
8. Ⓨ Ⓝ
9. Ⓨ Ⓝ
10. Ⓨ Ⓝ
11. Ⓨ Ⓝ
12. Ⓨ Ⓝ

___ / 12
Total

DAY 168

NAME: ______________________________

DIRECTIONS Solve each problem.

SCORE

1. Ⓨ Ⓝ
2. Ⓨ Ⓝ
3. Ⓨ Ⓝ
4. Ⓨ Ⓝ
5. Ⓨ Ⓝ
6. Ⓨ Ⓝ
7. Ⓨ Ⓝ
8. Ⓨ Ⓝ
9. Ⓨ Ⓝ
10. Ⓨ Ⓝ
11. Ⓨ Ⓝ
12. Ⓨ Ⓝ

___ / 12 Total

1. Add 168 and 43.

____

2. $80 \times 200 =$ _______

3. $5\overline{)150}$

4. $4^3 =$ _______

5. 10% of 650 = _______

6. Insert parentheses to make the equation true.

$48 \div 4 + 8 - 6 \times 2 = 16$

7. Distribute.

$3(x - 5) =$ ______________

8. Distribute.

$-3(x - 5) =$ ______________

9. Calculate the distance a train can travel in 3 hours at 65 mph.

____

10. Name a polygon with six sides.

____

11.

Box A	Box B
A	A
Z	A
Z	Z
Z	T
T	T
T	S
S	M
S	G
S	G

If you randomly choose a letter from one of these columns, from which column would you have a better probability of choosing a consonant?

____

12. Complete the magic square.

1		12	
14	11		
15	10		
4	5	9	

DAY 169

NAME: ____________________

DIRECTIONS Solve each problem.

1. Subtract 135 from 382.

____

2.

$$\begin{array}{r} 40 \\ \times\ 64 \\ \hline \end{array}$$

3. 167 ÷ 6 = ______

4. List the first four multiples of 10.

____

5. Is $\frac{9}{10}$ equal to $\frac{7}{8}$?

Circle: yes no

6. Insert parentheses to make the equation true.

48 ÷ 4 + 8 – 6 x 2 = –8

7. 5 x 6 + ☐ = 50

8. Find *e*. 10.8 – *e* = 5.4

e = ______

9. How many liters are in 8,450 milliliters?

____

10. Are opposite sides of a parallelogram always equal in length?

____

11. **Cookies Baked**

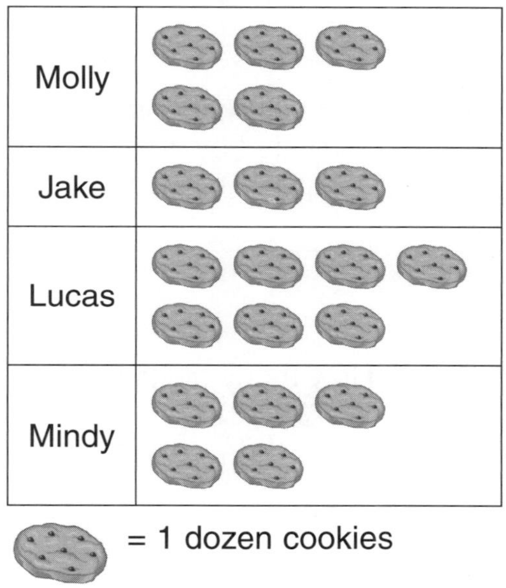

Molly gave half of her cookies to her neighbor. How many cookies did she give away?

____

12. Compare a decagonal pyramid with a decagonal prism.

	Faces	Edges	Vertices
Decagonal Pyramid			
Decagonal Prism			

SCORE

1. Ⓨ Ⓝ
2. Ⓨ Ⓝ
3. Ⓨ Ⓝ
4. Ⓨ Ⓝ
5. Ⓨ Ⓝ
6. Ⓨ Ⓝ
7. Ⓨ Ⓝ
8. Ⓨ Ⓝ
9. Ⓨ Ⓝ
10. Ⓨ Ⓝ
11. Ⓨ Ⓝ
12. Ⓨ Ⓝ

___ / 12 Total

DAY
170

NAME: ______________________________

DIRECTIONS Solve each problem.

SCORE

1. Ⓨ Ⓝ
2. Ⓨ Ⓝ
3. Ⓨ Ⓝ
4. Ⓨ Ⓝ
5. Ⓨ Ⓝ
6. Ⓨ Ⓝ
7. Ⓨ Ⓝ
8. Ⓨ Ⓝ
9. Ⓨ Ⓝ
10. Ⓨ Ⓝ
11. Ⓨ Ⓝ
12. Ⓨ Ⓝ

___ / 12
Total

1. Add 140 and 69.

____

2. $43 \cdot 30 =$ ______

3. What is the quotient when 5,627 is divided by 10?

____

4. How many digits are in 26,789,201?

____

5. Write the improper fraction for $2\frac{5}{6}$.

____

6. Write the next number in the sequence. 25, 36, 49,

____

7. $\frac{3}{4} = \frac{\square}{8}$

8. Find *p*. $p - 95 = 162$

$p =$ ______

9. How many millimeters are in 25.6 centimeters?

____

10. Is 68 degrees an *acute*, *obtuse*, *right*, or *straight* angle?

____

11. What is the mode for this set of data?
13, 11, 12, 15, 16, 15, 14,
15, 12, 12, 15, 15, 16, 13, 13

____

12. A tree grows about 4 inches each year. The tree is expected to be 25 feet tall. If it is 13 feet now, how many years will it take to reach its expected height?

____

NAME: ________________________________

DIRECTIONS Solve each problem.

1. Subtract 143 from 478.

____

2. 71 x 6 = ______

3. $5\overline{)285}$

4. What is the value of the digit 6 in 35,690?

____

5. Write one and two hundred fifty-six thousandths as a decimal.

____

6. 4 x 5 ☐ 12 = 32

7. Distribute.

25(11 + *h*) = ______________

8. Find *d*. $\frac{d}{12} = 10$

d = ______

9. How many grams are in 4.5 kilograms?

____

10. Which line is perpendicular to line G?

____

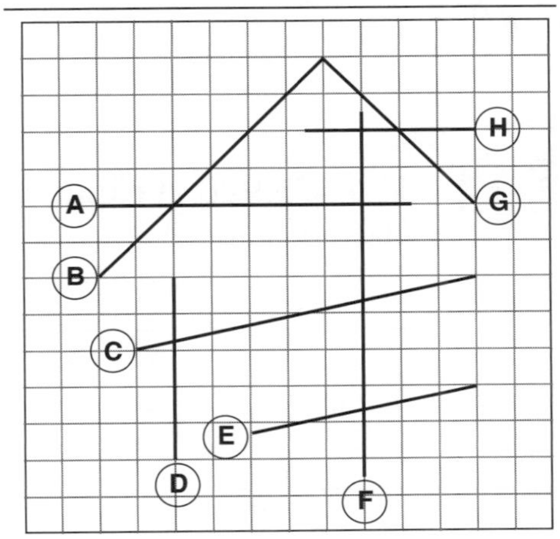

11. Record the data in the circle chart.

Twelve people were surveyed. Six like dogs. Three like cats. An equal number of people like cats and birds.

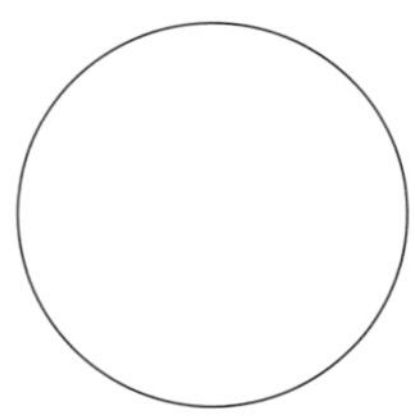

12. Soup is on sale at the store for 3 cans for $1.50. How much would it cost to buy 12 cans?

____

SCORE

1. Ⓨ Ⓝ
2. Ⓨ Ⓝ
3. Ⓨ Ⓝ
4. Ⓨ Ⓝ
5. Ⓨ Ⓝ
6. Ⓨ Ⓝ
7. Ⓨ Ⓝ
8. Ⓨ Ⓝ
9. Ⓨ Ⓝ
10. Ⓨ Ⓝ
11. Ⓨ Ⓝ
12. Ⓨ Ⓝ

___ / 12 Total

DAY 172

NAME: ______________________________

DIRECTIONS Solve each problem.

SCORE

1. Ⓨ Ⓝ
2. Ⓨ Ⓝ
3. Ⓨ Ⓝ
4. Ⓨ Ⓝ
5. Ⓨ Ⓝ
6. Ⓨ Ⓝ
7. Ⓨ Ⓝ
8. Ⓨ Ⓝ
9. Ⓨ Ⓝ
10. Ⓨ Ⓝ
11. Ⓨ Ⓝ
12. Ⓨ Ⓝ

___ / 12 Total

1. 147 + 652 = ______

2. 42 x 30 = ______

3. 463 ÷ 6 = ______

4. Write 475,926 in expanded notation.

____

____

____

____

5. 25% of 640 is ______.

6. Complete the table. Look for a pattern and write the rule.

Number of Squares	1	2	3	4	5
Number of Sides	4				

____

____

7. Write the expression for seventy-two more than a number *g*.

____

8. Find *j*. $5j = 65$

j = ______

9. 8 gallons = ______ pints

10. Name the triangle that has all angles equal to 60°.

____

11.

Student	Savings Amount
Jack	$144
Trevor	$137
Brandon	$85
Michael	$202

Jack earned his money by mowing lawns. If he charges $12.00 to mow a lawn, how many lawns did he mow in order to earn his savings?

____

12. Circle the factors of the given product.

Possible Factors									Product
9	3	5	2	10	6	15	13	16	156

DAY 173

NAME: ______________________________

DIRECTIONS Solve each problem.

1. 216 – 135 = ______

2.

$$\begin{array}{r} 81 \\ \times\ 5 \\ \hline \end{array}$$

3. Is 196 ÷ 6 greater than, less than, or equal to $32\frac{5}{6}$?

____

4. Round 345,498 to the nearest thousand.

____

5. Simplify $\frac{9}{12}$.

____

6. Write the next number in the pattern. –60, –45, –30,

____

7. Find *v*. $\frac{72}{v} = 8$

v = ______

8. Find *v*. 9*v* = 72

v = ______

9. Calculate the perimeter of a rectangle with dimensions measuring 3.2 m by 4.2 m.

____

10. What is the shape of a cross-section of a sphere?

____

11.

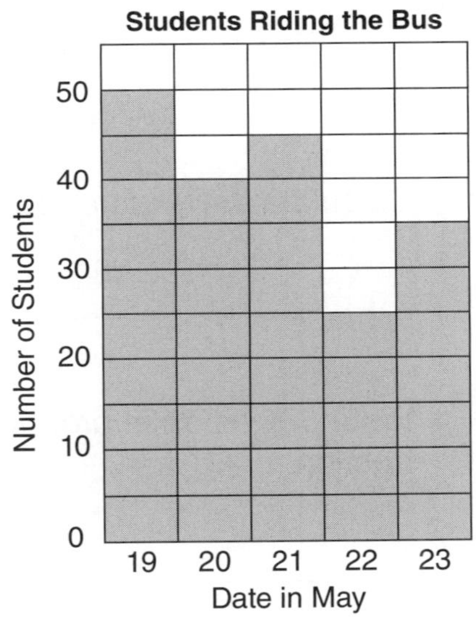

The bus company anticipates a 10% increase in the number of riders on the 24th from the number they had on the 19th. How many students will ride the bus on the 24th?

____

12. I am part of a whole. I am greater than one-half but less than two-thirds. I have a 0 in my hundredths place. What am I?

____

SCORE

1. Ⓨ Ⓝ
2. Ⓨ Ⓝ
3. Ⓨ Ⓝ
4. Ⓨ Ⓝ
5. Ⓨ Ⓝ
6. Ⓨ Ⓝ
7. Ⓨ Ⓝ
8. Ⓨ Ⓝ
9. Ⓨ Ⓝ
10. Ⓨ Ⓝ
11. Ⓨ Ⓝ
12. Ⓨ Ⓝ

___ / 12 Total

DAY 174

NAME: ______________________

DIRECTIONS Solve each problem.

SCORE

1. Ⓨ Ⓝ
2. Ⓨ Ⓝ
3. Ⓨ Ⓝ
4. Ⓨ Ⓝ
5. Ⓨ Ⓝ
6. Ⓨ Ⓝ
7. Ⓨ Ⓝ
8. Ⓨ Ⓝ
9. Ⓨ Ⓝ
10. Ⓨ Ⓝ
11. Ⓨ Ⓝ
12. Ⓨ Ⓝ

___ / 12 Total

1. $$\begin{array}{r} 106 \\ +\ 64 \\ \hline \end{array}$$

2. $23 \cdot 40 =$ ______

3. $422 \div 6 =$ ______

4. Calculate the square root of 36.

____

5. Write $3\frac{2}{5}$ as an improper fraction.

____

6. $40 - 32$ ☐ $6 = 14$

7. Distribute.
$21(a + 9) =$ ______________

8. Find p when $\frac{p}{7} = 8.1$.

$p =$ ______

9. How many meters are in 825 centimeters?

____

10. Complete the chart for the shape.

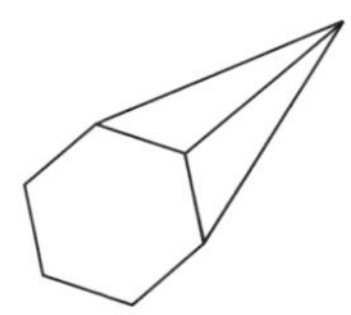

Name the figure.	
How many surfaces?	
How many vertices?	
Does it stack or roll?	
Is it a plane shape or a solid shape?	

11. The numbers 20 through 30 were written on individual cards and placed in a bag. If you pull a card from the bag, what is the probability that it will have a 3 on it?

____

12. A car gets 32 miles per gallon of gas. How many miles can you expect to travel on 14 gallons of gas?

____

NAME: ______________________

DIRECTIONS Solve each problem.

1. $\begin{array}{r} 137 \\ -\ 58 \\ \hline \end{array}$

2. 16 x 50 = ______

3. Divide 723 by 9.

____

4. What is the last odd number before 300,000?

____

5. $\frac{5}{6} - \frac{1}{3} =$ ______

6. Write the next number in the sequence. 160, 240, 320,

____

7. Write the expression for seven more than *x* squared.

____

8. Find *y*. $18y = 72$

$y =$ ______

9. 126 inches = ______ yards

10. How many total degrees are in three right angles?

____

11. What is the mode of this set of data?

2,216; 2,443; 2,341; 2,443; 2,401

____

12. The deep end of a swimming pool is 7 meters deep. If the shallow end is half as deep, how many centimeters deep is the shallow end?

____

SCORE

1. Ⓨ Ⓝ
2. Ⓨ Ⓝ
3. Ⓨ Ⓝ
4. Ⓨ Ⓝ
5. Ⓨ Ⓝ
6. Ⓨ Ⓝ
7. Ⓨ Ⓝ
8. Ⓨ Ⓝ
9. Ⓨ Ⓝ
10. Ⓨ Ⓝ
11. Ⓨ Ⓝ
12. Ⓨ Ⓝ

___ / 12 Total

DAY 176

NAME: ____________________

DIRECTIONS Solve each problem.

SCORE

1. Ⓨ Ⓝ
2. Ⓨ Ⓝ
3. Ⓨ Ⓝ
4. Ⓨ Ⓝ
5. Ⓨ Ⓝ
6. Ⓨ Ⓝ
7. Ⓨ Ⓝ
8. Ⓨ Ⓝ
9. Ⓨ Ⓝ
10. Ⓨ Ⓝ
11. Ⓨ Ⓝ
12. Ⓨ Ⓝ

___ / 12 Total

1. Calculate the sum of 146, 29, and 37.

____

2.

$$\begin{array}{r} 51 \\ \times\ 40 \\ \hline \end{array}$$

3. $6\overline{)492}$

4. What number is 10 less than zero?

____

5. 75% of 400 is ______.

6. (4 + 2) • (5 + 3) = ______

7. Distribute.

$8(20 - r) =$ ____________

8. Find y. $y - 7.8 = 11.5$

$y =$ ______

9. How many liters are in 4,500 milliliters?

____

10. True or false? A prism can have any polygon as its base.

____

11. What is the probability that the spinner will land on a sport that requires a bat or racket?

____

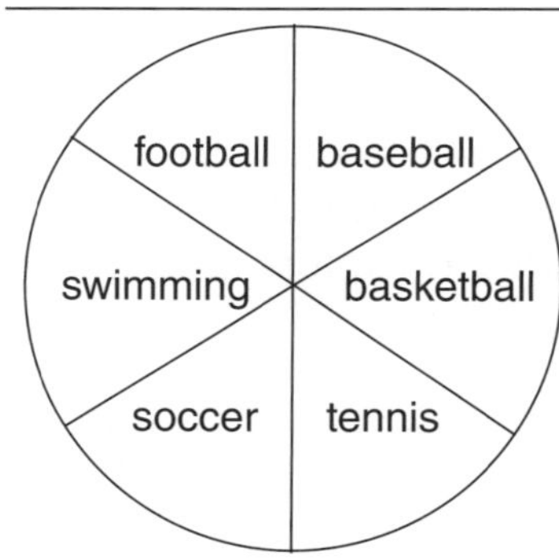

12. Count the number of blocks in this stack. How many more blocks are needed to make a cube that is 3 blocks high?

____

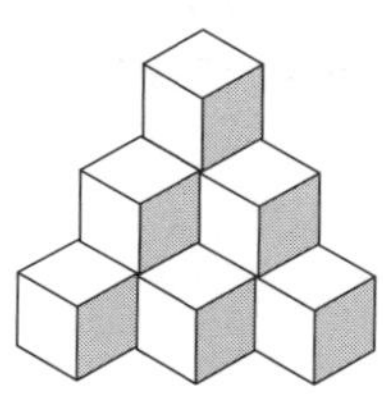

NAME: ______________________________

DIRECTIONS Solve each problem.

1. Subtract 108 from 273.

____

2. Calculate the product of 30 and 73.

____

3. 67 $\overline{)283}$

4. Write the factors of 30.

____

5. Write $3\frac{2}{3}$ as an improper fraction.

____

6. $3 + 4^2 - 5 \times 8 =$ ______

7. Distribute.
$9(h - 11) =$ ______________

8. Write the expression for the product of nineteen and *e*.

____

9. Find the area of a triangle with a base of 10 cm and a height of 14 cm.

____

10. How many vertices does the solid have?

____

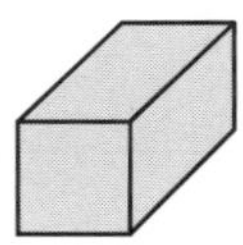

11. What is the mean of this set of data?

13, 11, 12, 15, 16, 15, 14,
13, 15, 12, 12, 15, 15, 16, 13

____

12. Tickets at a carnival cost $0.75 each. You want to go on the bumper car which costs 7 tickets. How much change will you get from a $20 bill?

____

SCORE

1. Ⓨ Ⓝ
2. Ⓨ Ⓝ
3. Ⓨ Ⓝ
4. Ⓨ Ⓝ
5. Ⓨ Ⓝ
6. Ⓨ Ⓝ
7. Ⓨ Ⓝ
8. Ⓨ Ⓝ
9. Ⓨ Ⓝ
10. Ⓨ Ⓝ
11. Ⓨ Ⓝ
12. Ⓨ Ⓝ

___ / 12
Total

DAY

178

NAME: ____________________

DIRECTIONS Solve each problem.

SCORE

1. Ⓨ Ⓝ
2. Ⓨ Ⓝ
3. Ⓨ Ⓝ
4. Ⓨ Ⓝ
5. Ⓨ Ⓝ
6. Ⓨ Ⓝ
7. Ⓨ Ⓝ
8. Ⓨ Ⓝ
9. Ⓨ Ⓝ
10. Ⓨ Ⓝ
11. Ⓨ Ⓝ
12. Ⓨ Ⓝ

___ / 12
Total

1. Calculate the sum of 154, 38, and 49.

____

2. 27 • 40 = ______

3. 422 ÷ 8 = ______

4. What number is 30 more than –16?

____

5. Write 90% as a fraction.

____

6. $17 - 2^2 \times 5 =$ ______

7. Find *k*. $k - \frac{3}{11} = \frac{4}{11}$

$k =$ ______

8. Find *r*. $r + \frac{1}{4} = \frac{3}{4}$

$r =$ ______

9. Calculate the distance a car can travel in 7 hours at 150 $\frac{\text{km}}{\text{h}}$.

____

10. Circle the regular shapes.

11. Inside a bag of candy are 16 lollipops, 12 pieces of chocolate, and 7 pieces of licorice. If you reach in the bag and grab a piece of candy, what is the probability that it will either be licorice or a lollipop?

____

12. A punch recipe calls for twice as much lemonade as lime soda. It calls for half as much ice cream as lime soda. If you use 2 gallons of lime soda, how much lemonade will you need and how much ice cream will you need?

____

____

NAME: ______________________________

DIRECTIONS Solve each problem.

1. Take 136 away from 378.

____

2. 73 x 20 = ______

3. 722 ÷ 10 = ______

4. How do you know that 3,050 is divisible by 5?

____

____

5. Arrange in ascending order.
2.5, 2.8, 2.6

____

6. $\square^2 = 36$

7. Write the expression for eighteen less than *n*.

____

8. Find *w*. $w^2 = 169$

w = ______

9. Record the line length.

____

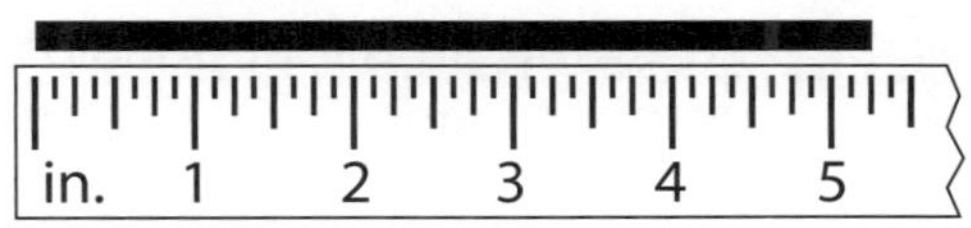

10. What is the diameter of a circle with a radius of 3.5 cm?

____

11. In a game, the probability of the spinner landing on white is 3:4. How many times would you expect to land on white if you spin the spinner 16 times?

____

12. Yuki has 14 kids at her party, including herself. Four people can sit at each table. How many tables does she need?

____

SCORE

1. Ⓨ Ⓝ
2. Ⓨ Ⓝ
3. Ⓨ Ⓝ
4. Ⓨ Ⓝ
5. Ⓨ Ⓝ
6. Ⓨ Ⓝ
7. Ⓨ Ⓝ
8. Ⓨ Ⓝ
9. Ⓨ Ⓝ
10. Ⓨ Ⓝ
11. Ⓨ Ⓝ
12. Ⓨ Ⓝ

___ / 12
Total

DAY

180

NAME: ____________________

DIRECTIONS Solve each problem.

SCORE

1. Ⓨ Ⓝ
2. Ⓨ Ⓝ
3. Ⓨ Ⓝ
4. Ⓨ Ⓝ
5. Ⓨ Ⓝ
6. Ⓨ Ⓝ
7. Ⓨ Ⓝ
8. Ⓨ Ⓝ
9. Ⓨ Ⓝ
10. Ⓨ Ⓝ
11. Ⓨ Ⓝ
12. Ⓨ Ⓝ

___ / 12 **Total**

1. 576 + 132 = ______

2. 54 x 32 = ______

3. $8\overline{)249}$

4. Write the smallest possible number using 6, 3, 8, and 4.

____

5. $\frac{3}{8} + \frac{2}{8} =$ ______

6. Write the next number in the sequence. 320, 400, 480,

____

7. Distribute.
6(*b* + *c*) = ____________

8. Find *x*. 17.5 + *x* = 22.1

x = ______

9. Calculate the area of the shape.

____

10. Is 91° an *acute* or *obtuse* angle?

____

11.

	Re gular Price	Discount
Pants	$32	25%
Shirts	$24	30%
Shoes	$45	35%
Socks	$4	10%

How much money do you save with the discount when buying the pants?

____

12. A palindrome is a number that is the same backwards or forwards, for example 242. The addition problems below are also palindromes. Complete the chart with palindromes.

Addition	Palindrome
	121
132 + 231	
623 + 326	
	767

ANSWER KEY

Day 1
1. 46
2. 56
3. 5
4. thousands
5. $\frac{31}{100}$
6. 1,775
7. 7
8. 52
9. 18 m^3
10. pentagon
11.

Day 1	Day 2	Day 3	Day 4
32	29	30	32

12.

8	3	4
1	5	9
6	7	2

Day 2
1. 52
2. 24
3. 9
4. 8,549
5. 3 tenths
6. 418
7. 89
8. 19
9. 1:22
10. equilateral triangle
11. $\frac{1}{3}$
12. 15 minutes

Day 3
1. 64
2. 20
3. 7
4. 1,700
5. less than
6. 12
7. x
8. 20
9. 6:35 P.M.
10. 3.9 cm
11. 40 students
12. large bag for $2.99

Day 4
1. 13
2. 28
3. 90
4. 36
5. 10%
6. 30
7. 77
8. +
9. 365 days; 366 days in a leap year
10. square; 4; 4; yes; plane shape
11. $\frac{1}{9}$
12. 0.3 feet

Day 5
1. 32
2. 81
3. 7
4. 15
5. 4
6. 3,276
7. 14
8. 40
9. 49 cm^2
10. 120°; obtuse
11. 37
12. 7 days

Day 6
1. 31
2. 42
3. 6
4. 416
5. equal to
6. 32
7. 78
8. 5
9. 38 minutes
10. Students should draw a circle.
11. Spinner A
12.

	Faces	Edges	Vertices
Triangular Pyramid	4	6	4
Triangular Prism	5	9	6

Day 7
1. 72
2. 48
3. 6
4. 1, 2, 4, 5, 8, 10, 20, 40
5. $\frac{61}{100}$
6. 28
7. 16
8. 3
9. 20 cm
10. 6 faces
11. $\frac{2}{7}$
12. 18 years old

Day 8
1. 29
2. 36
3. 70
4. 8,368
5. 5
6. add 3
7. –
8. 10
9. 9,500 grams
10. yes
11. 32
12. 2.5 gallons

Day 9
1. 44
2. 45
3. 7
4. 2, 4, 6, 8
5. no
6. multiply by 4
7. 11
8. +
9. 65 mm
10. 8.4 cm
11. Lucas
12. 18 hands

Day 10
1. 5
2. 54
3. 5
4. 5 digits
5. 70%
6. 116
7. 3
8. ÷
9. 4 cm
10. 70°
11. $\frac{1}{12}$
12.

+	22	26	33	35	41	46
19	41	45	52	54	60	65
29	51	55	62	64	70	75
39	61	65	72	74	80	85
49	71	75	82	84	90	95

Day 11
1. 126
2. 16
3. 8
4. 2
5. $2\frac{1}{4}$
6. 200
7. 2
8. +
9. 3:47 A.M.
10. 8 vertices
11. certain
12. $10.00

Day 12
1. 82
2. –27
3. 40
4. 10,000 + 5,000 + 700 + 20 + 9
5. 12
6. 10
7. 25
8. 10
9. 5 kg
10. 4 sides
11. $\frac{1}{3}$
12. $33.44

ANSWER KEY *(cont.)*

Day 13

1. −22
2. 48
3. 6
4. 8,000
5. 4 fifths
6. 7
7. 15
8. x
9. 16 cm^2
10. cone
11. Sunday
12. 0.4; 40%

Day 14

1. 76
2. 32
3. −8
4. yes
5. $3\frac{1}{3}$
6. add 4
7. 70
8. +
9. 64 cm^3
10. cylinder; 3; 0; stacks and rolls; solid
11. $\frac{10}{11}$
12. $4.50

Day 15

1. 16
2. 18
3. 9
4. 33
5. $2\frac{2}{35}$
6. 16
7. +
8. 3
9. 150 seconds
10. yes
11. blue pants, yellow shirt; orange skirt, yellow shirt
12. 1, 2, 5, 10

Day 16

1. 82
2. 30
3. 90
4. negative number
5. $4\frac{2}{3}$
6. 86
7. 20
8. 278
9. 1
10. An isosceles triangle should be drawn.
11. $\frac{1}{6}$
12. 183 inches

Day 17

1. 32
2. 20
3. 6
4. yes
5. 21
6. 0
7. 24
8. 146
9. 36 months
10. 8 vertices
11. Bag One
12. Answers may vary. See a sample answer below.

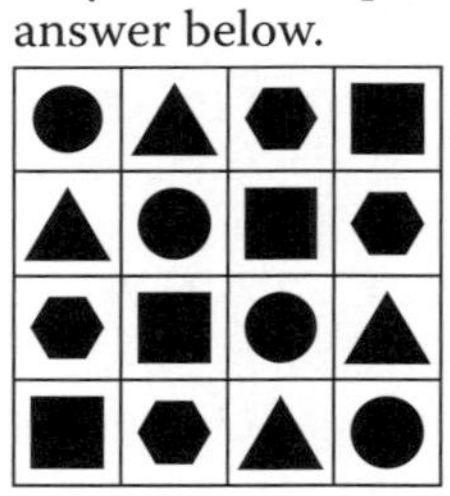

Day 18

1. 64
2. 42
3. −8
4. 88,257
5. $\frac{65}{100}$ or $\frac{13}{20}$
6. 40
7. 70
8. −
9. 18 cm
10. 2
11. $\frac{16}{35}$
12. $(15 - 3) \div 4 = 3$

Day 19

1. 27
2. 36
3. 8
4. yes
5. 45%
6. 5
7. 29
8. 30
9. 75 mm
10. no
11. 2 times
12. B

Day 20

1. 174
2. 25
3. 84
4. 23
5. $\frac{17}{5}$
6. 67
7. −
8. 3
9. 10:09 A.M.
10. acute
11. $\frac{1}{10}$
12. 10 different groups

Day 21

1. 55
2. 28
3. 6
4. thousands
5. $\frac{12}{5}$
6. 345
7. 4
8. ÷
9. 7:25
10. Line F
11.

Player	Home Runs
Mitch	3
Sam	2
Tim	0
Dale	3

12. $9.79

Day 22

1. 68
2. 8
3. 8
4. 548
5. .97
6. +1, +2, +3, +4, etc.
7. +
8. 40
9. 7,000 grams
10. 360°
11. $\frac{1}{3}$
12. Answers will vary. Possible answer: Clockwise from top: 1, 6, 8, 5, 4, 2, 9, 7, 3

Day 23

1. 58
2. −32
3. 9
4. 9,000
5. 54
6. 24
7. -
8. 15
9. 16 cm^3
10. The circle should be circled.
11. $\frac{3}{5}$
12. 6; 4; 3; 9; 2

Day 24

1. 100
2. 40 people
3. $118\frac{6}{8}$ or 118.75
4. 9
5. no
6. 11
7. −
8. 4
9. 750 m
10. triangle; 3; 3; yes; plane shape
11. 45 minutes
12. 3 pieces

ANSWER KEY *(cont.)*

Day 25

1. 27
2. 56
3. 5
4. 31st
5. yes
6. 113
7. 4.7
8. 32
9. 42 minutes
10. yes
11. 31
12.

2	9	4
7	5	3
6	1	8

Day 26

1. 43
2. 63
3. –6
4. yes
5. $\frac{17}{4}$
6. decreasing square numbers
7. 53
8. ÷
9. 40 cm^2
10. A square should be drawn.
11. yes
12. 4 ways

Day 27

1. 43
2. 24
3. 7
4. 1, 2, 4, 5, 10, 20
5. 0.8 or 0.80
6. 35
7. –
8. $\frac{2}{10}$ or $\frac{1}{5}$
9. 6:57
10. 0
11. $\frac{3}{7}$
12. $250.00

Day 28

1. 264
2. –36
3. 7
4. no
5. 15
6. 64
7. 133
8. 3
9. 16 cm
10. 4 sides
11. 73
12. B, C, A, D

Day 29

1. 26
2. 64
3. 4
4. 7, 14, 21
5. 2
6. 19; 43
7. +
8. 389
9. 370 cm
10. yes
11. 60 cookies
12. 2 quarts

Day 30

1. 91
2. 15
3. –9
4. 5 digits
5. greater than
6. 144
7. 2.5
8. 6
9. 31 days
10. 169°
11. $\frac{2}{12}$ or $\frac{1}{6}$
12. 7:28

Day 31

1. 326
2. 30
3. 8
4. 2 thousands or 2,000
5. yes
6. 4,000
7. 65
8. 42
9. 4:57 P.M.
10. heart
11. 1 blue section, 1 orange section, 2 red sections
12. $12.75

Day 32

1. –26
2. 54
3. 90
4. 500 + 70 + 3
5. $\frac{1}{6}$
6. 16
7. 49
8. x
9. 27 cm^3
10. 180°
11. $\frac{2}{3}$
12.

–	72	76	81	85	93	97
19	53	57	62	66	74	78
39	33	37	42	46	54	58
59	13	17	22	26	34	38
69	3	7	12	16	24	28

Day 33

1. 66
2. 72
3. 8
4. 7,260
5. $2\frac{1}{4}$ or $\frac{9}{4}$
6. subtract 5
7. 72
8. –
9. no
10. 1
11. $\frac{1}{6}$
12. 24 birds

Day 34

1. 283
2. 21
3. 5
4. yes
5. 0.9
6. 24
7. ÷
8. 52
9. 13:24
10. cube; 6; 8; stack; solid shade
11. Mrs. Hindi's class
12. 96 miles

Day 35

1. –2
2. 35
3. 6
4. 90
5. 0.57
6. 4
7. 15.8
8. 50
9. 366 days
10. no
11. mow, edge, pull; pull, edge, mow; mow, pull, edge; edge, mow, pull; edge, pull, mow; pull, mow, edge
12. 13 full groups

Day 36

1. 66
2. 50
3. 9
4. -2
5. equal to
6. 29
7. 154
8. x
9. 72
10. Students should draw a square or rectangle.
11. $\frac{5}{6}$
12. 0.80

ANSWER KEY *(cont.)*

Day 37

1. 69
2. 170
3. 6
4. yes
5. 1.45
6. add previous 2 numbers together
7. +
8. 347
9. circumference
10. 8 faces
11. $\frac{5}{11}$
12.

	Faces	Edges	Vertices
Pentagonal Pyramid	6	10	6
Pentagonal Prism	7	15	10

Day 38

1. 215
2. 63
3. 4
4. yes
5. 72%
6. 5,327
7. x
8. 25
9. 22 cm
10. isosceles triangle
11. $\frac{12}{35}$
12. C should be circled.

Day 39

1. 45
2. −160
3. 5
4. no
5. yes
6. 135
7. 43
8. 38
9. 81 m^2
10. yes
11. 3 points
12. 12, 19

Day 40

1. 183
2. 60
3. −10
4. 34
5. $2\frac{1}{4}$
6. 38
7. x
8. 50
9. 1,750 m
10. 50°
11. $12.45
12. (5 − 3) x 4 = 8

Day 41

1. 132
2. 140
3. 8
4. 4 thousands or 4,000
5. 3.79
6. −2
7. 23
8. 222
9. The clock should read 6:20.
10. false
11. 5 out of 9
12. 65, 66, 67, or 68 people

Day 42

1. 58
2. 360
3. 7
4. 67,403
5. no
6. $1\frac{1}{2}$
7. 3
8. −
9. 10.5 liters
10. 
11. $\frac{2}{3}$
12. $60

Day 43

1. 83
2. 130
3. 4
4. 2,400
5. 24
6. −3; −2
7. 50
8. +
9. 42 mm
10. hexagonal prism
11. 0
12. 10

Day 44

1. 6
2. 49
3. 4
4. odd number
5. yes
6. 10
7. −
8. 3
9. 195 minutes
10. hexagon; 6; 6; yes; plane shape
11. $\frac{1}{9}$
12. 5 swimmers

Day 45

1. 55
2. 610
3. 7
4. 16th
5. $\frac{76}{100}$ or $\frac{19}{25}$
6. 88
7. 140
8. 118
9. 90 cm^3
10. 180°
11. 60
12. 1, 2, 3, 6, 9, 18

Day 46

1. 54
2. −630
3. 17
4. false
5. $\frac{30}{60}$ or $\frac{1}{2}$
6. 10
7. 175
8. 46
9. 28 m^2
10. 
11. Spinner A
12. 6

Day 47

1. 38
2. 560
3. −6
4. 1, 2, 3, 6, 9, 18
5. 27
6. 1
7. 20
8. 124
9. 17:46
10. 2 edges
11. $\frac{2}{6}$ or $\frac{1}{3}$
12. 5, 3, 15, 9

Day 48

1. 169
2. 42
3. 9
4. 35
5. $\frac{21}{8}$
6. 11
7. $\frac{2}{5}$
8. 3
9. 9:05
10. solid shape
11. 91
12. Answers will vary; shading may include left half, right half, upper half, lower half, and the upper or lower halves of a diagonal split

ANSWER KEY *(cont.)*

Day 49

1. 62
2. 730
3. 138
4. 3, 6, 9, 12
5. 24
6. 1
7. 152
8. 5
9. 3.5 cm
10. yes
11. 10 times
12. $33

Day 50

1. 35
2. 350
3. 28
4. 6 digits
5. 9
6. 105
7. 40
8. 143
9. 2.5 cm
10. yes
11. $\frac{5}{12}$
12.

1	6	5
8	4	0
3	2	7

Day 51

1. 17
2. 360
3. 6
4. 9 ones or 9
5. less than
6. 17
7. 25
8. $\frac{2}{8}$ or $\frac{1}{4}$
9. 2 pints
10. line G
11.

Child's Name	Brother	Sister
Trish	2	1
Max	0	0
Melissa	2	0
Allison	0	1
Trent	1	1

12. 600 sheep

Day 52

1. 616
2. 260
3. –67
4. 4000 + 200+ 30+ 7
5. $-\frac{4}{11}$
6.

Input	42	52	62	72	82	92
Output	56	66	76	86	96	106

Rule: Add 14 to the input to get the output.

7. 6
8. 2
9. 16:39
10. rotated
11. $85, $137, $144, $202
12. 1976

Day 53

1. 33
2. 160
3. 7
4. 4,000
5. no
6. 2
7. ÷
8. 96
9. 750 cm
10. 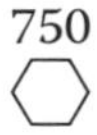
11. $\frac{1}{6}$
12. 3.5 pounds

Day 54

1. 95
2. 310
3. 8
4. yes
5. $\frac{7}{4}$
6. 5
7. 99
8. 24
9. 7 kg
10. sphere; 1; 0; roll; solid shape
11. $\frac{2}{11}$
12. 20 people

Day 55

1. 16
2. 130
3. 9
4. 5,839
5. no
6. 23
7. $\frac{1}{8}$ or 12.5%
8. $x + 12$
9. 4.58 liters
10. isosceles triangle
11. 48
12.

×	8	6	9	5	7	4
6	48	36	54	30	42	24
8	64	48	72	40	56	32
9	72	54	81	45	63	36
7	56	42	63	35	49	28

Day 56

1. 188
2. 650
3. 5
4. yes
5. $\frac{1}{2}$, $\frac{1}{3}$, $\frac{1}{4}$
6. 3
7. +
8. 35
9. 32 minutes
10. 180°
11. women, girls, boys, men
12. $9

Day 57

1. 33
2. 58
3. 79
4. yes
5. yes
6. 14
7. 15
8. 13
9. 564 cm
10. 8 vertices
11. $\frac{1}{11}$
12. $12.05; $7.95

Day 58

1. 24
2. –240
3. 10
4. 11, 13, 17, 19
5. 6
6. –9
7. 20
8. 42
9. 7,500 grams
10. 2 diagonals
11. $\frac{7}{35}$ or $\frac{1}{5}$
12. 30 years

Day 59

1. 29
2. 96
3. 61
4. no
5. 1.76
6. 5
7. 32
8. 2.5
9. 48 m
10. 3.1 cm
11. 60 points
12.

	Faces	Edges	Vertices
Rectangular Pyramid	5	8	5
Rectangular Prism	6	12	8

Day 60

1. 107
2. 270
3. 123
4. 9,762
5. $-\frac{3}{9}$ or $-\frac{1}{3}$
6. 630
7. 40
8. $7h$ or 7 x h
9. 250 m
10. less than
11. $\frac{8}{10}$ or $\frac{4}{5}$
12. 2:02

ANSWER KEY *(cont.)*

Day 61

1. 644
2. 540
3. –67
4. thousands
5. 5.94
6. 8
7. ÷
8. 2
9. 23:26
10. 5 faces
11. $\frac{4}{9}$
12. $84

Day 62

1. 75
2. 520
3. $2.50
4. 85,038
5. 12
6. 2
7. 100
8. 58
9. 5:50
10. 4 sides
11. $\frac{1}{1}$ or 100%
12. 3 + 4 + 5 = 12

Day 63

1. 46
2. 52
3. 21
4. 29,000
5. 3
6. 8
7. 90
8. 24
9. 90 mm
10. 2 axes of symmetry
11. $\frac{2}{5}$
12. 12 two-digit numbers: 12, 13, 14, 21, 23, 24, 31, 32, 34, 41, 42, and 43

Day 64

1. 7
2. 320
3. 203
4. 64
5. $\frac{5}{8}$
6. 16
7. –2
8. 40
9. 9,000 grams
10. pentagon; 5; 5; yes; plane shape
11. 15 minutes
12. 32 problems

Day 65

1. 161
2. 350
3. 67
4. 25th
5. 50%
6.

Input	37	47	57	67	77	87
Output	74	94	114	134	154	174

Rule: Multiply the input by 2 to get the output.

7. 24
8. $m + 10$
9. 36 m^2
10. straight angle; 180°
11. $1.60
12. 728,064

Day 66

1. 544
2. –335
3. 8
4. greater than
5. 8
6. –12
7. 30
8. 5 or –5
9. 56 cm^3
10. complementary angles
11. Spinner A
12. 60 miles

Day 67

1. 251
2. 230
3. 34
4. 1, 2, 3, 5, 6, 10, 15, 30
5. 2
6. 36
7. $\frac{1}{10}$ or 10% or 0.10
8. –3
9. 8 pints
10. 10 faces
11. $\frac{3}{7}$
12. 77 digits

Day 68

1. 32
2. 204
3. 3
4. 229,999
5. 20
6. 13
7. $\frac{27}{5}$
8. –7
9. 9.56 m
10. 4 vertices
11. 14
12. 25%

Day 69

1. 131
2. 1,470
3. 123
4. 5, 10, 15
5. 6.69
6. 10
7. 2.9
8. 13
9. 26 m
10. no
11. 45 cookies
12. 28 handshakes

Day 70

1. –10
2. 136
3. 21
4. 6 digits
5. $\frac{2}{8}$ or $\frac{1}{4}$
6. 408
7. 280
8. $r - 10$
9. 11:49
10. 60°
11. $\frac{1}{6}$
12. $2.50; $22.50

Day 71

1. 28
2. 105
3. $34\frac{1}{4}$ or 34.25
4. 5 hundreds
5. $5\frac{3}{5}$
6. 18
7. 6
8. 7 or –7
9. 9.5 liters
10. octagon
11. Sara: $15, Ang: $5, Ben: $25, Tina: $10
12. $5.00

Day 72

1. 143
2. –150
3. $39\frac{3}{7}$
4. 80,000 + 6,000 + 300 + 90 + 1
5. 22 tenths
6. 29
7. 36
8. 30
9. 2,525 grams
10. square and rhombus
11. $\frac{1}{3}$
12. 27 miles

ANSWER KEY *(cont.)*

Day 73

1. 24
2. 100
3. –66
4. 367,200
5. $\frac{10}{3}$
6. –1
7. 80
8. 168
9. 2:24
10. square pyramid
11. $\frac{3}{6}$ or $\frac{1}{2}$
12. 201 matches

Day 74

1. 94
2. 200
3. $39\frac{1}{2}$ or 39.5
4. odd number
5. 6
6. –20
7. 7,000
8. 8.8
9. 950 cm
10. rectangular prism, 6, 8, stack, solid shape
11. 56 students
12. (5 – 3) × 12 = 24; (12 – 4) × 3 = 24

Day 75

1. –4
2. 408
3. 72
4. 700
5. $\frac{4}{9}$
6. 37
7. 6
8. $\frac{a}{b}$ or a ÷ b
9. 72 m^2
10. acute angle
11. 67.5
12.

10	3	8
5	7	9
6	11	4

Day 76

1. 56
2. 125
3. $68\frac{1}{4}$ or 68.25
4. yes
5. $3\frac{1}{5}$
6. –36
7. 10
8. 15
9. 08:47
10. A square should be drawn.
11. $\frac{5}{6}$
12. 1, 2, 4, 5, 10, 20

Day 77

1. 54
2. 8,720
3. $40\frac{1}{7}$
4. no
5. $\frac{13}{3}$
6.

Input	78	68	58	48	38	28
Output	53	43	33	23	13	3

Rule: Subtract 25 from the input to get the output.

7. 6
8. 3
9. 4:12 A.M.
10. 12 edges
11. blue and black vehicles
12. $2.00

Day 78

1. 81
2. 3,720
3. $48\frac{5}{9}$
4. 71
5. equal to
6. –2
7. 8
8. 6
9. 144 cm^2
10. 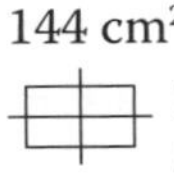 2 lines of symmetry
11. $\frac{19}{35}$
12. 20 double hamburgers

Day 79

1. 56
2. 5,880
3. $87\frac{5}{6}$ or 87.83
4. no
5. $\frac{8}{15}$
6. –11
7. 54
8. 50
9. 70 mm
10. 90°
11. 4 times
12. $48.90

Day 80

1. 781
2. –210
3. $36\frac{3}{8}$ or 36.375
4. 3,589
5. 30%
6. 2,365
7. 80
8. $x - 2$
9. 72 cm^2
10. obtuse
11. $3.60
12. 23 weeks

Day 81

1. 624
2. 156
3. $63\frac{2}{3}$ or 63. 67
4. 9 hundred thousands or 900,000
5. $2\frac{3}{5}$
6. 3
7. 3
8. 12 or –12
9. 53 minutes
10. Line A
11. Mark: 3; Eric: 5
12. $135.00

Day 82

1. 54
2. 3,160
3. $75\frac{4}{7}$
4. 9,736
5. $2\frac{3}{10}$
6. Table: Gram: 3,750; 5,250; Kilogram: 4.5; 6; Rule: Divide the gram value by 1,000 to get the kilogram value.
7. 6
8. –21
9. 3,500 grams
10. 48°
11. $\frac{2}{3}$
12. $37.50

Day 83

1. 39
2. 7,200
3. $117\frac{5}{7}$
4. 46,000
5. $-\frac{3}{8}$
6. 51
7. 3
8. 2
9. 47 minutes
10. A pentagon should be drawn.
11. June 19th
12. $36.00

Day 84

1. –5
2. 4,630
3. $63\frac{1}{2}$ or 63.5
4. no
5. $\frac{26}{10}$ or $\frac{13}{5}$
6. 3
7. 2
8. 54
9. 61 days
10. supplementary angles
11. $\frac{6}{9}$ or $\frac{2}{3}$
12. 15 necklaces

ANSWER KEY *(cont.)*

Day 85

1. 681
2. 1,260
3. $65\frac{1}{4}$ or 65.25
4. 12th
5. 9
6. 9
7. 1
8. $2y + 4$
9. 9.5 liters
10. no
11. 95
12. C should be circled.

Day 86

1. 138
2. 1,200
3. $57\frac{1}{6}$
4. true
5. 9.53
6. 4
7. 7.2
8. 2
9. 6.25 km
10. A rectangle should be drawn.
11. Spinner A
12. 21 bananas

Day 87

1. 867
2. 1,240
3. $67\frac{1}{8}$
4. 1, 5, 7, 35
5. $\frac{21}{140}$ or $\frac{3}{20}$
6. −11
7. 5
8. 132
9. 9.56 m
10. 12 vertices
11. $\frac{2}{7}$
12. 30 girls

Day 88

1. 721
2. 90
3. 7
4. yes
5. 0.75
6. 4
7. 30
8. 160
9. 84 cm^3
10. no
11. Box B
12. 8 boxes

Day 89

1. 80
2. 430
3. $59\frac{1}{4}$ or 59.25
4. 6, 12, 18, 24
5. 6
6.

Input	1	2	3	4	5	6
Output	1	4	9	16	25	36

Rule: Square the input to get the output.

7. 11
8. 46
9. 5.8 cm
10. no
11. $10.80
12. 11:25 A.M.

Day 90

1. 58
2. 1,000
3. $104\frac{5}{6}$
4. 3 digits
5. 1
6. 81
7. 4.5
8. 7
9. 18 m
10. greater than
11. $\frac{8}{12}$ or $\frac{2}{3}$
12.

Addition	Palindrome
423 + 324	747
514 + 415	929
314 + 413	727
142 + 241	383

Day 91

1. 29
2. −230
3. 4
4. 5 ten thousands
5. $\frac{4}{8}$ or $\frac{1}{2}$
6. 9
7. 9
8. −7
9. 35 minutes
10. 30 cm^2
11. Friday
12. 5 yards

Day 92

1. 32
2. 450
3. $28\frac{7}{8}$
4. 50,000 + 6,000 + 700 + 20 + 9
5. $\frac{3}{100}$
6. −30
7. 4
8. −10
9. 500 cm
10. 4 right angles
11. $\frac{1}{4}$ green, $\frac{3}{4}$ yellow
12.

	Faces	Edges	Vertices
Hexagonal Pyramid	7	12	7
Hexagonal Prism	8	18	12

Day 93

1. 35
2. 940
3. −9
4. 4,500
5. 9 eighths
6. 40
7. 21
8. $12 - d$
9. 4 kg
10. 1 axis of symmetry
11. $2,700
12. 150 seconds or 2 minutes 30 seconds

Day 94

1. 283
2. 200
3. $75\frac{1}{6}$
4. 121
5. 16
6. 0
7. 20
8. −16
9. 6,500 mL
10. triangular pyramid; 4; 4; no; solid shape
11. $\frac{3}{11}$
12. 32 minutes

Day 95

1. 149
2. 160
3. 90
4. 3,665
5. $2\frac{2}{5}$
6. 19
7. 16
8. 16
9. 4 cm^2
10. 180°
11. $4.35
12.

−	64	68	73	76	81	85
19	45	49	54	57	62	66
29	35	39	44	47	52	56
39	25	29	34	37	42	46
49	15	19	24	27	32	36

Day 96

1. −4
2. 1,700
3. 4
4. negative number
5. 31.25
6. 16
7. 8
8. −29
9. 250 grams
10. 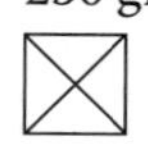
11. $\frac{2}{6}$ or $\frac{1}{3}$
12. 15 ÷ 3 + 5 = 10

ANSWER KEY *(cont.)*

Day 97

1. 183
2. 315
3. 50
4. yes
5. 12
6. 40
7. 24
8. 3 or −3
9. 7:21 P.M.
10. 6 faces
11. 2 vehicles
12. 4, 2

Day 98

1. 75
2. 180
3. 32
4. 357,037
5. yes
6. 11
7. 15
8. $\frac{17}{b}$ or 17 ÷ b
9. 12:26 P.M.
10. The square and octagon should be circled.
11. $\frac{23}{35}$
12. 3 hours and 45 minutes

Day 99

1. 425
2. 2,400
3. $48\frac{3}{5}$
4. yes
5. 7 halves
6. 18
7. 75
8. 13
9. 30 cm
10. true
11. 9 2-point shots
12. 19 cars

Day 100

1. 109
2. 84
3. 5
4. 34,569
5. 3.5, 6.3, 6.8
6. 64
7. 32
8. 56
9. 2
10. 45°
11. shoes
12.

1	8	13	12
14	11	2	7
4	5	16	9
15	10	3	6

Day 101

1. 33
2. 240
3. 50
4. 6 hundreds or 600
5. 6.9
6.

Millimeter	50	85	120	155
Centimeter	5	8.5	12	15.5

Rule: Divide the mm value by 10 to get the cm value.

7. 24
8. $2x + 2$
9. 72 cm^3
10. triangle
11. $\frac{1}{2}$ cars, $\frac{1}{4}$ trucks, $\frac{1}{8}$ motorcycles, $\frac{1}{8}$ minivans
12. 96 inches

Day 102

1. 482
2. 185
3. 5
4. 68,391
5. 6%
6. (3 + 5) x 2 = 16
7. 45
8. 12
9. 2
10. A circle should be drawn.
11. 3 equal sections; 1 red, 2 yellow
12. 134.9 cm should be circled.

Day 103

1. 186
2. 2,100
3. $71\frac{5}{8}$
4. 4,000
5. $\frac{10}{3}$ or $3\frac{1}{3}$
6. −17
7. 11
8. $20 + 4x$
9. 12 cm
10. rectangular pyramid
11. $\frac{3}{5}$
12. 48 flowers

Day 104

1. 78
2. 245
3. $71\frac{1}{4}$ or 71.25
4. odd number
5. 0.58
6. 6
7. 4
8. $t + 7$
9. 45 miles per hour
10. octagon, 8, 8, yes, plane shape
11. $\frac{8}{9}$
12. $8.00

Day 105

1. 12
2. 90
3. 60
4. 39th
5. $\frac{5}{6}$
6. 4
7. 22
8. 4
9. 0.5 or $\frac{1}{2}$
10. 90°
11. 93
12. 102 matches

Day 106

1. 45
2. 520
3. $14\frac{8}{9}$ or 14.89
4. greater than
5. 11 eighths
6. 8
7. 40
8. $5p - 10$
9. yes
10. hexagon
11. Spinner B
12. 0.8; 80%

Day 107

1. 22
2. 830
3. $108\frac{1}{2}$
4. 1, 2, 4, 5, 8, 10, 20, 40
5. 90%
6. 2
7. 100
8. $b = 132$
9. 56.25 cm^2
10. 1 edge
11. $\frac{2}{7}$
12. 1, 2, 4, 8, 16, 32

ANSWER KEY *(cont.)*

Day 108

1. 97
2. 630
3. 70
4. 3, 5, 7
5. 10
6. 3
7. 2
8. 5
9. 165 miles
10. octagon
11. Box B
12. $12.30; $7.70

Day 109

1. 322
2. 230
3. $87\frac{5}{7}$
4. 4, 8, 12
5. 5
6. 20
7. 7
8. $\frac{1}{2} + s$
9. 35 mm
10. 6.9 cm
11. 5 times
12. center: 9; clockwise from top: 1, 4, 3, 2, 8, 5, 6, 7

Day 110

1. 99
2. 430
3. $21\frac{4}{6}$ or 21.67
4. 7 digits
5. $\frac{9}{5}$
6. 255
7. 5.7
8. 37.5
9. 6 cm^2
10. greater than
11. 81
12. 57,892

Day 111

1. 106
2. 610
3. $4\frac{3}{5}$ or 4.6
4. 20 thousands or 20,000
5. true
6. 100
7. 53
8. 5.2
9. 3,500 mL
10. parallelogram
11. CA: 4 shaded boxes, OR: 5 shaded boxes, WA: 7 shaded boxes
12. 20 people

Day 112

1. 416
2. 350
3. $52\frac{7}{8}$
4. 300,000 + 40,000 + 8,000 + 100 + 9
5. $\frac{6}{100}$ should be circled.
6.

Number of Hexagons	1	2	3	4	5
Number of Sides	6	12	18	24	30

Rule: Multiply the number of hexagons by six to get the number of sides.

7. 5.2
8. 20
9. 3
10. yes
11. The spinner should be divided into three equal parts: $\frac{1}{3}$ labeled blue, $\frac{2}{3}$ labeled orange
12. 2 CDs

Day 113

1. 86
2. 255
3. 36
4. 98,460
5. $\frac{18}{5}$
6. 123
7. 54
8. 126
9. 22 m
10. A square should be drawn.
11. $\frac{1}{6}$
12. 3 cookies

Day 114

1. 100
2. 2,400
3. 8 group of eight
4. 8
5. no
6. 2,100
7. 34
8. 7.1
9. 61 km per hour
10. cone; 2; 0; roll; solid shape
11. $\frac{1}{11}$
12. 7 years old

Day 115

1. 84
2. −325
3. 46.2
4. 11
5. no
6. 46
7. 90
8. −0.5
9. 49 cm^2
10. 302°; reflex
11. soccer and basketball; soccer and swimming; soccer and tennis; basketball and swimming; basketball and tennis; swimming and tennis
12. 6 classrooms

Day 116

1. 333
2. 730
3. 39
4. -5
5. $12\frac{3}{5}$
6. 22
7. 9
8. 3
9. 60 m^3
10. square
11. men
12.

×	9	4	7	5	8	6
10	90	40	70	50	80	60
20	180	80	140	100	160	120
30	270	120	210	150	240	180
40	360	160	280	200	320	240

Day 117

1. 321
2. 210
3. $7\frac{2}{3}$
4. 1, 5, 7, 35
5. 3.568
6. 106
7. 681
8. 500
9. 1,500 grams
10. none
11. 6
12. 104 pieces of candy

Day 118

1. 175
2. 390
3. $5\frac{8}{9}$
4. 2,999,999
5. $\frac{2}{3}$
6. 22
7. 5
8. 7,200
9. 520 km
10. true
11. $\frac{28}{35}$ or $\frac{4}{5}$
12. $(15 - 12) \times 3 = 9$

ANSWER KEY *(cont.)*

Day 119

1. 75
2. −335
3. 29
4. yes
5. $\frac{3}{10}$
6. 13
7. +
8. $7x - 63$
9. 750 cm^3
10. yes
11. 14.3 points
12. 10 cubes

Day 120

1. 38
2. 730
3. $9\frac{17}{20}$ or 9.85
4. 87,642
5. 6% should be circled.
6. 957
7. 7
8. 4
9. 4,700 g
10. greater than
11. $15.75
12. 39 bottles

Day 121

1. 321
2. 240
3. 82
4. ten thousands
5. $\frac{5}{3}$
6.

Centimeter	300	500	700	900	1,100
Meter	3	5	7	9	11

Rule: Divide centimeters by 100 to convert to meters.

7. 8
8. 2
9. 5.275 liters
10. line F
11. 10
12. 21 cm

Day 122

1. −106
2. 2,400
3. 46
4. 49,068
5. 5
6. 88
7. 90
8. 40
9. 20:17
10. isosceles triangle
11. $\frac{1}{2}$ blue, $\frac{1}{4}$ green, $\frac{1}{4}$ orange
12. 5, 3, 15

Day 123

1. 84
2. 215
3. $29\frac{4}{5}$ or 29.8
4. 13,000
5. 4.053
6. 34
7. −
8. 52
9. 8,475 m
10.  1 lines of symmetry
11. $\frac{1}{5}$
12. $20

Day 124

1. 159
2. 160
3. $13\frac{4}{7}$
4. The product of an integer (3 or −3) and itself equals 9.
5. $\frac{4}{10}$ or $\frac{2}{5}$
6. 1
7. 5
8. 3
9. 45 mph
10. decagon; 10; 10; yes; plane shape
11. 15 minutes
12. 96 cards

Day 125

1. 137
2. 300
3. 19
4. 20th
5. 5
6. $(8 + 9) \times 3 - 1 = 50$
7. 3
8. 210
9. 24 m^3
10. equilateral triangle
11. heads and tails; heads and heads; tails and tails
12. $64.20

Day 126

1. 168
2. 240
3. $82\frac{4}{5}$ or 82.8
4. less than
5. $12\frac{95}{100}$ or $12\frac{19}{20}$
6. $8 + 9 \times (3 - 1) = 26$
7. 5
8. 10
9. 4.5 cm^2
10. pentagon
11. Spinner B
12. 300 feet

Day 127

1. 140
2. 85
3. 91
4. 1, 2, 4, 7, 8, 14, 28, 56
5. 60
6. 44
7. 90
8. 147
9. 18:58
10. 5 faces
11. $\frac{5}{7}$
12. 17 chickens

Day 128

1. 45
2. 468
3. $47\frac{1}{6}$
4. 3^3
5. 4
6. $7 \times (8 - 4) \times 3 = 84$
7. 872
8. 8 or −8
9. 110 miles
10. 360°
11. 251 and 722
12. 3,101

Day 129

1. 78
2. 800
3. $87\frac{8}{9}$
4. 8, 16, 24, 32, 40
5. $2\frac{38}{100}$ or $2\frac{19}{50}$
6. 4
7. 3
8. $96 - 12n$
9. 350 cm^3
10. no
11. 24 cookies
12.

	Faces	Edges	Vertices
Octagonal Pyramid	9	16	9
Octagonal Prism	10	24	16

Day 130

1. 185
2. 145
3. $47\frac{1}{2}$ or 47.5
4. 6 digits
5. $\frac{7}{10}$
6. 2,025
7. 900
8. $17s$ or $17 \times s$
9. 250 grams
10. 81 degrees
11. 31
12.

13	8	10	7
14	3	17	4
9	12	6	11
2	15	5	16

ANSWER KEY *(cont.)*

Day 131

1. 124
2. 455
3. $92\frac{3}{5}$
4. 4 thousands or 4,000
5. $\frac{9}{12}$ or $\frac{3}{4}$
6. 1
7. 7
8. 11
9. 1:01 A.M.
10. rhombus
11.

Family	Milk	Juice	Water
Kims	3	1	4
Bergs	4	2	4

12. 33 marbles

Day 132

1. −188
2. 320
3. $38\frac{1}{7}$
4. 1,000,000 + 300,000 + 50,000 + 600 + 7
5. $\frac{21}{8}$
6. Number of Sides: 20, 30, 40, 50; Rule: Multiply the number of decagons by 10 to get the number of sides.
7. $5b + 20$
8. 20
9. 6
10. reflected
11. 3 equal sections labeled with 1, 2, and 3.
12. 17 hours and 30 minutes

Day 133

1. 217
2. 150
3. 57
4. 45,000
5. 84%
6. 64
7. 97
8. 41
9. 14 m
10. cylinder
11. $\frac{3}{6}$ or $\frac{1}{2}$
12. 25%

Day 134

1. 77
2. 150
3. $57\frac{2}{3}$
4. 7 or −7
5. 5
6. −88
7. 65
8. $4x - 84$
9. 50 km per hour
10. triangular prism; 5; 6; stack; solid
11. $\frac{3}{11}$
12. Answers may vary. Possible answer: $\frac{7}{15}$

Day 135

1. 28
2. 300
3. $70\frac{7}{8}$
4. 3,975
5. 18
6. *3,246*
7. 70
8. 0.1
9. 500 cm^3
10. 180°
11. 501
12. $4.00

Day 136

1. 130
2. 2,400
3. 66
4. positive number
5. 4
6. −40
7. $4\frac{1}{4}$
8. $g - 49$
9. 09:26
10. yes
11. yes
12. $6.00

Day 137

1. 294
2. 120
3. $115\frac{1}{2}$ or 115.5
4. 1, 3, 9, 27
5. $\frac{11}{4}$
6. 14
7. 518
8. $q = 192$
9. 3,900 g
10. 12 edges
11. $\frac{6}{11}$
12. 1, 2, 3, 5, 6, 10, 15, 30

Day 138

1. 114
2. 2,000
3. 48
4. 12, 14, 15, 16, 18
5. $\frac{8}{3}$
6. 8
7. 5
8. $52 - 13h$
9. 24 months
10. 5 sides
11. $\frac{28}{35}$ or $\frac{4}{5}$
12. 1 cup

Day 139

1. 317
2. 1,200
3. $153\frac{2}{3}$
4. no
5. 3.58
6. −15
7. 60
8. 14
9. 9.3 km
10. 2.28 m
11. 50 times
12. 9 people

Day 140

1. 101
2. 36,000
3. 132
4. 1,248
5. 5
6. 1,860
7. $\frac{5}{10}$ or $\frac{1}{2}$
8. 8
9. 3 cm
10. reflex
11. $105
12. $12 \div 4 + 3 = 6$; $15 \div 5 + 3 = 6$

Day 141

1. 31
2. 76
3. $47\frac{1}{3}$
4. hundreds
5. .55
6. 23
7. 120
8. 216
9. 4
10. 7.5 cm^2
11. Wednesday
12. rectangular prism

ANSWER KEY *(cont.)*

Day 142
1. 277
2. 2,400
3. $39\frac{3}{7}$
4. 87,461
5. 70%
6. Chart: Meter: 5,250; 7,750 Kilometer: 4; 6.5 Rule: Divide the meter value by 1,000 to get the kilometer.
7. $18a + 36$
8. 4.4
9. 33 in.^{2}
10. 6 angles
11. half section for 1, quarter section for each 2 and 3
12. 1 hour, 45 minutes

Day 143
1. 286
2. 2,100
3. $75\frac{4}{9}$
4. 70,000
5. $\frac{17}{6}$
6. $(3 + 5) \times 8 - 2 \times 10 = 44$
7. 22
8. 8
9. 3,250 g
10. circle or triangle
11. $\frac{1}{5}$
12.

×	20	30	40	50	60	70
6	120	180	240	300	360	420
9	180	270	360	450	540	630
7	140	210	280	350	420	490
8	160	240	320	400	480	560

Day 144
1. 354
2. 340
3. $66\frac{5}{7}$
4. yes
5. $\frac{4}{8}$ or $\frac{1}{2}$
6. $3 + 5 \times (8 - 2) \times 10 = 303$
7. 164
8. $x - 25$
9. 9
10. parallelogram; 4; 4; no; plane shape
11. 2 hours 52 minutes
12. 3 gallons

Day 145
1. 217
2. 2,900
3. $68\frac{1}{4}$ or 68.25
4. 51st
5. $1\frac{3}{6}$ or $1\frac{1}{2}$
6. 2,914
7. 20
8. 9
9. 48 cm^3
10. obtuse
11. 611
12. $\frac{1}{8}$

Day 146
1. 487
2. 200
3. $29\frac{4}{5}$ or 29.8
4. no
5. $\frac{3}{5}$
6. 144
7. 4
8. $700 - 100p$
9. 56 m^2
10. hexagon
11. Spinner A
12. 16 steps

Day 147
1. 483
2. 1,800
3. $9\frac{5}{8}$
4. 1, 2, 3, 4, 5, 6, 10, 12, 15, 20, 30, 60
5. $2\frac{2}{3}$
6. 29
7. 4
8. 4
9. 7.5 liters
10. 4 vertices
11. $\frac{4}{7}$
12. 2, 4

Day 148
1. 322
2. 1,500
3. 20.5 or $20\frac{1}{2}$
4. 156,790
5. 45
6. 5
7. 13
8. $10b + 78$
9. 110 miles
10. no
11. Box B
12. 873.48

Day 149
1. 126
2. 720
3. $49\frac{1}{2}$ or 49.5
4. 9, 18, 27
5. 72
6. –45
7. 6
8. 200
9. 250 cm^3
10. yes
11. 6 dozen cookies or 72 cookies
12. 168 trading cards

Day 150
1. 98
2. 600
3. 38
4. 6 digits
5. $1\frac{7}{100}$
6. 176
7. 39
8. $-2x - 6$
9. 3,800 m
10. straight
11. 45
12. 60 minutes

Day 151
1. 43
2. 204
3. 50
4. 8 ones or 8
5. $1\frac{1}{10}$
6. 11
7. –
8. 110
9. 48 cm^3
10. line E
11. 41.86 or 41.9
12. 9 runs

Day 152
1. 323
2. 125
3. 60
4. 400 + 60 + 1
5. 4
6. Output: 15, 20, 25; Rule: Multiply the input by 5 to get the output.
7. 30
8. $m \div 34$ or $\frac{m}{34}$
9. 10:47
10. 360°
11. half circle for 1, quarter circle for each 2 and 3
12. 6 miles

ANSWER KEY *(cont.)*

Day 153

1. 485
2. 24,000
3. 29
4. 359,000
5. 75
6. –7
7. 4
8. $14t - 140$
9. 9
10. 2 axes of symmetry
11. $75
12. 9 pieces of gum

Day 154

1. 277
2. 1,500
3. 40
4. odd number
5. $\frac{2}{3}$
6. 41
7. $\frac{5}{8}$
8. 43
9. 60 km per hour
10. pentagonal prism; 7; 10; stack; solid
11. 0
12.

Ten	1,673,420
Hundred	1,673,400
Thousand	1,673,000
Ten thousand	1,670,000
Hundred thousand	1,700,000
Million	2,000,000

Day 155

1. 286
2. 225
3. $70\frac{2}{7}$
4. 88,257
5. $\frac{5}{100}$ should be circled.
6. 875
7. 1
8. 10 or –10
9. 144 cm^2
10. right triangle
11. dishwasher, trash, dog; dishwasher, dog, trash; trash, dishwasher, dog; trash, dog, dishwasher; dog, dishwasher, trash; dog, trash, dishwasher
12. $7.50 for twenty tickets

Day 156

1. 812
2. 384
3. 70
4. –9
5. 50
6. 24
7. 75
8. 131
9. 21:26
10. triangle or rectangle
11. $\frac{1}{6}$
12. 12 kids

Day 157

1. 412
2. 2,400
3. 479
4. 1, 2, 13, 26
5. 3.5, 3.6, 3.8
6. 6.4
7. 6
8. $2x + 32$
9. 90 minutes
10. 3 faces
11. $\frac{6}{11}$
12. $\frac{3}{8}$ of the square is yellow.

Day 158

1. 106
2. 35,000
3. 30
4. 3
5. 6.564
6. 9.1
7. 3.8
8. 5
9. 250 km
10. 10 sides
11. $\frac{19}{35}$
12. 6 hours

Day 159

1. 22
2. 2,400
3. less than
4. yes
5. 62%
6. 52.5
7. 6
8. $81 + 27u$
9. 950 cm^3
10. yes
11. 64 times
12. 23 cars

Day 160

1. 183
2. 6,400
3. $85\frac{1}{6}$ or 85.17
4. 98,542
5. less than
6. 80
7. 8
8. $\frac{1}{2}$ or 0.5
9. 2,250 grams
10. 40°
11. $73.65
12.

5	8	6	11
2	15	1	12
9	4	10	7
14	3	13	0

Day 161

1. 116
2. 4,300
3. 30
4. 4 ten thousands or 40,000
5. $7\frac{4}{100}$ or $7\frac{1}{25}$
6. +
7. 60
8. 326
9. 6.24 m
10. 60 m
11. $\frac{1}{2}$
12. $0.85; $2.65; $3.90; $1.65; $2.55; $1.30; Total: $12.90; Change: $7.10

Day 162

1. 247
2. 750
3. 20
4. 35,982
5. 1.6, 1.4, 1.3
6.

Gram	9,000	8,500	8,000	7,500
Kilogram	9	8.5	8	7.5

Rule: Divide the gram value by 1,000 to get the kg value.

7. $3x + 27$
8. 1 or –1
9. 9 $ft.^2$
10. 
11. 4 equal sections: red, green, yellow, and orange
12. $16.25 per hour

ANSWER KEY *(cont.)*

Day 163

1. 66
2. 4,300
3. 149.6
4. 27,000
5. $\frac{2}{5}$
6. 7
7. 3.2
8. 48
9. 14 cm
10. triangular prism
11. 400 trucks
12.

×	20	30	40	50	60	70
10	200	300	400	500	600	700
20	400	600	800	1,000	1,200	1,400
30	600	900	1,200	1,500	1,800	2,100
40	800	1,200	1,600	2,000	2,400	2,800

Day 164

1. 1,730
2. 1,200
3. $38\frac{2}{5}$ or 38.4
4. yes
5. 6
6. −38
7. 14
8. $900q$ or $900 \times q$
9. 24 cm
10. 60°
11. 15 minutes
12. 20 days

Day 165

1. 333
2. 4,300
3. 71
4. 47th
5. equal to
6. 1,080
7. 3
8. 2.5 or $2\frac{1}{2}$
9. 1,000 cm^3
10. 50°, acute
11. $\frac{2}{8}$ or $\frac{1}{4}$
12. 21 cups of water

Day 166

1. 231
2. 7,100
3. 39
4. less than
5. 63
6. +
7. $5x + 10$
8. $-5x - 10$ or $-5x + (-10)$
9. 55 mm
10. yes
11. spinner A
12. $(5 + 4) \times 3 = 27$
    $(4 + 5) \times 3 = 27$

Day 167

1. 128
2. 24,000
3. equal to
4. 1, 2, 4, 5, 8, 10, 20, 40
5. $\frac{1}{2}$
6. 8
7. $d - 8$
8. $8 - d$
9. 950 cm^3
10. 8 edges
11. $\frac{5}{7}$
12. 1, 2, 3, 4, 6, 8, 12, 24

Day 168

1. 211
2. 16,000
3. 30
4. 64
5. 65
6. $48 \div 4 + (8 - 6) \times 2 = 16$
7. $3x - 15$
8. $-3x + 15$
9. 195 miles
10. hexagon
11. Box A
12.

1	8	12	13
14	11	7	2
15	10	6	3
4	5	9	16

Day 169

1. 247
2. 2,560
3. $27\frac{5}{6}$
4. 10, 20, 30, 40
5. no
6. $48 \div (4 + 8) - 6 \times 2 = -8$
7. 20
8. 5.4
9. 8.45 L
10. yes
11. 30 cookies
12.

	Faces	Edges	Vertices
Decagonal Pyramid	11	20	11
Decagonal Prism	12	30	20

Day 170

1. 209
2. 1,290
3. 562.7
4. 8 digits
5. $\frac{17}{6}$
6. 64
7. 6
8. 257
9. 256 mm
10. acute angle
11. 15
12. 36 years

Day 171

1. 335
2. 426
3. 57
4. 6 hundreds or 600
5. 1.256
6. +
7. $275 + 25h$
8. 120
9. 4,500 g
10. line B
11. Divide circle into 4 equal sections: 2 sections for dogs, 1 section for birds, 1 section for cats
12. $6.00

Day 172

1. 799
2. 1,260
3. $77\frac{1}{6}$
4. 400,000 + 70,000 + 5,000 + 900 + 20 + 6
5. 160
6.

Number of Squares	1	2	3	4	5
Number of Sides	4	8	12	16	20

Rule: Multiply the number of squares by 4 to get the number of sides.

7. $g + 72$
8. 13
9. 64 pints
10. equilateral triangle
11. 12 lawns
12. 3, 2, 6, 13

Day 173

1. 81
2. 405
3. less than
4. 345,000
5. $\frac{3}{4}$
6. −15
7. 9
8. 8
9. 14.8 m
10. circle
11. 55 students
12. 0.60

Day 174

1. 170
2. 920
3. $70\frac{1}{3}$
4. 6 or −6
5. $\frac{17}{5}$
6. +
7. $21a + 189$
8. $p = 56.7$
9. 8.25 m
10. hexagonal pyramid; 7; 7; none; solid
11. $\frac{2}{11}$

ANSWER KEY *(cont.)*

12. 448 miles

Day 175

1. 79
2. 800
3. $80\frac{1}{3}$
4. 299,999
5. $\frac{3}{6}$ or $\frac{1}{2}$
6. 400
7. $x^2 + 7$
8. 4
9. 3.5
10. 270°
11. 2,443
12. 350 cm

Day 176

1. 212
2. 2,040
3. 82
4. –10
5. 300
6. 48
7. $160 - 8r$
8. 19.3
9. 4.5 liters
10. true
11. $\frac{2}{6}$ or $\frac{1}{3}$
12. 17 blocks

Day 177

1. 165
2. 2,190
3. $4\frac{15}{67}$ or 4.22
4. 1, 2, 3, 5, 6, 10, 15, 30
5. $\frac{11}{3}$
6. –21
7. $9h - 99$
8. $19e$ or 19 x e
9. 70 cm^2
10. 8 vertices
11. 13.8
12. $14.75

Day 178

1. 241
2. 1,080
3. $52\frac{3}{4}$ or 52.75
4. 14
5. $\frac{9}{10}$
6. –3
7. $\frac{7}{11}$
8. $\frac{2}{4}$ or $\frac{1}{2}$
9. 1,050 km
10. The hexagon and pentagon should be circled.
11. $\frac{23}{35}$
12. 4 gallons of lemonade and 1 gallon of ice cream

Day 179

1. 242
2. 1,460
3. $72\frac{1}{5}$ or 72.2
4. Any number ending in 0 is divisible by 5.
5. 2.5, 2.6, 2.8
6. 6 or –6
7. $n - 18$
8. 13 or –13
9. $5\frac{1}{4}$ inches
10. 7 cm
11. 12 times
12. 4 tables

Day 180

1. 708
2. 1,728
3. $31\frac{1}{8}$ or 31.125
4. 3,468
5. $\frac{5}{8}$
6. 560
7. $6b + 6c$
8. 4.6
9. 27 cm^2
10. obtuse angle
11. $8
12.

Addition	Palindrome
56 + 65	121
132 + 231	363
623 + 326	949
235 + 532	767

REFERENCES CITED

Kilpatrick, J., J. Swafford, and B. Findell, eds. 2001. *Adding it up: Helping children learn mathematics.* Washington, DC: National Academies Press.

Marzano, R. 2010. When practice makes perfect...sense. *Educational Leadership* 68 (3): 81–83.

McIntosh, M. E. 1997. Formative assessment in mathematics. *Clearing House* 71 (2): 92–96.

DIGITAL RESOURCES

Accessing the Digital Resources

The digital resources can be downloaded by following these steps:

1. Go to www.tcmpub.com/digital
2. Use the ISBN number to redeem the digital resources.
3. Respond to the question using the book.
4. Follow the prompts on the Content Cloud website to sign in or create a new account.
5. The content redeemed will now be on your My Content screen. Click on the product to look through the digital resources. All resources are available for download. Select files can be previewed, opened, and shared. For questions and assistance with your license key card, or to report a lost card, please contact Shell Education.

   mail: customerservice@tcmpub.com
   phone: 800-858-7339

CONTENTS OF THE DIGITAL RESOURCES

Teacher Resources

- Practice Page Item Analysis Chart
- Student Item Analysis Chart

Student Resources

- Practice Pages